Schooling in a Corporate Society

EDUCATIONAL POLICY, PLANNING AND THEORY

Series Editor: DON ADAMS

Schooling in a Corporate Society

The political economy of education in America

Edited by
MARTIN CARNOY
Stanford University

DAVID McKAY COMPANY, INC.
NEW YORK

SCHOOLING IN A CORPORATE SOCIETY

To my mother and father

Acknowledgements

THE EDITOR would like to thank the authors, periodicals, and publishers for their kind permission to reprint the following copyrighted material:

"The Channeling Colony" by Marcus Raskin is reprinted from *Being and Doing*, by Marcus Raskin (New York: Random House, 1971) by permission of the author and Random House.

"Unequal Education and the Reproduction of the Social Division of Labor" by Samuel Bowles. Copyright © 1971 by Samuel Bowles. It also appears in the *Review of Radical Economics*. By permission of the author.

"Economic Theories of Racism" by Michael Reich. Copyright © 1970 by Michael Reich. It also appears, in a somewhat different version, in *The Political Economy of Urban Problems*, edited by David M. Gordon (Lexington, Mass.: D. C. Heath, 1971). By permission of the author.

"Job Discrimination and Education" by Philip Blair is reported more fully in *Job Discrimination and Education: An Investment Analysis — A Case Study of Mexican-Americans in Santa Clara County, California* (New York: Praeger, 1972).

"Rational Income Decisions of Blacks and Everybody Else" by Stephan Michelson is reprinted from *Industrial and Labor Relations Review*, Vol. 23, no. 1 (October 1969). Copyright © 1969 by Cornell University. All rights reserved.

"The Case for Community Control of the Schools" by Henry M. Levin is from James W. Guthrie and Edward Wynne, editors, *New Models for American Education* © 1971. Reprinted by permission of Prentice-Hall, Inc., Englewood Cliffs, New Jersey.

"The Rise of the 'Free School' " by Bonnie Barrett Stretch is reprinted from *Saturday Review*, June 20, 1970, copyright © 1970 Saturday Review, Inc. By permission of the author and *Saturday Review*.

"Education Vouchers: A Proposal for Diversity and Choice" by Judith Areen and Christopher Jencks is reprinted from *Teachers College Record*, 72, no. 3 (February 1971) by permission of the authors and *Teachers College Record*.

"Why We Must Disestablish School" by Ivan Illich is reprinted from *Deschooling Society* by Ivan Illich (New York: Harper and Row, 1971). Copyright © 1970 by Ivan Illich. Originally appeared in *The New York Review of Books*, and reprinted by permission of Harper & Row, Publishers, Inc.

"Cuban Education and the Revolutionary Ideology" by Samuel Bowles. Copyright © 1971 by Samuel Bowles. The same article appeared in *Harvard Educational Review*, 41, no. 4 (Fall 1971). By permission of the author.

The Denver Post for cartoons captioned "Into the bus, off the bus, into the bus, off the bus—Man, what an education!" and "Of course, this forced busing is only a temporary measure while we learn to love one another, or something..." by Patrick Oliphant in *The Denver Post* (September 1, 1971) and February 17, 1972, © The Los Angeles Times Syndicate, reprinted by permission of the artist.

Contributors

Judith Areen is a fellow at the Center for the Study of Public Policy in Cambridge, Massachusetts and instructor at Boston University School of Law.

Philip Blair is associate professor of mechanical engineering at San Jose State College.

Samuel Bowles is associate professor of economics at Harvard University.

Philip Brenner is presently a graduate student at Johns Hopkins University in Baltimore. He was co-director of the Washington Mini-School.

Martin Carnoy is associate professor of education and economics at Stanford University.

Ivan Illich is director of the International Center for Documentation (CIDOC) in Cuernavaca, Mexico.

Christopher Jencks is co-director of the Center for the Study of Public Policy in Cambridge and associate professor of education at Harvard University.

Henry Levin is associate professor of education and economics at Stanford University.

Stephan Michelson is research associate in the Center for Educational Policy Research, Harvard University.

Marcus Raskin is co-director of the Institute for Policy Studies in Washington, D.C.

Michael Reich is assistant professor of economics at Boston University and research associate at the National Bureau of Economic Research.

Thomas Ribich is associate professor of economics, University of North Carolina, Chapel Hill.

Bonnie Barrett Stretch was formerly associate editor for education of the *Saturday Review.*

Contents

xii   *Contents*

Introduction

MARTIN CARNOY

THROUGHOUT THE history of educational research in the United States, educators and, more recently, social scientists, have tacitly assumed that the goal of both the socioeconomic and educational systems of the United States is the maximization of every individual's potential. This view is consistent with both the concept of education as a liberator of men's minds and with the later idea that the modern, industrial state requires a socially mobile population. The meritocratic ideal, in which the "best," most "intelligent" men rise to the top, and on which the U.S. school system is based, pervades this research, and indeed, almost all popular writing on education. In a meritocracy, the individual is assumed to have "free will," able to go as high as his motivation, desire, and ability take him. Any individual who does not achieve success has only himself to blame, since he did not take advantage of the means available to him.

These are deeply ingrained beliefs. It is not surprising that those who are successful in any society orient their thinking to praise the system that allowed them to succeed, rather than question or condemn it. Thus, public education and the American "classless," melting-pot society have been characterized by the image makers— all successful products of the system—as an ideal, consistent with the rags-to-riches American dream and equal opportunity for all. Research has therefore assumed away the issues of goals, the institutional structure of schools, and the *reasons* for public education.

1

Starting from visionary American "ideals," the research has taken as its primary aim to improve the efficiency of *achieving* these ideals. The existence of "distortions" and inefficiencies in the school system were (and are) taken as impediments to *desirable* objectives. It is these impediments, not the goals of the socioeconomic and educational structures, that are the object of past research.

But what if these ideals are *not* the goals of the system? Perhaps the real goals are not the "maximization" of everyone's potential, but only the potential of a few—the elite, or ruling class. The American dream of social mobility may become a reality for a limited percentage of low- and middle-income families, while the majority are held in place, to a large extent by the school system itself. If these are the goals of the system, "distortions" and inefficiencies as seen by those who have assumed the objective of the American dream would not necessarily be distortions at all, but rational and efficient parts of a system with very different desired outputs.

Marcus Raskin describes the system as a "channeling colony," teaching children how to operate "properly" in real-world hierarchies by recreating those hierarchies in the schools. Children are taught to respond to certain rewards and punishments, to learn the criteria for success and failure, and to be highly sensitive to their "record," that vague, never-seen file which follows them—constantly growing thicker—throughout their lives. The values and culture transmitted in the schools largely reflect the ideology of the upper echelons of the hierarchy. Today's school is the result of an elite rule that has dictated the role of the schools from the nineteenth century until now.

If the educational system in the United States was developed to fill the needs of capitalists in a growing economy, as Samuel Bowles argues in the first of his two essays of this collection, schools have fulfilled their function admirably. They took immigrants from many foreign cultures (if not the immigrants themselves, at least their children) and trained them in the norms of hard work, saving, showing up on time, respect for the hierarchy, loyalty to the elite of the new land, and in the basic rudiments of the new language. Schooling was provided free of charge to all children, and the average number of years in school per member of the labor force rapidly became the highest in the world. Literacy, in terms of being able to read and write, became almost universal. The schools provided an increasingly sophisticated business and industrial structure with an increasingly schooled, if not necessarily more skilled, labor force.

Between 1880 and 1910, the period of the second great wave of immigration, professional educators and businessmen moved successfully to take the control of urban schools away from political wards dominated by politicians and working-class ethnics and to transfer it to city-wide school boards controlled by business interests.[1] The educator-philosophers made this move in the name of homogenizing urban schooling, of ensuring quality control of the schools' socialization processes, and taking the political "corruption" out of the public schools. At the same time, however, business and intellectual elites established control over what was taught in the schools and over school hierarchies. This hierarchy of control is essentially the same one that is being challenged today. Now, much more than at the turn of the century, it is the society's primary instrument to channel children into social and economic roles. Bowles presents evidence that, contrary to the American dream, the school system helps *preserve* the status structure from generation to generation rather than helping to generate interclass mobility.

If the analyses of Raskin and Bowles are correct, why has the massive criticism of the schools by minority groups, intellectuals, and students themselves occurred only in the last ten years?[2] Schools have certainly not become more hierarchical or less successful in teaching children basic skills. Nor have they become more joyless, frightening places than in the past.[3] The reasons for the present, widespread onslaught appears to be a combination of (1) a change in

[1]David Tyack, "Centralization of Control in City Schools at the Turn of the Century," in *The Organizational Society*, ed. Jerry Israel (Chicago: Quadrangle Books, 1971).

[2]There have of course been earlier attacks on the schools. But these—the progressive school movement, for example—came entirely from intellectuals and represented conflicts among educational philosophies that had little to do with today's political and social criticisms. John Dewey and his followers wanted to change the joylessness of the schools, but they also wanted to make school the dominant or even the only transmitter of culture in the society. Although they probably failed on the first count, they did succeed in putting added stress on long-term schooling and developing the "whole man." See John Dewey, *Democracy and Education* (New York: Collier Books, 1969).

[3]In 1909, a factory inspector did an informal survey of 500 working children in 20 factories. She found that 412 of them would rather work in the terrible conditions of factories than return to school. Helen Todd, "Why Children Work," *McClure's Magazine* (April 1913): 68–69.

society's concept of equality, shifting from equal access to schooling to equal schooling outcomes for various socioeconomic groups; (2) higher expectations on the part of parents from schooling in a society where average real family income has more than doubled in the last generation and where real expenditures on schooling have more than tripled since 1930; and (3) a changing concept in certain segments of the society of the type of socialization that should take place in the school: students themselves, for example, are rejecting the hierarchy of traditional education.

If earlier reforms are today the subject of attack, it is in part because substantial segments of the society no longer believe in centralism as an effective response to human needs, no longer trust in professionalism, no longer accept the inevitability or justice of the distribution of power and wealth along existing class and racial lines, and no longer think that technological change implies progress.[4]

In an existential revolution in which colonized groups such as blacks and browns, the young, and women are questioning the social roles in which they have been cast, the school system, perhaps more than any other single institution, has come under fire. Blacks and browns attack the schools because they have not fulfilled their ideal of equal opportunity and have attempted to impose a white middle-class culture; youth no longer accept oppression and contradiction; and women resent being socialized into roles of second-class citizens.

Still, this does not explain why the schools have been attacked more than other institutions, for example, the large corporations, the family, or private property. Why schools? After all, the reality of any society is that schools are not generally the originators, but the transmitters of values and norms. Despite this reality, however, schools are viewed by parents as important agents of socialization and as allocators of economic and social roles. Most children stay in school more and more years. The relationships developed there, described by Raskin, have become an increasing fraction of their societal experience. Simultaneously, a rapid evolution in hiring practices has occurred. A degree from school, certifying completion of a schooling level, has become the single most important criterion of getting first and subsequent jobs. How far someone gets in school,

[4]David Tyack, *New York Times*, 11 January 1971, p. 48.

therefore, determines much more now than in the past what kind of work he will do. Schools are also attacked because they are the institution closest to the people who see themselves as oppressed. These people may also recognize corporate oppression, but they are not in corporations; and if they were, they could not do very much about it without jeopardizing their economic position. On the other hand, students are required to be in school, and so they can stop schools without fear of reprisal.

The conflict of ideas outside the schools with the current hierarchical socialization process inside leads to one kind of obvious dissention. A much subtler problem is faced by the poor. As the number of people getting a given degree rises more rapidly than the demand for them, job requirements are upgraded by raising the certificate necessary to get the job. This process begins at the lowest levels of schooling and moves upward.[5] Ten years ago, for example, a high school diploma was the entrée to almost any skilled blue-collar job; today, many of these jobs require some junior college training or even a junior college degree. A high school dropout is guaranteed long periods of unemployment in his working lifetime. For the most part, however, certificate requirements have little to do with the actual performance of workers on the job once they are hired.[6] Requiring school certification for a job is apparently even unconstitutional.[7] But employers use certification as a convenient screening device that is highly correlated with the hierarchical rules. In the employer's mind, a high school graduate (as opposed to a dropout) will be more likely to show up daily, submit to orders, and not cause trouble. The screening process works against those who were last to arrive into the urban economy, since they are the least schooled and least enculturated, although not necessarily the least productive. These groups, in today's labor force the blacks and the browns, see the biased educational system as the impediment to jobs.

Thus the schools become the focal point for different frustrations in American society. To come to grips with these frustrations, various

---

[5]For a description of this process, see Martin Carnoy, "The Political Economy of Education," mimeographed (Stanford: Stanford University, 1970).

[6]Ivar Berg, *Education and Jobs: The Great Training Robbery* (New York: Frederick A. Praeger, 1970).

[7]Ivan Illich, "Abolishing Schools," *New York Times*, 3 and 4 May 1971, pp. 35, 45.

groups in society are attempting to gain control of their children's schools and change their form and content to suit group needs. Paradoxically, two generations of Dewey-influenced professional educators must now pay the price for having convinced us of the schools' role in shaping our lives. But there is real question whether simply changing the schools will have much effect on the dominant economic, social, and political institutions of American society. Inversely, it may be impossible to change the public school system, the channeling system, without changing the dominant social values and structures. These are the implications of both Bowles' and Raskin's essays.

The source of jobs and income is in the hands of the elite; thus, even with the elite's loss of the schools, it is conceivable that graduates would end up discontent but still accepting the established economic and social structure. In that case, disenfranchised groups would be satisfied with the illusion of control, but in reality they would still be locked into the hierarchy. This is particularly true for the disenfranchised minorities, who along with their need for cultural identity and independence from white middle-class rule, are still seeking higher incomes through higher degrees. Although some minority subgroups have stressed total independence or, conversely, alliances with radical whites to change the entire economic structure, the overwhelming majority in the black and brown communities wants to take over the schools so that their children can succeed in the *present* economic system.

On the other hand, high-income whites are apparently beginning to reject the corporate structure altogether, and are therefore willing to reject dependency by giving up the traditional norms of success. For this group, creating new kinds of schools is a means to achieving a child-centered school environment rather than a subject-matter focus; to generate relationships among children and between children and teachers that stress emotional welfare and humanness rather than scholastic achievement.

Both movements gain psychically from making desired changes in their schools and having direct control over how and what their children are taught. Nevertheless, no amount of school control by blacks, browns, or women will create equality of opportunity in a racist and sexist economic and social structure. No amount of local control will attack the suburban preserves of the elite public schools. Control may provide the type of leadership that, if it is not coopted, may in turn create economic counter-institutions to employ and serve the community. This "community mercantilism" is a real potential threat to the established structure, and it is the reason why liberal corporations are already trying to influence the community control movement.[8] For the upper-income whites, liberation has not come through establishing counter-schools, but through rejecting the traditional norms for success. The "free school" is the means of transmitting and expanding this liberation to their children.

The problem of independence, control, or even simply assuring equal opportunity cannot be settled merely by changing the schools: schools simply reflect and inculcate the values of a larger society. These are the foci of the essays in this collection that discuss equal opportunity; they challenge the concept of reforming American society and American schools without changing basic institutional structures in the society. They also try to show that equal access to the school or the marketplace does not imply that people have free choice in those institutional structures; to the contrary, the individual is dominated by institutions and the relationships imposed by them. These relationships and the individual's understanding of them, not his personal motivation or desire, are the key factors determining his behavior.

The essays analyzing discrimination are based on certain concepts of equality of opportunity. On the labor market side, the concept is straightforward: people with equal qualifications for work should receive equal pay and access to the same type of jobs. Michael Reich argues that racism is rooted in the economic system—in capitalist and imperialist ideology, not in the attitudes of the white working class as commonly assumed. Reich's model as extended to the educational system is consistent with Bowles' and Raskin's analyses: those in control of the school system (certainly the white working class does not control the schools) have used it to reinforce children into social roles which place blacks and Mexican-Americans at the bottom of the heap.

[8] See Rick Greenspan, "Secondary Education: The Corporations Move In," *Pacific Research and World Empire Telegram* (Palo Alto) 2, no. 1 (November 1970): 10–16.

This analysis applies equally to women. Women are cast in social roles which make them secretaries instead of professionals and teach them to accept lower salaries for the same work. Since most women in the United States are white, they do not generally face the same school and economic survival problems as blacks and Mexican-Americans. But even though sexism seems more acceptable to our society (by both men and women), this merely demonstrates its cultural depth. Women have been effectively socialized by their *families* as well as by schools to be passive players in a male-dominated society.[9]

Philip Blair and Stephan Michelson test the effect of discrimination against blacks and Mexican-Americans in the labor market and consider how this discrimination influences their investment in schooling. Blair uses a series of estimates to measure discrimination, all in the traditional economic mode. He finds that Mexican-Americans are worse off than Anglos in the income they receive, even if they have the same amount of schooling. They also have a much higher unemployment rate. But Blair's most important result indicates that Mexican-Americans receive a much higher rate of return to investing in schooling at noncompletion levels than at degree levels. Euro-Americans, on the other hand, receive higher rates at completion than at dropout levels. Furthermore, these results would change negligibly if the relative public expenditures on Mexican-Americans were raised considerably, say by 20 percent. Blair concludes that investing more in Mexican-American schooling will do little to change the economic incentives to stay in school. The key to such change appears to be ethnic discrimination in the labor market itself.

Michelson develops a model of educational investment behavior in which the poor acquire more schooling because they want to reach certain *minimum* levels of income. In order to reach a given income goal, they must have more schooling than Euro-Americans. Blair shows that, *on the average*, going to school of itself does not produce equal income for minority groups. Michelson says that the poor will

[9]"Girls are so socialized to accept their limited roles that few of them protest. Don McNeilly III, a student at the University of California at Santa Cruz, has discovered that even very young girls are aware that powerful social roles are not for them. . . . The sex barrier to aspirations was at least as high as the barrier between white and Mexican-American students, and in some cases higher." *Transaction* 8, no. 4 (February 1971): 10.

go to school anyway. This is the real strength of the system: it gets the poor to enter the socializing institution voluntarily, without having to pay them equal wages at the end of the process. The socializing institution provides the best (legal) strategy for minority income, even if it is not very good. Michelson stresses that the poor are not responding as much to rates of return on investment in schooling as to a demand for goods. The only way they see to obtain their desired standard of living is through additional schooling.

The concept of equality of opportunity in schooling, unlike labor market discrimination, has recently changed. The responsibility of schooling for equal outcomes of different groups goes far beyond anything that Horace Mann or John Dewey had in mind. Thomas Ribich's essay discusses the many levels of meaning of "equality of opportunity." Educational philosophy has always put primary responsibility on the individual to succeed; schooling is made available to him, but he must prove himself worthy of continuing in school. In the past, equality of opportunity meant that primary and secondary schools, and more recently colleges, were available free of charge. Today, economists show that, at the secondary and higher levels of schooling (and a generation ago, even at the primary level), the "free of charge" doctrine is fallacious: students forgo income while attending school and this affects their decision to continue. Ribich challenges the neoclassical economic analysis that equal access to schooling would occur if capital markets were perfect. People with different conceptions of their social roles (imposed by society) will not take equal amounts of schooling even if the cost of borrowing capital and the return to it were the same. At the same time he argues that equality of output in the schools—that all groups end up equal at the end of the schooling period—may be a very inefficient approach to economic growth or even income distribution optimization. He concludes that the efficiency and ethical arguments result in an ambiguous case for equal school outcomes.

In Ribich's essay, compensatory schooling as a philosophical goal must rest on the past performance of society to the poor: if poor parents have been systematically prevented from accumulating and transferring either physical or human capital to their children, then compensatory schooling today is a way of compensating the poor for the past. Bowles' data support this contention of past discrimination in the school system. Reich's analysis also implies that the deck has been consistently stacked against minorities, not only in the labor market, but in schools: the institution that develops human capital operates to hinder blacks and browns from doing as well as whites.

This is the subject of my essay and also of Michelson's equal-opportunity contribution. Both show that schools are currently structured in a way that precludes equalizing average outcomes of students from different subcultures within the society. Equalization is especially difficult for those groups most unlike the dominant white upper-middle class. Although Michelson and I start our discussions with much the same issues as those treated by Ribich, our concern is not with the economic and ethical basis of equality of opportunity. In effect, these essays begin where Ribich leaves off and deal with the actual allocation of resources to schools (Michelson) and with the structure of schooling and what that implies for the goal of equal outcomes (Carnoy). Students not only forgo income while in school, but minority students, who generally get less resources for schooling, do worse in school and find it more difficult and less psychically rewarding. They start out behind white middle-class children in the first grade and the very nature of schooling (as part of the certification structure) denies them equality. Part of this failure of schooling to equalize outcomes is in the smaller amount of resources devoted to the schooling of lower-class and minority children than to the children of the white elite or middle class. But my argument is that, even if resources are equal or greater for minorities, the relationship between teacher and student is apparently such that average outcomes among groups would still not be equal at the end of primary school. Reform for achieving this new type of equality of opportunity has concentrated on increasing resources to ghetto schools. Michelson implies that, unless the tax base for financing schooling is drastically altered, resource equality will not be achieved. My essay, in addition to the discouraging evaluations of the early 1960s,[10] indicates that, even if resources *are* equalized, the resource compensation strategy is unlikely to succeed.

What, then, is the way out? Society is influenced and to a large degree controlled by an elite with certain norms. Those norms are

[10]See Thomas Ribich, *Education and Poverty* (Washington: Brookings Institution, 1968).

accepted by a high percentage of the populace. The economic, political, and cultural institutions of the society are built on hierarchical models that suit the needs of the elite, although in the case of the United States, they have also managed to provide a high material consumption to most of the population. On the edges of the elite and among the masses, dissatisfied groups begin to attack this system, all seeking to liberate themselves from the hierarchical norms of the elite, but varying greatly in their needs and demands. The schools, as the primary instrument in transmitting American mythology and elite hierarchical models to the masses, are a major focal point of attack by these groups.

The attack is on the *structure* of the schools, to change drastically the form and/or the content of what is taught.

In a more general framework, we see two significant challenges to the existing social order. First, there are demands that the schools satisfy their rhetorical goals of providing equal educational opportunities (read as equal educational outcomes) for all groups in the society, rich and poor, black and white, Chicano and Anglo. This objective has implications for the financing, heterogeneity of enrollments, and educational offering of the schools. Second, the schools are being pressured to be client-oriented rather than professionally oriented, child-centered rather than adult-centered. This goal has implications for the number and nature of alternatives that must be available to satisfy the needs of students with substantially different talents, personalities, abilities, and interests.[11]

The accent that different groups put on these challenges is very different: equal outcomes are primarily the concern of those who perceive themselves at the bottom of the hierarchy—the blacks and Mexican-Americans. Client-orientation is a pressure coming from white upper-middle-income parents who are alienated from the general goals of the society and, specifically, from the rules and regulations laid down by school boards and professional educators in the district to implement those goals in the schools. Minority groups are usually conservative toward what is taught in the schools, even though they may demand changes in the composition of school boards so that their children can have an equal chance to go to a university. A clear separation has to be made between the demand to be able to make it

[11]Henry M. Levin, *An Economic Analysis of Education Vouchers* (in process, 1971), chap. 1.

in the system as it is and the demand to change the goals, objectives, and structure of the whole system.

Most blacks and browns are demanding that the schools make them more *employable* in the present economic structure; that they make them more suitable for dependency status in that structure. Much of the community-control movement, which Henry M. Levin describes in his contribution, fits into the challenge of equal school outcomes: blacks and browns believe correctly that white Anglo control has created schools in which their children *cannot* do as well as those of the controlling interest; therefore, control is essential to equal opportunity to learn in the schools. "Control," however, is a tricky, many-leveled word. Where blacks have gained control of the boards of ghetto schools, for example, they have found that they do not control the state legislature, which distributes state aid to education and sets curriculum and other requirements. But even if blacks could get equal funds out of the legislature, even if they could alter curriculum, even if they could produce equal outcomes through community control, Michelson and I must argue that they still would not control the economy and the requirements for jobs. They would remain dependent for the definition of social roles on a society that has continually ensured them the bottom rung on its ladder.

Levin counters this argument by pointing out the important psychological effects of winning at least some control over one's own destiny, especially for a people who have been oppressed during their entire history in this country. Political and social learning as a result of community control may not be the end point of a liberation period, but the beginning of something much more extensive and profound. This depends on who controls the community-control movement. Cooptation by establishment blacks and Chicanos would ensure that the building of self-identity and the use of the schools for real community social change and political development would be subverted to the needs of the corporate structure. In that case, blacks and browns would successfully maintain their undesirable social roles through their "own" school boards. The results of community control of schools, then, are inexorably tied to the dependency of the community on decisions presently out of its control.

High-income whites, on the other hand, have controlled school boards since the centralization of schools at the turn of the century.

Alienation within this group, when it occurs, is not concerned with opportunity but with the *meaning* of opportunity. To this segment of the affluent, liberation means rejecting the employment mentality, rejecting the accouterments of success, and rejecting the concept that increasing complexity and technification of society is progress. In no sense is this liberation of any higher level or in any way more profound than the demand to control the community school. Both are struggles for freedom.

The "free schools" are the result of this white "liberation." The cost to parents of experimenting with new educational forms is hardly high; surrounded by a learning environment outside the school, parents and children can always change their minds and be successful in the traditional ways. Although no real research has been done on what happens to children after they leave the free schools, the desired result is to increase their propensity to choose life rather than death.[12] This choice would manifest itself in the ways in which an individual works and lives, especially in the relations he has with those around him, as well as the kinds of products and services he produces and consumes. Since our affluent society allows for considerable variance in behavior as long as it poses no threat to the established order, free school graduates (and others) can presently reject the employment scene and live simple and fulfilling lives. Not surprisingly, having parents who disapprove of super-consumption and having been in a free school rather than public school environment apparently makes this transition to life less painful. But we will not understand the impact of free schools on American culture for a long time.

As is the case with community control, however, the full impact of free schooling in the experimental and innovative form described by Bonnie Barrett Stretch and Philip Brenner may never be felt. Already, public schools are incorporating elements of free-school style into the traditional classroom. Silberman's infatuation with the North Dakota "experiment" of child-oriented classrooms as the solution to our schooling problem shows the direction that professional educators may take to maintain control.[13] Children can un-

---

[12]Eric Fromm, *The Revolution of Hope* (New York: Harper & Row, 1970).

[13]Charles Silberman, *Crisis in the Classroom* (New York: Random House, 1970).

doubtedly gain as a result of North Dakota-type schools, with their sensitized teachers and more joyful atmosphere, but the end result will still be competitive achievement tests[14] and socialization into corporate society. Nevertheless, incorporating such state-controlled changes into public schools will undoubtedly slow the growth of free schooling.

How far public schools can go in coopting Brenner's minischool concept is more difficult to predict. A social studies-oriented curriculum that questions the entire institutional structure may generate an individual politization which contradicts the whole basis for present public schools. The "usual" free school is supposed to develop a more sensitive person, at best ready to commit social change through, in the words of David Harris, "revolutionary love."[15] But the minischool graduate is to be trained to question all structures in terms of fulfilling human needs and, if necessary, to build new ones in their place. The demands of high school students for relevant social studies material have already resulted in some curricular changes, but the use of this new material is carefully controlled by public school employees. In the minischool, students are encouraged to go beyond the teacher's control in their quest for innovative reconstruction. For the minischool, obsolescence may come from a different direction: the student and community-control movements may make the minischool obsolete by destroying the present structure of the schools.

The voucher plan would make all these experiments (community control, free school, minischool, Minot, North Dakota, etc.) possible. The article by Judith Areen and Christopher Jencks differs from the others in this section in that it presents an alternative *financial* arrangement for American schooling, rather than a structural change in the schools themselves. Vouchers would decentralize control of the schools and would allow families to satisfy their own tastes. For the majority of the population, socialized to believe in material success, achievement scores, and as much formal schooling as you can

---

[14]Minot, North Dakota (the site of the state experimental schools) children are already being tested to compare their test results with children in traditional schools. The main concern of the parents is whether their children are learning, i.e., scoring high on achievement tests.

[15]Address at Stanford University, March 24, 1971.

get, vouchers will change little in the schools except, possibly, average achievement. Schools that have to compete for pupils on the basis of such scores will be even more inclined to teach children how to take exams, rather than teach them to love learning. Nevertheless, the voucher system will greatly encourage experimentation for those seeking liberation from the traditional structure.

Vouchers have been criticized by everyone. The reasons behind the fears of professional educators and teachers' unions are obvious, but radicals also come out against vouchers because they fear a takeover of the schools by big corporations. Some evidence exists of economies of scale that would make large schools more profitable to run than moderately small schools, but the evidence is not overwhelming.[16] Why would "chain schools" be run any more efficiently, given parental involvement, complaints, pressures, etc., than the state school systems are run now? This does not mean that private corporations will not enter the school business. In many instances they are already involved directly; indirectly, as the radicals should recognize most of all, they control the ideology and output of the system. The voucher plan is counterrevolutionary in the sense that it dispels radical change of the whole school system. On the other hand, given the conditions of U.S. society, it may provide the best means to give financial stimulation to black and brown community schools and free schools, all struggling for independence.

As has been pointed out again and again in this introduction, however, all these solutions must be regarded as second-bests. No alteration of the school structure can be divorced from the economic and social structures of the society in which the change takes place. The last two essays in this collection present their solutions in this integrated context. Ivan Illich calls for the total abolishment of schools. I once asked Illich why he picked on the schools rather than other institutions in the society which were equally pernicious in their dehumanization. He answered that the schools are so beyond criticism and have become so essential to the ritual of the modern pyramidal social structure that his choice fell to them. Illich's piece should be read understanding that reasoning. Abolition of formal schooling with its hierarchy of degrees, bias against *learning* and

---

[16]See Stephan Michelson, "Economics in the Courts: Equal School Resource Allocation," mimeographed, June 1971.

toward *teaching*, and socialization into lifetime dependency, means to Illich the abolition of overmodernized, overspecialized, and over-mystified society. Illich believes in man; modern society does not. It is not a military, dictatorial society that Illich is criticizing. It is liberal, pluralistic "democracy." Modern, dehumanizing capital-intensive technology, the corporate form, and universal schooling are all products of England and America, among the freest societies the world has ever known (according to English and American history books). In the name of increasing consumption per capita, the United States has exported these structures all over the world, helping local elites destroy whatever alternatives might have arisen from the un-schooled—and therefore incompetent—masses.

Cuba is not deschooling education, but it is one of the few countries of the world to attempt drastic changes in its education system as part of revolutionary changes in its society. Cuba is accomplishing this by converting schools from places to gain social status to places to learn skills and socialist ideology. In addition, there is a strong element of using the schools to eliminate the dichotomy between learning and work: children in school—especially high school students—spend part of the school year performing productive tasks. Schooling (training) has been distributed much more equitably by greatly ex-panding rural schools relative to urban. Adult education, a necessary part of spreading revolutionary ideology, has all but eliminated illit-eracy. In line with Illich's argument that it is possible to give decent health care, literacy, and nutritional requirements to everyone in the world today without any increase in per capita expenditures on edu-cation,[17] Cuba has attempted to deprofessionalize tasks to make the study of medicine, agronomy, engineering, etc. possible for a much higher percentage of the population.

Nevertheless, Bowles says that this process of reducing elitism in the schools has been slower than the liberation and income-distribu-tion objectives of the Cuban revolution would dictate. In order to meet economic growth objectives, more accent has been put on tech-nical training, and technical schools still retain elite status. In addi-tion, the revolutionary change in education has not taken place primarily *within* the schools but in the distribution of education be-

[17]Ivan Illich, "Outwitting the 'Developed' Countries," *New York Review of Books*, 6 November 1969.

tween schools and other educational forms. Thus, the hierarchical relation of students to teacher is for the most part maintained in the school classroom, but time is now allocated to collective study periods with student teachers. Less time is spent by the teacher on socialization and this socialization has been moved to summer camps and to youth organizations. The hierarchical structure of the classroom is apparently not amenable to the formation of the collective society, while other structures are.

Bowles' essay raises many important questions about alternative schooling in the United States. Does the philosophy of schooling represented by the free schools produce an individual who loves man but prefers to remain outside all institutional structures? Should educational structures be inherently different in affluent societies from those that require discipline—either collective or individual—for economic growth? Is socialization by the schools bad per se, even within a rigid structure, or is it the *particular kind* of socialization in the schools today which must be changed? Is the *structure* of school inacceptable or is it the *control* of the school? What happens in a society in which some groups in the population are development-minded and others are liberation-minded? Is that the pattern in the United States today? What kind of economic and social structure will allow both or either of these objectives to be maximized?

These questions should be kept in mind in reading the volume. The reader should not count on finding in it definitive plans to save the United States, or even more modestly, American education. Rather, it brings together some recent thinking on education and educational research by social scientists and educators. The essays are not answers, but analyses and ideas. Their main purpose is to stimulate the pursuit of these ideas beyond their present boundaries and constraints.

I

Schooling and Equal Opportunity

SHUT UP AND LEARN, KID!

'INTO THE BUS, OFF THE BUS, INTO THE BUS, OFF THE BUS — MAN, WHAT AN EDUCATION!'

A. SOCIAL MOBILITY

.1. *The Channeling Colony*

MARCUS G. RASKIN

AT ANY one time there are 55 million Americans in school, higher school, lower school, universities. What are they learning? Is it truth, beauty, scientific method to relate apparently unrelated phenomena, facts, wisdom and knowledge? Is it preparation for the next higher academic level? Or are these 55 million in the channeling process for more profound purposes which appear as the trivia of life, but which in effect structure the political, social, and economic order? On all levels in the school, whether public or private, progressive or traditional, the young person is expected to learn the *basic* economic and political lessons which the modern nation-state teaches and requires so that it may remain authoritarian and pyramidal. The school thus serves as the training instrument for the state. The substance of what is learned—Plato, zoology, *Silas Marner*, quadratics, woodwork, and music appreciation—is less indelible in the young person's mind than other lessons which are taught and internalized. The student is taught and usually learns the importance of identification papers, records, tardy slips, no whispering to your neighbor, the acceptable dress, signatures, forms, and tests. He comes to learn and respect the idea that in the colonized society authority dictates and individuals internalize the notion that papers are more important than the person himself. The physical and mental refugee of the twentieth century, whether he is trying to get out of a concentration camp, prison, hospital, school, or corporation, knows that the papers about himself are the key to his being and to his escape. Papers are the means by which the modern state says that every individual's place in the world depends on the authorized organs of the state. There is a German phrase which makes clear the nature of this state authoritarianism on the individual: "Unless your life is certified with official stamp and seal, let me tell you, brother, it's a tough and dirty deal."[1]

Persons without citizenship papers do not exist, nor do people without passports. Stamps of approval are necessary from the colonizing agencies in the body politic for personal existence. Through keeping records and issuing papers, Authority legitimates *its* power. The individual is hounded by the relentless memory of the strokes which others have made of him for purposes of reinforcing colonized relationships. It is the task of the school to prepare and involve the student in such a relationship.

In school, students are readied for adult life through the synthetic process of tension with themselves about whom they are supposed to be in the pyramid. They are in dialectic with their records and profiles, which they come to believe are the definition of who they are. Since record-keeping and profiles do not describe the subjective feeling and potentiality of people, even if that is what such records say, and since the records and profile are to serve the needs of the authority system and describe where such an individual might fit (court fool, house radical, etc.), the young are taught bad faith. Students are urged to fulfill an achievement profile of themselves which is primarily derived from requirements and functions set by the colonizer's needs. Although the needs of the colonized system may be tempered by the interests and learning of the student, the standards applied to students which then become their profile are more accurately the reflection and descriptive judgment of the needs of standards which the colonies require. But even knowing that the records and papers of a system tell us more about the system than the people who are stamped with them, the student seems unable to escape the image created for him—as him—through the hierarchic other.

The profile is the young's mocking shadow of the individual which pursues him and ultimately dictates his being. The student accepts the intrusion of "measurement" of his self made known to him by the

---

[1]John K. Dickenson, *German and Jew* (New York: Quadrangle Press, 1967), p. 194.

colonizer. Schools continue this process by creating barriers to reinforce the "soundness" of the objective measure or profile that is created for the individual. (For example, the track system, "basic" subjects, etc. as a way of typing a young person for life.) Children in a colonized world find themselves on the bed of Procrustes through administrative determinations which are based on considerations they are not expected to know or to be cognizant of. They are expected to be tools of forces that they cannot see, understand, or control. They are not supposed to know, for example, that poor textbooks in most schools are related to arrangements of convenience between book manufacturers and the bureaucracy of a school system. Or the issue of record-keeping of the child or student may be related to having bought a computer which is only economic if it is operating continuously at some record-keeping task! The last concern is the child.

Two forces pertain. The individual student is in school for reasons not relevant to himself as a person, and he generally learns things not relevant to him or to a subject matter that one would want to know. And, he learns that he is now secondary to the records and profiles about himself. His personal insecurity is intensified because of the dissonance he feels between what he believes himself to be and wants, and what others want or expect of him from pressures which they believe are on *them*. They are slaves to the hierarchic other which becomes part of themselves.

Needless to say, such determination by the pyramidal system is the individual's impediment to self-definition and control of his future within the limits and boundaries which he consciously and freely sets with others. Thus, the school as a colonizing function is important for what is *informally* learned. The student learns that others, who have little interest in him and no lasting human relationship with him, set standards, rewards, and payoffs for him. As he gets older, personality and achievement tests are taken with him as the object, which may decide his job, whether he goes into the army, whether he qualifies for places that then have their standards, qualifications, and records. Officials of the profile system readily admit the meaningless or cynical nature of tests and records. It is not unusual for the professor and the education administrator to say that grades don't matter while using grades as their sole criterion for judging when they are asked for recommendations. Of course, this situation makes the student's position even more ambiguous and intolerable.

Take a more profound and homologous case. Children are taught and told by their parents and caretakers what to do and what not to do in terms that are clearly for the good of the children. "Don't touch the hot stove, don't run in the street," etc. are the bases for acting forcefully with the child to limit the possibility of certain physical injury if the event occurs. This system of telling carries over into the general structure of how the child relates on all other matters which have to do with the interest of the authority or the colony. This process is seen in the classroom early in the grades.

Before he gets to school the child begins to find out about life by testing limits. The teacher and other school authorities become the arbiters and interpreters of these limits. They can give pleasure or pain, anxiety or approbation to the student. Thus, a very subtle game begins. The bright student and the dull student may find themselves dissembling or faking their understanding in return for approbation. (This system of relationships tends to bad faith—that is, the acceptance of role or function even though the person views that function as mad or meaningless.) Both of them may become expert at the system of mock understanding and knowing how to internalize dumbness so that they will more easily accept the hierarchic other and end up colonized.

John Holt, in his brilliant book *How Children Fail*, gives examples of the strategy of faking. The teacher asks a question. The child raises his hand when others do, making believe that he knows the answer, hoping and betting on the laws of chance that he won't get called on. If someone else is called on he will have appeared to have known the answer in the mind of the teacher and his classmates. The child may become a body and lip reader, guessing what the teacher is answering in the question she or he is asking. The student watches the teacher's lips to see if she is giving the right answer.[2] (Of course the great teacher could teach probability theory and lip reading to his students from the strategy of teacher-student faking!) However, the unspoken interest of the channeling system is to get children to think defensively in terms of tests, right answers, or neatness per se.

[2]John Holt, *How Children Fail* (New York: Delta Books, 1964).

Other values such as creativity or analysis from student-formulated assumptions are eschewed because they cannot be easily contained in the pyramidal authority since the values and facts created from that social structure would come under scrutiny. Children learn and are taught an operational language or command and instruction, then in defense they attempt to create a private language for self and friend.

Once the student accepts the school treadmill, profilism,[3] and the informal lessons of the pyramidal structure, he usually finds that to survive he must become a master at the strategy of faking or totally internalize the channeling colony's view of where he will fit into the colonized reailty. The price of the student internalizing the system's profile and expectation as mediated through the schools is very costly

[3]Since the society is enmeshed in the fact of investigator and investigated, one is no longer giving away his external self, but his very being, which comes to mean the external actions of the other to my colonized being. Since 1966, an important issue on records has occupied the attention of various members of Congress and the technocratic/bureaucratic part of the academic community. Carl Kaysen, the director of the Institute for Advanced Study, has argued for the importance of a centralized data-gathering center which in his mind would *not* include police dossiers, FBI reports, and personal records. According to his Task Force Report, the "center would assemble in a single facility all large-scale systematic bodies of demographic, economic and social data generated by the present collection of administrative processes of the federal government—integrate the data to the maximum feasible extent, and in such a way as to preserve as much as possible of the original information content of the whole body of records, and provide ready access to the information, within the laws governing disclosure, to all users of the government, and where appropriate to qualified users outside the government on suitable compensatory terms." (Carl Kaysen, "Data Banks and Dossiers," *Public Interest*, no. 7 (Spring 1967): 52–61.)

Kaysen's theory is that the present statistics do not help us make informed judgments about policy questions because they are spread about in dislocated and decentralized form. While he advocates greater centralization of data about people, he does not see the centralization of data as an extension of the principle of centralization of people. Unfortunately, the control mechanisms in a colonized society are related to welfare and education as well as the police. Invariably, all these functions are intertwined. Consequently, the assurances of the technocrat that he does not want to use the information for control purposes misses the point of what amounts to control in modern life. Furthermore, there is a certain amount of Pollyanna thinking which goes into an analysis that believes that data will protect along the lines one assumes in his proposal. An idea for change must be understood within a historical, political context. While efficiency of material-gathering may appear in and of itself to be good, and may help the technocrats in their rise to political power, the fact is that within the context of a pyramidal state where emphasis is on stability and control, mechanisms attending proposals such as Kaysen's add to the momentum of authoritarianism. In this sense, his idea fits as an attempt to rationalize the vertical structure.

since the young person is in danger of giving up the choices and projects he can potentially initiate through his own doing or in association with others. Under the theory of delayed payoff (study hard to get the good job or get to graduate school), the young person is mortgaging his future to activities of the pyramid from which he cannot easily extricate himself. The choices are not his but rather those structured for him.

There is a further irony in these matters. The student may fail at what the school wants him to be. Indeed, it may expel him even though he attempts to stifle his own sense of doing and intends to internalize the authority's purposes in himself to the extent that he is prepared to seek actively or imbibe supinely what the system wants and demands of him. For example, young people who are creative attempt to get Ph.D.s. They swallow hard the arid academism of the classroom and find that they fail at turning themselves over to the colony either because the schools don't want them for economic reasons—too many Ph.Ds—or the field of knowledge they have undertaken would be "poorly" served if the potential Ph.D. or high school diplomate graduated. The result is that the person, on any level, may now accept the results of what is given about him by others and is conditioned to attempt to meet the "standards" which the channeling system requires of him.

Until recently the phrases, "Is it going down on your record?" or "Don't spoil your record" were enough to strike horror in the hearts of the young. The schools, corporations, and the state needed the records to know whom to reward and whom to punish. The young believed, and it was true in one framework, that they were giving up their chance at success if they did not bend to the will of the colonizing structure. Whole systems of organization and knowledge were to be predicated on the acceptance by the young of this pyramidal structure. The young were to learn that by accepting this system they would be giving away more than their external selves.

In first seeing the pervasiveness of channeling in Western industrialized society, I thought that this system was the way in which the young were initiated to the secrets of the industrial culture. However, the industrial system seems to be the exact opposite of ancient rites of initiation. In the ancient rite the individual attained the status of human being. There was a change in his existential condition because the basis of his culture, its guiding purposes and myths were revealed to him in a profoundly religious and basic way. As a result of what was revealed to him, the individual was able to locate his place in the cosmos. He found himself to be rooted in that cosmos. The person became another—a whole person. The situation is profoundly different in an industrial culture. Nothing is revealed to the individual and the possibility of his wholeness is explicitly denied through the Channeling Colony where the individual learns that he is to see himself functionally in the performance of a specialized series of tasks. Records, profiles, and identity papers help the individual to make the adjustment to the anti-initiatory rite of seeing himself as less than a human being.

Even the Jews who have attempted to maintain some meaning in initiatory rites find that they are unable to withstand the pressures of profilism. There is a humorous story about a Jewish boy of thirteen at his Bar Mitzvah. Historically, the act of Bar Mitzvah signified the transformation of a boy into a man. His responsibilities and place among the Jews were revealed to him at that time. When this thirteen-year-old boy gives his Bar Mitzvah speech, he says—presumably because of all the gifts he has received—"Ladies and gentlemen, today I am a fountain pen." Taken literally, the boy is saying: Today I have become a tool, an instrument in the hands of others. I have been characterized into something other than I am which I have no relationship to. (Obviously, there are psychosexual aspects to the story as well as that of the Jewish emphasis on learning as a trade, but they are secondary.) I have left my place as a human being to become a thing, the very reverse of ancient rites of initiation.

Politically, there are ways of changing profilism and of controverting the process whereby "selves" are reduced to "things." On the university level, which must now be viewed as a *body politic*, students would begin to organize against testing, grading and record keeping. In the Middle Ages the peasants demanded that records related to their serfdom and their reduction into property be burned. From such demands new movements emerged which gave rise to the roots of Anabaptist and Mennonite thought. They set the stage for the reassertion of individual meaning and conscience which unite the prophetic spirit with the social gospel.

In the Channeling Colony, students are essentially in the same position as the peasants of the Middle Ages. While somewhat unbecoming, parents of middle-class children may find themselves demanding that records about their children be destroyed, since they are an impediment to the idea of teaching and the freedom of the child. Parents and children, as well as older students, will come to see that the power of the pyramidal structure is in the records kept by it, and in the controls which it exercises through the profiles it creates of others. Another's idea of the young person's being may be his occupation, but it dares not dictate the fate of the young person.

Is there a way to decolonize from the present structure of the school? Let us continue with the example of records and testing. When we analyze cheating[4] and cooperating, we find that it does not take a great leap in imagination to see that behaviorally such actions may be the same. The difference is the attitude brought to the relationship and the fact that the individual's motive is thought by him to be irrelevant. (This sense of irrelevance can only be changed through externally changing the person's sense of guilt, which the person feels because of his dissonance with an apparently "correct" external value.) Generally, students cheat because they have internalized the values of the hierarchic other. Thus, they use the system's methods of dealing with that failure. The individual senses the stupidity of what he is expected to know and then acts in bad faith by committing actions which reinforce the values of the system as they are. His guilt is most likely a political one. He accepted the colonizer's conception of himself as the student who is to be trained to be an opportunistic individual who cannot work with or borrow from another.

By professors, students, and campus ministers arguing and engaging the school in a dialogue which makes clear that the university is not concerned with awarding place for the army or corporation—that is, the vertical structure—but is interested in knowledge and inquiry per se, they engage the vertical organization in the humane purpose of transforming itself into achieving community and cooperation in scholarship. Their political stand will change scholarship so that it fulfills the purpose of inquiry. If such a challenge is successful, the university will be impeded in its attempts to fulfill an external colonizing purpose which requires the awarding of status and place. An example of this limited success was the Columbia Student Movement,

---

[4]Cheating is not faking.

forcing that university to drop its plans for building a gym for itself at the living expense of the Harlem residents. Another was the MIT administration's suspending work on certain war research contracts.

If the schools did not grade and profilize youngsters for the corporation and the state, competitive relationships would give way to the practice of free inquiry in which students would borrow and learn from one another in groups, projects and experimentation. Consequently, they would be able to concentrate on the new practice of building community schools rather than acting as winnower and sifter of personnel for the corporate hierarchic machine or the state.

FROM CHANNELING COLONY TO EDUCATING SOCIETY

When we begin to think about the purpose and utility of the modern school, whether it is elementary, high school, or college, we must be aware of the functions it serves which are not immediately apparent. Besides acting as a control mechanism, compulsory attendance "frees" a parent from worry about the child during a six- or seven-hour period. In that period, the parents may work or engage in other activities. This is not a bad thing. It is only to say that there are many motivations for school. As Philippe Aries has pointed out, the historical justification for the school in Catholic countries was to teach morals to the young who were influenced by their parents in the ways of the profane. The children were taken out of the home to learn the ABC's of morality.[5]

The moral criterion is no longer applicable since the definitions of who or what is moral seem to be under scrutiny by the children rather than the adults or the schools. Schools and adults have lost their authority to set out the basis of moral definitions and limits; that is, they are no longer believed just because authority says so. Once the mock definitions of morality are broken because of this onslaught on authority (knowing your opportunity, and minding your p's and q's in the way the Channeling Colony laid out the framework of the p's and q's) we are left with other justifications for the school that are real but not as "high-minded." An economic justification remains.

[5]Philippe Aries, *Centuries of Childhood* (New York: Vintage, 1965).

It is the accepted dictum that the more children there are in school, the smaller will be the burden on the economic system for jobs which it might be unable to provide or give training for. The hope is that the longer people remain in school the likelihood is that they will someday be able to get jobs because of their education. There may now be evidence to suggest that this view is merely myth, for while it may be correct in the particular, it no longer seems to hold true as a general practice because of the profound shifts in requirements of the society. So long as there is stability in the society, what is needed seems set in concrete. Where the goals are no longer determined and the structures themselves are under attack, the jobs that one plans for appear foolish. Thus, the screening and channeling which the school may do for the corporate system is no longer a viable function in its own terms as the economic basis of the society comes under scrutiny and profound change.

Once the Channeling Colony begins to deteriorate as a well-oiled machine because there might be too many children in school, or the authority systems in the school are under challenge because the knowledges taught seem empty as compared to what can be learned informally and by personal experience, the brightest children reject the school and the sorts of education that would lead them to the Plantation Colony. They begin to use the society as a place to study and change, rejecting the more contented idea of their parents and the authorities that the school and learning in it are for the purpose of mediating oneself into a priori notions of what "reality" demands. Children and their teachers begin to act on the basis of what they see, the contradiction between the schools (higher and lower) as a place to learn and what goes on becomes virtually impossible to contain in the old structures. Perhaps because of the great social movements of the 1960s, the civil rights movement, the attempt on the part of some educators to recapture the idea of spontaneity in education, certain truths were rediscovered by children, students, and teachers. These truths, when acted upon, subvert the framework of the Channeling Colony with its extrinsic rewards and delayed payoff assumptions. It is no longer possible to deny the obvious.

A child or person who wants to learn and think does so either in isolation or in discourse and play with friends and adults whom he respects. Persons use private moments in the bathtub or on the toilet to explore questions that are important to subjective understanding.

It is in such situations that a person turns questions over in his mind and considers avenues of investigation and thought. For a child the experience of learning is in the context of play and playfulness. The child learns physical and mental activities, language and walking, in an atmosphere of love and self-testing and personal experimentation. He tests his being in the world. He finds what is useful to him, to his parents and peers by this system of testing. In his play where rules emerge between himself and others they are of the kind that he accepts because he enjoys the activity that the rules make possible, as in checkers or marbles.

In games such as tag football he believes that the actions are negotiable. Consequently, he undertakes to negotiate the actions on the field against the rules. Before his beside himself is developed the child learns and attempts to find his being in the world through love and rule making which flows from the activity he undertakes. Such activities can have useful content. Where children and young people are organized in terms of tasks which they learn about and work at in the community, the malaise of not having "something to do" or feeling useful could become unknown. Real work and learning—not mock disciplined work as in many Montessori schools—becomes an attainable and immediate activity where results are felt in children's time.

Given this measure as the standard of how to learn, it is no surprise to note that the schools are utterly incapable of providing this framework. In the last decade the breakdown of the schools (except in terms of offering anything but the sort of "excellence" which was required to beat the Russians to the moon) generated considerable discussion of innovation. They included massive doses of federal legislation and money which were to shore up the Channeling Colony. The practical result of this interest was an increase in jobs for those with guidance and other social-control training. It also meant the extension of the economic corporation into the field of "education." Such firms as Xerox and Time-Life undertook to get a piece of the education market with government funds. In this process they undertook to challenge the school bureaucracies and administrators who saw a challenge to their power from teachers who know equipment, and from equipment that might need different (or no) teachers. But little changed for the students except that they became pawns in the struggle between the old administrators, the new learning technique people, and the young Peace Corps-type idealist. The fundamental institutional result of those efforts has been to build the importance of the school within the community as a central place for the teaching of hierarchy, competition, and submissiveness to the young while serving as an employment and opportunity market for adults not otherwise gainfully employed.[6] These opportunities are not very meaningful to the young. The schools still remain the encapsulating instrument against them—especially in the cities.

There are ways of turning schools around. We might begin by changing the "have to" quality of them by repealing the compulsory attendance laws. These laws operate to keep the children in line, off the streets, and out of the factories and teach them how to be punctual and deny to their parents the right of educating their young in the way they choose. That is to say, the compulsory laws are an instrument to rationalize pyramidal discipline in the body politic.

There is no need for compulsory attendance of children when parents and children (as they get older) agree upon what a child is supposed to know after a certain length of time. Parents and those nominated as "teachers of the community" would work through a program for children which the parents could join as aides and resources. Parents and teachers would prepare materials and places where the child could learn what was mutually agreed upon for and with the child. In this situation, the school would merely be an occasional meeting place but not the place where a child is expected to learn. The teachers of the community would be paid by the community either to organize much smaller new schools, start neighborhood science library centers where small groups of children could attach themselves, and prepare teaching plans and materials to show how quickly and thoroughly

[6]During this period I served as a member of the Panel on Educational Research and Development. I first suggested that the universities should take over the schools in the cities on a contract basis from the local boards of education. They would be responsible to local boards of parents. Thus the schools of New York City (Manhattan) or other cities where there were great universities would operate the schools, setting up curriculum with the parents who would be on school boards—one or two schools to a board. I had hoped that this would have the effect of bringing back the whites into the public school system while at the same time offering an exciting radical educational experience for children. I had hoped that education by such a system would not necessarily mean merely educating for the next rung in the ladder, although this was a naive view on my part. On the other hand, the idea itself very quickly came to be changed until it was unrecognizable in practice.

areas of knowledge can be taught to children. The teachers of the community would work out of a school or television station, a cooperative house of young people who gave up on family life, a university, art gallery, and would serve to organize learning and action experiences to show children how to bring about change in the society while comprehending and appreciating nature. Their classroom would be the institutions of the society and the natural phenomena of life.

.2. Unequal Education and the Reproduction of the Social Division of Labor*

SAMUEL BOWLES

THE IDEOLOGICAL defense of modern capitalist society rests heavily on the assertion that the equalizing effects of education can counter the disequalizing forces inherent in the free-market system. That educational systems in capitalist societies have been highly unequal is generally admitted and widely condemned. Yet educational inequalities are taken as passing phenomena, holdovers from an earlier, less enlightened era, which are rapidly being eliminated.

The record of educational history in the United States, and scrutiny of the present state of our colleges and schools, lend little support to this comforting optimism. Rather, the available data suggest an alternative interpretation. In what follows I argue (1) that schools have evolved in the United States not as part of a pursuit of equality, but rather to meet the needs of capitalist employers for a disciplined and skilled labor force, and to provide a mechanism for social control in the interests of political stability; (2) that as the economic importance of skilled and well-educated labor has grown, inequalities in the school system have become increasingly important in reproducing the class structure from one generation to the next; (3) that the U.S. school system is pervaded by class inequalities, which have shown little

*Many of the ideas in this essay have been worked out jointly with Herbert Gintis and other members of the Harvard seminar of the Union for Radical Political Economics. I am grateful to them and to Janice Weiss and Christopher Jencks for their help.

sign of diminishing over the last half century; and (4) that the evidently unequal control over school boards and other decision-making bodies in education does not provide a sufficient explanation of the persistence and pervasiveness of inequalities in the school system. Although the unequal distribution of political power serves to maintain inequalities in education, the origins of these inequalities are to be found outside the political sphere, in the class structure itself and in the class subcultures typical of capitalist societies. Thus, unequal education has its roots in the very class structure which it serves to legitimize and reproduce. Inequalities in education are part of the web of capitalist society, and are likely to persist as long as capitalism survives.

THE EVOLUTION OF CAPITALISM AND THE RISE OF MASS EDUCATION

In colonial America, and in most pre-capitalist societies of the past, the basic productive unit was the family. For the vast majority of male adults, work was self-directed, and was performed without direct supervision. Though constrained by poverty, ill health, the low level of technological development, and occasional interferences by the political authorities, a man had considerable leeway in choosing his working hours, what to produce, and how to produce it. While great inequalities in wealth, political power, and other aspects of status normally existed, differences in the degree of autonomy in work were relatively minor, particularly when compared with what was to come.

Transmitting the necessary productive skills to the children as they grew up proved to be a simple task, not because the work was devoid of skill, but because the quite substantial skills required were virtually unchanging from generation to generation, and because the transition to the world of work did not require that the child adapt to a wholly new set of social relationships. The child learned the concrete skills and adapted to the social relations of production through learning by doing within the family. Preparation for life in the larger community was facilitated by the child's experience with the extended family, which shaded off without distinct boundaries, through uncles and fourth cousins, into the community. Children learned early how to deal with complex relationships among adults other than their parents, and children other than their brothers and sisters.[1]

Children were not required to learn a complex set of political principles or ideologies, as political participation was limited and political authority unchallenged, at least in normal times. The only major socializing institution outside the family was the church, which sought to inculcate the accepted spiritual values and attitudes. In addition, a small number of children learned craft skills outside the family, as apprentices. The role of schools tended to be narrowly vocational, restricted to preparation of children for a career in the church or the still inconsequential state bureaucracy.[2] The curriculum of the few universities reflected the aristocratic penchant for conspicuous intellectual consumption.[3]

The extension of capitalist production, and particularly the factory system, undermined the role of the family as the major unit of both socialization and production. Small peasant farmers were driven off the land or competed out of business. Cottage industry was destroyed. Ownership of the means of production became heavily concentrated in the hands of landlords and capitalists. Workers relinquished control over their labor in return for wages or salaries. Increasingly, production was carried on in large organizations in which a small management group directed the work activities of the entire labor force. The social relations of production—the authority structure, the prescribed types of behavior and response characteris-

[1]This account draws upon two important historical studies: P. Aries, *Centuries of Childhood* (New York: Vintage, 1965); and B. Bailyn, *Education in the Forming of American Society* (Chapel Hill: University of North Carolina Press, 1960). Also illuminating are anthropological studies of education in contemporary pre-capitalist societies. See, for example, J. Kenyatta, *Facing Mount Kenya* (New York: Vintage Books, 1962) pp. 95–124. See also Edmund S. Morgan, *The Puritan Family: Religion and Domestic Relations in Seventeenth Century New England* (New York: Harper and Row, 1966).

[2]Aries, *Centuries of Childhood.* In a number of places, e.g., Scotland and Massachusetts, schools stressed literacy so as to make the Bible more widely accessible. See C. Cipolla, *Literacy and Economic Development* (Baltimore: Penguin Books, 1969); and Morgan, *Puritan Family,* chap. 4. Morgan quotes a Massachusetts law of 1647 which provided for the establishment of reading schools because it was "one chief project of that old deluder, Satan, to keep men from knowledge of the Scriptures."

[3]H. F. Kearney, *Scholars and Gentlemen: Universities and Society in Pre-Industrial Britain* (Ithaca, N.Y.: Cornell University Press, 1971).

tic of the work place—became increasingly distinct from those of the family.

The divorce of the worker from control over production—from control over his own labor—is particularly important in understanding the role of schooling in capitalist societies. The resulting social division of labor—between controllers and controlled—is a crucial aspect of the class structure of capitalist societies, and will be seen to be an important barrier to the achievement of social-class equality in schooling.

Rapid economic change in the capitalist period led to frequent shifts of the occupational distribution of the labor force, and constant changes in the skill requirements for jobs. The productive skills of the father were no longer adequate for the needs of the son during his lifetime. Skill training within the family became increasingly inappropriate.

And the family itself was changing. Increased geographic mobility of labor and the necessity for children to work outside the family spelled the demise of the extended family and greatly weakened even the nuclear family.[4] Meanwhile, the authority of the church was questioned by the spread of secular rationalist thinking and the rise of powerful competing groups.

While undermining the main institutions of socialization, the development of the capitalist system created at the same time an environment—both social and intellectual—which would ultimately challenge the political order. Workers were thrown together in oppressive factories, and the isolation which had helped to maintain quiescence in earlier, widely dispersed peasant populations was broken down.[5] With an increasing number of families uprooted from the land, the workers' search for a living resulted in large-scale labor migrations. Transient, even foreign, elements came to constitute a major segment of the population, and began to pose seemingly insurmountable problems of assimilation, integration, and control.[6] In-

[4]See Bailyn, *Education in the Forming of American Society;* N. Smelser, *Social Change in the Industrial Revolution* (Chicago: University of Chicago Press, 1959).

[5]F. Engels and K. Marz, *The Communist Manifesto* (London, England: G. Allen and Unwin, 1951); K. Marx, *The 18th Brumaire of Louis Bonaparte* (New York: International Publishers, 1935).

[6]See, for example, S. Thernstrom, *Poverty and Progress: Social Mobility in a 19th Century City* (Cambridge: Harvard University Press, 1964).

equalities of wealth became more apparent, and were less easily justified and less readily accepted. The simple legitimizing ideologies of the earlier period—the divine right of kings and the divine origin of social rank, for example—fell under the capitalist attack on the royalty and the traditional landed interests. The general broadening of the electorate—first sought by the capitalist class in the struggle against the entrenched interests of the pre-capitalist period—threatened soon to become an instrument for the growing power of the working class. Having risen to political power, the capitalist class sought a mechanism to ensure social control and political stability.[7]

An institutional crisis was at hand. The outcome, in virtually all capitalist countries, was the rise of mass education. In the United States, the many advantages of schooling as a socialization process were quickly perceived. The early proponents of the rapid expansion of schooling argued that education could perform many of the socialization functions that earlier had been centered in the family and, to a lesser extent, in the church.[8] An ideal preparation for factory work was found in the social relations of the school: specifically, in its emphasis on discipline, punctuality, acceptance of authority outside the family, and individual accountability for one's work.[9] The social relations of the school would replicate the social relations of the work place, and thus help young people adapt to the social division of labor. Schools would further lead people to accept the authority of the state and its agents—the teachers—at a young age, in part by

[7]B. Simon, *Studies in the History of Education, 1780-1870,* vol. 1 (London, England: Lawrence and Wishant, 1960).

[8]Bailyn, *Education in the Forming of American Society.*

[9]A manufacturer, writing to the Massachusetts State Board of Education from Lowell in 1841 commented:

> I have never considered mere knowledge . . . as the only advantage derived from a good Common School education. . . . (Workers with more education possess) a higher and better state of morals, are more orderly and respectful in their deportment, and more ready to comply with the wholesome and necessary regulations of an establishment. . . . In times of agitation, on account of some change in regulations or wages, I have always looked to the most intelligent, best educated and the most moral for support. The ignorant and uneducated I have generally found the most turbulent and troublesome, acting under the impulse of excited passion and jealousy.

Quoted in Michael B. Katz, *The Irony of Early School Reform* (Cambridge, Mass.: Harvard University Press, 1968), p. 88. See also David Isaac Bruck, "The Schools of Lowell, 1824-1861: A Case Study in the Origins of Modern Public Education in America" (Senior thesis, Harvard College, Department of Social Studies, April 1971).

fostering the illusion of the benevolence of the government in its relations with citizens.[10] Moreover, because schooling would ostensibly be open to all, one's position in the social division of labor could be portrayed as the result not of birth, but of one's own efforts and talents.[11] And if the children's everyday experiences with the structure of schooling were insufficient to inculcate the correct views and attitudes, the curriculum itself would be made to embody the bourgeois ideology.[12] Where pre-capitalist social institutions, particularly

[10]In 1846 the annual report of the Lowell, Mass., School Committee concluded that universal education was "the surest safety against internal commotions" (*1846 School Committee Annual Report*, pp. 17–18). It seems more than coincidental that, in England, public support for elementary education—a concept which had been widely discussed and urged for at least half a century—was legislated almost immediately after the enfranchisement of the working class by the electoral reform of 1867. See Simon, *Studies in the History of Education, 1780–1870.* Mass public education in Rhode Island came quickly on the heels of an armed insurrection and a broadening of the franchise. See F. T. Carlton, *Economic Influences upon Educational Progress in the United States, 1820–1850* (New York: Teachers College Press, 1966)

[11]Describing the expansion of education in the nineteenth century, Katz concludes:

... a middle class attempt to secure advantage for their children as technological change heightened the importance of formal education assured the success and acceptance of universal elaborate graded school systems. The same result emerged from the fear of a growing, unschooled proletariat. Education substituted for deference as a source of social cement and social order in a society stratified by class rather than by rank. (M. B. Katz, "From Voluntarism to Bureaucracy in U.S. Education," mimeograph, 1970.)

[12]An American economist, writing just prior to the "common school revival," had this to say:

Education universally extended throughout the community will tend to disabuse the working class of people in respect of a notion that has crept into the minds of our mechanics and is gradually prevailing, that manual labor is at present very inadequately rewarded, owing to combinations of the rich against the poor; that mere mental labor is comparatively worthless; that property or wealth ought not to be accumulated or transmitted; that to take interest on money let or profit on capital employed is unjust.... The mistaken and ignorant people who entertain these fallacies as truths will learn, when they have the opportunity of learning, that the institution of political society originated in the protection of property. (Thomas Cooper, *Elements of Political Economy* [1828], quoted in Carlton, *Economic Influences upon Educational Progress in the United States, 1820–1850*, pp. 33–34.

Political economy was made a required subject in Massachusetts high schools in 1857, along with moral science and civic polity. Cooper's advice was widely but not universally followed elsewhere. Friedrich Engels, commenting on the tardy growth of mass education in early nineteenth-century England, remarked: "So shortsighted, so stupidly narrow-minded is the English bourgeoisie in its egotism, that it does not even take the trouble to impress upon the workers the morality of the day, which the bourgeoisie has patched together in its own interest for its own protection." (Engels, *The Condition of the Working Class in England* [Stanford, Calif.: Stanford University Press, 1968].)

the church, remained strong or threatened the capitalist hegemony, schools sometimes served as a modernizing counter-institution.[13]

The movement for public elementary and secondary education in the United States originated in the nineteenth century in states dominated by the burgeoning industrial capitalist class, most notably in Massachusetts. It spread rapidly to all parts of the country except the South.[14] In Massachusetts the extension of elementary education was in large measure a response to industrialization, and to the need for social control of the Irish and other non-Yankee workers recruited to work in the mills.[15] The fact that some working people's movements had demanded free instruction should not obscure the basically coercive nature of the extension of schooling. In many parts of the country, schools were literally imposed upon the workers.[16]

The evolution of the economy in the nineteenth century gave rise to new socialization needs and continued to spur the growth of education. Agriculture continued to lose ground to manufacturing; simple manufacturing gave way to production involving complex interrelated processes; an increasing fraction of the labor force was employed in producing services rather than goods. Employers in the most rapidly growing sectors of the economy began to require more than obedience and punctuality in their workers; a change in motivational outlook was required. The new structure of production provided little built-in motivation. There were fewer jobs such as farming and piece-rate work in manufacturing in which material reward was tied directly to effort. As work roles became more complicated and interrelated, the evaluation of the individual worker's performance became increasingly difficult. Employers began to look for

[13]See Thernstrom, *Poverty and Progress*. Marx said this about mid-nineteenth-century France:

The modern and the traditional consciousness of the French peasant contended for mastery ... in the form of an incessant struggle between the schoolmasters and the priests. (Marx, *The 18th Brumaire of Louis Bonaparte*, p. 125.)

[14]Janice Weiss and I are currently studying the rapid expansion of southern elementary and secondary schooling which followed the demise of slavery and the establishment of capitalist economic institutions in the South.

[15]Based on the preliminary results of a statistical analysis of education in nineteenth-century Massachusetts being conducted jointly with Alexander Field.

[16]Katz, *Irony of Early School Reform* and "From Voluntarism to Bureaucracy in U.S. Education."

workers who had internalized the production-related values of the firm's managers.

The continued expansion of education was pressed by many who saw schooling as a means of producing these new forms of motivation and discipline. Others, frightened by the growing labor militancy after the Civil War, found new urgency in the social-control arguments popular among the proponents of education in the antebellum period.

A system of class stratification developed within this rapidly expanding educational system. Children of the social elite normally attended private schools. Because working-class children tended to leave school early, the class composition of the public high schools was distinctly more elite than the public primary schools.[17] And as a university education ceased to be merely training for teaching or the divinity and became important in gaining access to the pinnacles of the business world, upper-class families used their money and influence to get their children into the best universities, often at the expense of the children of less elite families.

Around the turn of the present century, large numbers of working-class and particularly immigrant children began attending high schools. At the same time, a system of class stratification developed within secondary education.[18] The older democratic ideology of the common school—that the same curriculum should be offered to all children—gave way to the "progressive" insistence that education

[17]Katz, *Irony of Early School Reform.*

[18]Sol Cohen describes this process in "The Industrial Education Movement, 1906–1917," *American Quarterly* 20 no. 1 (Spring 1968): 95–110 Typical of the arguments then given for vocational education is the following, by the superintendent of schools in Cleveland:

It is obvious that the educational needs of children in a district where the streets are well paved and clean, where the homes are spacious and surrounded by lawns and trees, where the language of the child's playfellows is pure, and where life in general is permeated with the spirit and ideals of America—it is obvious that the educational needs of such a child are radically different from those of the child who lives in a foreign and tenement section. (William H. Elson and Frank P. Bachman, "Different Course for Elementary School," *Educational Review* 39 (April 1910): 361–63.

See also L. Cremin, *The Transformation of the School; Progressivism in American Education, 1876–1957* (New York: Alfred A. Knopf, 1961), chap. 2, and David Cohen and Marvin Lazerson, "Education and the Industrial Order," mimeograph, 1970.

should be tailored to the "needs of the child."[19] In the interests of providing an education relevant to the later life of the students, vocational schools and tracks were developed for the children of working families. The academic curriculum was preserved for those who would later have the opportunity to make use of book learning, either in college or in white-collar employment. This and other educational reforms of the progressive education movement reflected an implicit assumption of the immutability of the class structure.

The frankness with which students were channeled into curriculum tracks, on the basis of their social-class background, raised serious doubts concerning the "openness" of the social-class structure. The relation between social class and a child's chances of promotion or tracking assignments was disguised—though not mitigated much— by another "progressive" reform: "objective" educational testing. Particularly after World War I, the capitulation of the schools to business values and concepts of efficiency led to the increased use of intelligence and scholastic achievement testing as an ostensibly unbiased means of measuring the product of schooling and classifying students.[20] The complementary growth of the guidance counseling profession allowed much of the channeling to proceed from the students' own well-counseled choices, thus adding an apparent element of voluntarism to the system.

The legacy of the progressive education movement, like the earlier reforms of the mid-nineteenth century, was a strengthened system of class stratification within schooling which continues to play an important role in the reproduction and legitimation of the social division of labor.

The class stratification of education during this period had proceeded hand in hand with the stratification of the labor force. As large bureaucratic corporations and public agencies employed an in-

---

[19]The superintendent of the Boston schools summed up the change in 1908:

Until very recently (the schools) have offered equal opportunity for all to receive *one kind* of education, but what will make them democratic is to provide opportunity for all to receive such education as will fit them *equally well* for their particular life work. (Boston, *Documents of the School Committee, 1908*, no. 7, p. 53; quoted in Cohen and Lazerson, "Education and the Industrial Order.")

[20]R. Callahan, *Education and the Cult of Efficiency* (Chicago: University of Chicago Press, 1962); Cohen and Lazerson, "Education and the Industrial Order"; and Cremin, *Transformation of the School*.

creasing fraction of all workers, a complicated segmentation of the labor force evolved, reflecting the hierarchical structure of the social relations of production. A large middle group of employees developed, comprising clerical, sales, bookkeeping, and low-level supervisory workers.[21] People holding these occupations ordinarily had a modicum of control over their own work; in some cases they directed the work of others, while themselves under the direction of higher management. The social division of labor had become a finely articulated system of work relations dominated at the top by a small group with control over work processes and a high degree of personal autonomy in their work activities, and proceeding by finely differentiated stages down the chain of bureaucratic command to workers who labored more as extensions of the machinery than as autonomous human beings.

One's status, income, and personal autonomy came to depend in great measure on one's place in the work hierarchy. And in turn, positions in the social division of labor came to be associated with educational credentials reflecting the number of years of schooling and the quality of education received. The increasing importance of schooling as a mechanism for allocating children to positions in the class structure played a major part in legitimizing the structure itself.[22] But at the same time, it undermined the simple processes which in the past had preserved the position and privilege of the upperclass families from generation to generation. In short, it undermined the processes serving to reproduce the social division of labor.

In pre-capitalist societies, direct inheritance of occupational position is common. Even in the early capitalist economy, prior to the segmentation of the labor force on the basis of differential skills and education, the class structure was reproduced generation after generation simply through the inheritance of physical capital by the offspring of the capitalist class. Now that the social division of labor is differentiated by types of competence and educational credentials as well as by ownership of capital, the problem of inheritance is not

[21]See M. Reich, "The Evolution of the U.S. Labor Force," in *The Capitalist System*, ed. R. Edwards, M. Reich, and T. Weisskopf (Englewood Cliffs, N.J.: Prentice-Hall, Inc., 1971).

[22]The role of schooling in legitimizing the class structure is spelled out in S. Bowles, "Contradictions in U.S. Higher Education," mimeograph, 1971.

nearly so simple. The crucial complication arises because education and skills are embedded in human beings; unlike physical capital, these assets cannot be passed on to one's children at death. In an advanced capitalist society in which education and skills play an important role in the hierarchy of production, then, the absence of confiscatory inheritance laws is not enough to reproduce the social division of labor from generation to generation. Skills and educational credentials must somehow be passed on within the family. It is a fundamental theme of this essay that schools play an important part in reproducing and legitimizing this modern form of class structure.

CLASS INEQUALITIES IN U.S. SCHOOLS

Unequal schooling reproduces the social division of labor. Children whose parents occupy positions at the top of the occupational hierarchy receive more years of schooling than working-class children. Both the amount and the content of their education greatly facilitates their movement into positions similar to those of their parents.

Because of the relative ease of measurement, inequalities in years of schooling are particularly evident. If we define social-class standing by the income, occupation, and educational level of the parents, a child from the 90th percentile in the class distribution may expect on the average to achieve over four and a half more years of schooling than a child from the 10th percentile.[23] As can be seen in Table 2.1, social-class inequalities in the number of years of schooling received arise in part because a disproportionate number of children from poorer families do not complete high school.[24] Table 2.2 indicates that these inequalities are exacerbated by social-class inequalities in college attendance among those children who did graduate from high school: even among those who had graduated from high school, chil-

[23]The data for this calculation refer to white males who were aged 25–34 in 1962. See S. Bowles, "Schooling and Inequality from Generation to Generation" (Paper presented at the Far Eastern Meetings of the Econometric Society, Tokyo, 1970).

[24]Table 2.1 understates the degree of social-class inequality in school attendance because a substantial portion of upper-income children not enrolled in public schools attend private schools. Private schools provide a parallel educational system for the upper class. I have not given much attention to these institutions as they are not quantitatively very significant in the total picture. Moreover, to deal extensively with them might detract attention from the task of explaining class inequalities in the ostensibly egalitarian portion of our school system.

Table 2.1.   Percentage of Male Children Aged 16–17 Enrolled in Public School, and Percentage at Less than the Modal Grade Level, by Parent's Education and Income, 1960[a]

Parent's Education	Enrolled in Public School	Below Modal Level
Less than 8 years		
Family income:		
less than $3,000	66.1	47.4
$3,000–4,999	71.3	35.7
$5,000–6,999	75.5	28.3
$7,000 and over	77.1	21.8
8–11 years		
Family income:		
less than $3,000	78.6	25.0
$3,000–4,999	82.9	20.9
$5,000–6,999	84.9	16.9
$7,000 and over	86.1	13.0
12 years or more		
Family income:		
less than $3,000	89.5	13.4
$3,000–4,999	90.7	12.4
$5,000–6,999	92.1	9.7
$7,000 and over	94.2	6.9

SOURCE: U.S. Bureau of the Census, *Census of Population, 1960*, vol. PC-(2)5a, Table 5.

[a]According to Census definitions, for 16-year-olds 9th grade or less and for 17-year-olds 10th grade or less define as below the modal level. Father's education is indicated if father is present; otherwise mother's education is indicated.

dren of families earning less than $3,000 per year were over six times as likely *not* to attend college as were the children of families earning over $15,000.[25]

Because schooling, especially at the college level, is heavily subsidized by the general taxpayer, those children who attend school longer have access for this reason alone to a far larger amount of public resources than those who are forced out of school or who drop out early.[26] But social-class inequalities in public expenditure

[25]For recent evidence on these points, see U.S. Bureau of the Census, *Current Population Reports* (Series P–20), nos. 183 and 185.

[26]W. L. Hansen and B. Weisbrod, "The Distribution of Costs and Direct Benefits of Public Higher Education: the Case of California," *Journal of Human Resources* 5, no. 3 (Summer 1970): 361–370.

Table 2.2.   College Attendance in 1967 among High School Graduates, by Family Income [a]

Family Income [b]	Percent Who Did Not Attend College
less than $3,000	80.2
$3,000–3,999	67.7
$4,000–5,999	63.7
$6,000–7,499	58.9
$7,500–9,999	49.0
$10,000–14,999	38.7
$15,000 and over	13.3

SOURCE: U.S. Bureau of the Census, *Current Population Report*, Series P-20, no. 185, 11 July 1969, p. 6. College attendance refers to both two- and four-year institutions.

[a] Refers to individuals who were high school seniors in October 1965 and who subsequently graduated from high school. 53.1 percent of all such students did not attend college.

[b] Family income for 12 months preceding October 1965.

on education are far more severe than the degree of inequality in years of schooling would suggest. In the first place, per-student public expenditure in four-year colleges greatly exceeds that in elementary schools; those who stay in school longer receive an increasingly large *annual* public subsidy.[27] Second, even at the elementary level, schools attended by children of the poor tend to be less well endowed with equipment, books, teachers, and other inputs into the educational process. Evidence on the relationship between the level of school inputs and the income of the neighborhoods that the schools serve is presented in Table 2.3.[28] The data in this table indicate that both school expenditures and more direct measures of school quality vary directly with the income levels of the communities in which the school is located.

Inequalities in schooling are not simply a matter of differences in years of schooling attained or in resources devoted to each student per year of schooling. Differences in the internal structure of schools

[27] In the school year 1969–70, per-pupil expenditures of federal, state, and local funds were $1,490 for colleges and universities and $747 for primary and secondary schools. U.S. Office of Education, *Digest of Educational Statistics, 1969* (Washington, D.C.: Government Printing Office, 1969).

[28] See also P. C. Sexton, *Education and Income* (New York: Viking Press, 1961).

Table 2.3.   Inequalities in Elementary School Resources: Percent Difference in Resource Availability Associated with a One Percent Difference in Mean Neighborhood Family Income

Resource	Within Cities 1	Between Cities 2
Current real education expenditure per student	n.a.	.73[b]
Average real elementary schoolteacher salary	.20[a]	.69[b]
Teacher-student ratio	.24[a]	n.a.
Real expenditure per pupil on teacher salary	.43[a]	n.a.
Verbal ability of teacher	.11[a]	1.20[a]

SOURCES: [a]John D. Owen, "The Distribution of Educational Resources in Large American Cities," *Journal of Human Resources* 7, no. 1 (Winter 1972): 26–38.
[b]John D. Owen, "Towards a Public Employment Wage Theory: Some Econometric Evidence on Teacher Quality," *Industrial Labor Relations Review* 25, no. 2 (January 1972): 213–222.

themselves and in the content of schooling reflect the differences in the social-class compositions of the student bodies. The social relations of the educational process ordinarily mirror the social relations of the work roles into which most students are likely to move. Differences in rules, expected modes of behavior, and opportunities for choice are most glaring when we compare levels of schooling. Note the wide range of choice over curriculum, life style, and allocation of time afforded to college students, compared with the obedience and respect for authority expected in high school. Differentiation occurs also within each level of schooling. One needs only to compare the social relations of a junior college with those of an elite four-year college,[29] or those of a working-class high school with those of a wealthy suburban high school, for verification of this point.[30]

[29]See J. Binstock, *"Survival in the American College Industry"* mimeograph, 1971.
[30]E. Z. Friedenberg, *Coming of Age in America* (New York: Random House, 1965). It is consistent with this pattern that the play-oriented, child-centered pedagogy of the progressive movement found little acceptance outside of private schools and public schools in wealthy communities. See Cohen and Lazerson, "Education and the Industrial Order."

The various socialization patterns in schools attended by students of different social classes do not arise by accident. Rather, they stem from the fact that the educational objectives and expectations of both parents and teachers, and the responsiveness of students to various patterns of teaching and control, differ for students of different social classes.[31] Further, class inequalities in school socialization patterns are reinforced by the inequalities in financial resources documented above. The paucity of financial support for the education of children from working-class families not only leaves more resources to be devoted to the children of those with commanding roles in the economy; it forces upon the teachers and school administrators in the working-class schools a type of social relations which fairly closely mirrors that of the factory. Thus, financial considerations in poorly supported working-class schools militate against small initimate classes, against a multiplicity of elective courses and specialized teachers (except disciplinary personnel), and preclude the amounts of free time for the teachers and free space required for a more open, flexible educational environment. The lack of financial support all but requires that students be treated as raw materials on a production line; it places a high premium on obedience and punctuality; there are few opportunities for independent, creative work or individualized attention by teachers. The well-financed schools attended by the children of the rich can offer much greater opportunities for the development of the capacity for sustained independent work and the other characteristics required for adequate job performance in the upper levels of the occupational hierarchy.

Much of the inequality in American education exists between schools, but even within a given school different children receive different educations. Class stratification within schools is achieved through tracking, differential participation in extracurricular activities, and in the attitudes of teachers and guidance personnel who expect working-class children to do poorly, to terminate schooling early, and to end up in jobs similar to those of their parents.[32]

[31]That working-class parents seem to favor more authoritarian educational methods is perhaps a reflection of their own work experiences which have demonstrated that submission to authority is an essential ingredient in one's ability to get and hold a steady, well-paying job.

[32]See, for example, A. B. Hollingshead, *Elmtown's Youth* (New York: John Wiley, 1949); W. L. Warner and P. S. Lunt, *The Social Life of a Modern Community*

Not surprisingly, the results of schooling differ greatly for children of different social classes. The differing educational objectives implicit in the social relations of schools attended by children of different social classes has already been mentioned. Less important but more easily measured are differences in scholastic achievement. If we measure the output of schooling by scores on nationally standardized achievement tests, children whose parents were themselves highly educated outperform children of parents with less education by a wide margin. A recent study revealed, for example, that among white high school seniors, those whose parents were in the top education decile were on the average well over three grade levels ahead of those who parents were in the bottom decile.[33] Although a good part of this discrepancy is the result of unequal treatment in school and unequal educational resources, much of it is related to differences in the early socialization and home environment of the children.

Given the great social-class differences in scholastic achievement, class inequalities in college attendance are to be expected. Thus one might be tempted to argue that the data in Table 2.1 are simply a reflection of unequal scholastic achievement in high school and do not reflect any *additional* social-class inequalities peculiar to the process of college admission. This view, so comforting to the admissions personnel in our elite universities, is unsupported by the available data, some of which is presented in Table 2.4. Access to a college education is highly unequal, even for children of the same measured "academic ability."

The social-class inequalities in our school system and the role they play in the reproduction of the social division of labor are too evident to be denied. Defenders of the educational system are forced back on the assertion that things are getting better, that inequalities of the past were far worse. And, indeed, some of the inequalities of the past have undoubtedly been mitigated. Yet, new inequalities have

---

(New Haven: Yale University Press, 1941); R. Rosenthal and L. Jacobson, *Pygmalion in the Classroom* (New York: Holt, Rinehart, and Winston, 1968); and W. E. Schafer, C. Olexa, and K. Polk, "Programmed for Social Class: Tracking in High School," *Trans-action* 7, no. 12 (October 1970): pp. 39–46.

[33]Calculation based on data in James S. Coleman et al. *Equality of Educational Opportunity*, vol. 2 (Washington, D.C.: U.S. Office of Education, 1966), and methods described in S. Bowles, "Schooling and Inequality from Generation to Generation."

Table 2.4.   **Probability of College Entry for a Male
who has Reached Grade 11**

| | | Socioeconomic Quartiles[a] | | | |
		Low 1	2	3	High 4
Ability Quartiles[a]	Low 1	.06	.12	.13	.26
	2	.13	.15	.29	.36
	3	.25	.34	.45	.65
	High 4	.48	.70	.73	.87

SOURCE: Based on a large sample of U.S. high school students as reported in John C. Flannagan and William W. Cooley, *Project TALENT, One-Year Follow-Up Studies*, Cooperative Research Project No. 2333, School of Education, University of Pittsburgh, 1966.

[a] The socioeconomic index is a composite measure including family income, father's occupation and education, mother's education, etc. The ability scale is a composite of tests measuring general academic aptitude.

apparently developed to take their place, for the available historical evidence lends little support to the idea that our schools are on the road to equality of educational opportunity. For example, data from a recent U.S. Census survey reported in Table 2.5 indicate that graduation from college has become increasingly dependent on one's class background. This is true despite the fact that the probability of high school graduation is becoming increasingly equal across social classes. On balance, the available data suggest that the number of years of schooling attained by a child depends upon the social-class standing of his father at least as much in the recent period as it did fifty years ago.[34]

The argument that our "egalitarian" education compensates for inequalities generated elsewhere in the capitalist system is so patently fallacious that few persist in maintaining it. But the discrepancy between the ideology and the reality of the U.S. school system

[34]See P. M. Blau and O. D. Duncan, *The American Occupational Structure* (New York: Wiley, 1967). More recent data do not contradict the evidence of no trend toward equality. A 1967 Census survey, the most recent available, shows that among high school graduates in 1965, the probability of college attendance for those whose parents had attended college has continued to rise relative to the probability of college attendance for those whose parents had attended less than eight years of school. See U.S. Bureau of the Census, *Current Population Reports* (Series P-20), no. 185, 11 July 1969.

Table 2.5. Among Sons Who had Reached High School, Percentage Who Graduated from College, by Son's Age and Father's Level of Education

Son's Age in 1962	Likely Dates of College Graduation[a]	Father's Education						
		Less than 8 Years	Some High School		High School Graduate		Some College or More	
			Percent Graduating	Ratio to <8	Percent Graduating	Ratio to <8	Percent Graduating	Ratio to <8
25–34	1950–59	7.6	17.4	2.29	25.6	3.37	51.9	6.83
35–44	1940–49	8.6	11.9	1.38	25.3	2.94	53.9	6.27
45–54	1930–39	7.7	9.8	1.27	15.1	1.96	36.9	4.79
55–64	1920–29	8.9	9.8	1.10	19.2	2.16	29.8	3.35

SOURCE: Based on U.S. Census data as reported in William G. Spady, "Educational Mobility and Access: Growth and Paradoxes," *American Journal of Sociology* 73, no. 3 (November 1967): 273–86.
[a] Assuming college graduation at age 22.

is far greater than would appear from a passing glance at the above data. In the first place, if education is to compensate for the social-class immobility caused by the inheritance of wealth and privilege, education must be structured so as to yield a negative correlation between social-class background of the child and the quantity and quality of his schooling. Thus the assertion that education compensates for inequalities in inherited wealth and privilege is falsified not so much by the extent of the social-class inequalities in the school system as by their very existence, or, more correctly, by the absence of compensatory inequalities.

Moreover, if we turn from the problem of intergenerational immobility to the problem of inequality of income at a given moment, a similar argument applies. In a capitalist economy, the increasing importance of schooling in the economy exercises a disequalizing tendency on the distribution of income even in the absence of social-class inequalities in quality and quantity of schooling. To see why this is so, consider a simple capitalist economy in which only two factors are used in production: uneducated and undifferentiated labor, and capital, the ownership of which is unequally distributed among the population. The only source of income inequality in this society is the unequal distribution of capital. As the labor force becomes differentiated by type of skill or schooling, inequalities in labor earnings contribute to total income inequality, augmenting the inequalities inherent in the concentration of capital. This will be the case even if education and skills are distributed randomly among the population. The disequalizing tendency will of course be intensified if the owners of capital also acquire a disproportionate amount of those types of education and training which confer access to high-paying jobs.[35] A substantial negative correlation between the ownership of

[35]A simple statistical model will elucidate the main relationships involved.

Let y (individual or family income) be the sum of w (earnings from labor, including embodied education and skills, L) and k (earnings from capital, K), related according to the equation $y = w + k = aK^A L^B$. The coefficients A and B represent the relative importance of capital and labor as sources of income. The variance of the logarithm of income (a common measure of inequality) can then be represented by the following expression:

$$\text{var} \log y = A^2 \text{var} \log K + B^2 \text{var} \log L + 2AB \text{ covar } (\log L, \log K).$$

The first term on the right represents the contribution of inequalities in capital ownership to total inequality, the second measures that part of total income in-capital and the quality and quantity of schooling received would have been required merely to neutralize the disequalizing effect of the rise of schooling as an economic phenomenon. And while some research has minimized the importance of social-class biases in schooling,[36] nobody has yet suggested that class and schooling were inversely related!

CLASS CULTURE AND CLASS POWER

The pervasive and persistent inequalities in American education would seem to refute an interpretation of education that asserts its egalitarian functions. But the facts of inequality do not by themselves suggest an alternate explanation. Indeed, they pose serious problems of interpretation. If the costs of education borne by students and their families were very high, or if nepotism were rampant, or if formal segregation of pupils by social class were practiced, or if educational decisions were made by a select few whom we might call the power elite, it would not be difficult to explain the continued inequalities in U.S. education. The problem of interpretation, however, is to reconcile the above empirical findings with the facts of our society as we perceive them: public and virtually tuition-free education at all levels, few legal instruments for the direct implementation of class segregation, a limited role for "contacts" or nepotism

---

equality due to inequalities of education and skills embodied in labor, and the third represents the contribution to income inequality of social class inequalities in the supply of skills and schooling. Prior to the educational differentiation of the labor force, the variance of labor was zero. All workers were effectively equal. The variance of the logarithm of income would then be due entirely to capital inequality and would be exactly equal to A^2var log K. The rise of education as a source of income and labor differentiation will increase the variance of the logarithm of embodied labor unless all workers receive identical education and training. This is true even if the third term is zero, indicating no social class inequalities in the provision of skills and education.

To assert the conventional faith in the egalitarian influence of the rising economic importance of education, one would have to argue that the rise of education is likely to be associated with either (1) a fall in A, the relative importance of capital as a source of earnings; (2) a decrease in the size of the covariance of the logarithms of capital and labor; (3) a decrease in the inequality of capital ownerships; or (4) an increase in equality in the supply of education. While each is possible, I see no compelling reason why education should *produce* these results.

[36]See, for example, Robert Hauser, "Educational Stratification in the United States," *Sociological Inquiry* 40 (Spring 1970): 102–29.

in the achievement of high status or income, a commitment (at the rhetorical level at least) to equality of educational opportunity, and a system of control of education which, if not particularly democratic, extends far beyond anything resembling a power elite. The attempt to reconcile these apparently discrepant facts leads to a consideration of the social division of labor, the associated class cultures, and the exercise of class power.

I will argue that the social division of labor—based on the hierarchical structure of production—gives rise to distinct class subcultures. The values, personality traits, and expectations characteristic of each subculture are transmitted from generation to generation through class differences in family socialization and complementary differences in the type and amount of schooling ordinarily attained by children of various class positions. These class differences in schooling are maintained in large measure through the capacity of the upper class to control the basic principles of school finance, pupil evaluation, and educational objectives. This outline, and what follows, is put forward as an interpretation, consistent where testable with the available data, though lacking as yet in firm empirical support for some important links in the argument.

The social relations of production characteristic of advanced capitalist societies (and many socialist societies) are most clearly illustrated in the bureaucracy and hierarchy of the modern corporation.[37] Occupational roles in the capitalist economy may be grouped according to the degree of independence and control exercised by the person holding the job. Some evidence exists that the personality attributes associated with the adequate performance of jobs in occupational categories defined in this broad way differ considerably, some apparently requiring independence and internal discipline, and others emphasizing such traits as obedience, predictability, and willingness to subject oneself to external controls.[38]

[37]Max Weber referred to bureaucracy as the "most rational offspring" of discipline, and remarked: "... military discipline is the ideal model for the modern capitalist factory...." See "The Meaning of Discipline," reprinted in H. H. Gerth and C. W. Mills, eds. *From Max Weber: Essays in Sociology* (New York: Oxford University Press, 1958), p. 261.

[38]For a survey of the literature see J. P. Robinson, R. Athanasiou, and K. Head, "Measures of Occupational Attitudes and Occupational Characteristics" (Survey Research Center, University of Michigan, February 1969).

These personality attributes are developed primarily at a young age, both in the family and, to a lesser extent, in secondary socializing institutions such as schools.[39] Because people tend to marry within their own class (in part because spouses often meet in our class-segregated schools), both parents are likely to have a similar set of these fundamental personality traits. Thus, children of parents occupying a given position in the occupational hierarchy grow up in homes where child-rearing methods and perhaps even the physical surroundings tend to develop personality characteristics appropriate to adequate job performance in the occupational roles of the parents.[40] The children of managers and professionals are taught self-reliance within a broad set of constraints;[41] the children of production-line workers are taught obedience.

Although this relation between parents' class position and child's personality attributes operates primarily in the home, it is reinforced by schools and other social institutions. Thus, to take an example introduced earlier, the authoritarian social relations of working-class high schools complement the discipline-oriented early socialization patterns experienced by working-class children. The relatively

[39]See, for example, Benjamin Bloom, *Stability and Change in Human Characteristics* (New York: Wiley, 1964).

[40]Note, for example, the class differences in child rearing with respect to the importance of obedience. See M. Kohn, "Social Class and Parental Values," in *The Family*, ed. R. Coser (New York: St. Martin's Press, 1964); and L. Dolger and J. Ginandes, "Children's Attitudes towards Disciplines as Related to Socioeconomic Status," *Journal of Experimental Education* 15, no. 2 (December 1946): 161–165. See also the study of differences in child-rearing practices in families headed by bureaucrats as opposed to entrepreneurs by D. Miller and G. Swanson, *The Changing American Parent* (New York: Wiley, 1958). Also, E. E. Maccoby, P. K. Gibbs, et al., "Methods of Child-Rearing in Two Social Classes," in *Readings in Child Development*, ed. W. E. Martin and C. B. Stendler (New York: Harcourt Brace, 1954). While the existence of class differences in child rearing is supported by most of the available data (but see H. Lewis, "Child-Rearing Among Low-Income Families," in *Poverty in America*, ed. L. Ferman et al. (Ann Arbor, Michigan: University of Michigan Press, 1965)), the stability of these differences over time has been questioned by U. Bronfenbrenner, "Socialization and Social Class through Time and Space," in *Education and Society*, ed. W. W. Kallenbach and H. M. Hodges (Columbus, Ohio: C. E. Merrill, 1963).

[41]See M. Winterbottom, "The Sources of Achievement Motivation in Mothers' Attitudes toward Independence Training," in *The Achievement Motive*, ed. D. C. McClelland et al. (New York: Appleton-Century-Crofts, 1953); and M. Kohn, "Social Class and Parent-Child Relationships: An Interpretation," *American Journal of Sociology* 68, no. 4 (January 1963): 471–480.

greater freedom of wealthy suburban schools extends and formalizes the early independence training characteristic of upper-class families.

Schools reinforce other aspects of family socialization as well. The aspirations and expectations of students and parents concerning both the type and the amount of schooling are strongly related to social class.[42] The expectations of teachers, guidance counselors, and school administrators ordinarily reinforce those of the students and parents. Schools often encourage students to develop aspirations and expectations typical of their social class, even if the child tends to have "deviant" aspirations.

It is true that to some extent schools introduce common elements of socialization for all students regardless of social class. Discipline, respect for property, competition, and punctuality are part of the implicit curriculum of virtually all schools. Yet, given the existing institutional arrangements, the ability of a school to change a child's personality, values, and expectations is severely limited. The responsiveness of children to different types of schooling seems to depend importantly upon the types of personality traits, values, and expectations developed through the family. Furthermore, children spend a small amount of time in school—less than one-quarter of their waking hours over the course of a year. Thus schools are probably more effective when they attempt to complement and reinforce rather than to oppose the socialization processes of the home and neighborhood. It is not surprising, then, that social-class differences in scholastic achievement and other measures of school success are far greater than would be accounted for by differences in the measured school financial resources and other inputs (quality and quantity of teachers, etc.) alone.[43]

In this interpretation class differences in the total effect of schooling are primarily the result of differences in what I have called class subculture. The educational system serves less to change the results of the primary socialization in the home than to ratify them and

[42]See, for example, S. M. Lipset and R. Bendix, *Social Mobility in Industrial Society* (Berkeley, Calif.: University of California Press, 1959); and T. Iwand and J. Stoyle, "Social Rigidity: Income and Occupational Choice in Rural Pennsylvania," *Economic and Business Bulletin* 22 (Spring-Summer 1970): 25–30.

[43]S. Bowles, "Toward an Educational Production Function," in *Education, Income, and Human Capital*, ed. W. L. Hansen (New York: National Bureau of Economic Research, 1970).

render them in adult form. The complementary relationship between family socialization and schools serves to reproduce patterns of class culture from generation to generation.

The operation of the labor market translates differences in class culture into income inequalities and occupational hierarchies. The personality traits, values, and expectations characteristic of different class cultures play a major role in determining an individual's success in gaining a high income or prestigious occupation. The apparent contribution of schooling to occupational success and higher income seems to be explained primarily by the personality characteristics of those who have higher educational attainments.[44] Although the rewards to intellectual capacities are quite limited in the labor market (except for a small number of high-level jobs), mental abilities are important in getting ahead in school. Grades, the probability of continuing to higher levels of schooling, and a host of other school success variables are positively correlated with "objective" measures of intellectual capacities. Partly for this reason, one's experience in school reinforces the belief that promotion and rewards are distributed fairly. The close relationship between educational attainments and later occupational success thus provides a meritocratic appearance to mask the mechanisms that reproduce the class system from generation to generation.

So far, the perpetuation of inequality through the schooling system has been represented as an almost automatic, self-enforcing mechanism, operating only through the medium of class culture. An important further dimension of the interpretation is added if we note that positions of control in the productive heirarchy tend to be associated with positions of political influence. Given the disproportionate share of political power held by the upper class and their capacity to determine the accepted patterns of behavior and procedures, to define the national interest, and in general to control the ideological and institutional context in which educational decisions are

---

[44]This view is elaborated in H. Gintis, "Education, Technology, and Worker Productivity," *American Economic Association Proceedings* 61, no. 2 (May 1971): 266–279. For other studies stressing the noncognitive dimensions of the schooling experience, see T. Parsons, "The School Class as a Social System: Some of its Functions in American Society," *Harvard Educational Review* 29, no. 4 (Fall 1959): 297–318; and R. Dreeben, *On What Is Learned in School* (Reading, Mass.: Addison-Wesley, 1968).

made, it is not surprising to find that resources are allocated unequally among school tracks, between schools serving different
classes, and between levels of schooling. The same configuration
of power results in curricula, methods of instruction, and criteria of
selection and promotion that confer benefits disproportionately on
the children of the upper class.

It is not asserted here that the upper class controls the main decision-making bodies in education, although a good case could probably
be made that this is so. The power of the upper class is hypothesized
as existing in its capacity to define and maintain a set of rules of
operation or decision criteria—"rules of the game"—which, though
often seemingly innocuous and sometimes even egalitarian in their
ostensible intent, have the effect of maintaining the unequal system.

The operation of two prominent examples of these rules of the
game will serve to illustrate the point. The first important principle
is that excellence in schooling should be rewarded. Given the capacity
of the upper class to define excellence in terms on which upper-
class children tend to excel (e.g., scholastic achievement), adherence
to this principle yields inegalitarian outcomes (e.g., unequal access
to higher education) while maintaining the appearance of fair
treatment.[45] Thus the principle of rewarding excellence serves to
legitimize the unequal consequences of schooling by associating
success with competence. At the same time, the institution of objectively administered tests of performance serves to allow a limited
amount of upward mobility among exceptional children of the lower
class, thus providing further legitimation of the operations of the
social system by giving some credence to the myth of widespread
mobility.

The second example is the principle that elementary and secondary
schooling should be financed in very large measure from local
revenues. This principle is supported on the grounds that it is neces-

---

[45]Those who would defend the "reward excellence" principle on the grounds of
efficient selection to ensure the most efficient use of educational resources might ask
themselves: Why should colleges admit those with the highest college entrance examination board scores? Why not the lowest, or the middle? According to conventional standards of efficiency, the rational social objective of the college is to render the
greatest *increment* in individual capacities ("value added," to the economist), not to
produce the most illustrious graduating class ("gross output"). Yet if incremental
gain is the objective, it is far from obvious that choosing from the top is the best policy.

sary to preserve political liberty. Given the degree of residential segregation by income level, the effect of this principle is to produce an unequal distribution of school resources among children of different classes. Towns with a large tax base can spend large sums for the education of their disproportionately upper-class children, without suffering a higher-than-average tax rate.[46] Because the main resource inequalities in schooling thus exist between, rather than within, school districts,[47] and because no effective mechanism exists for redistribution of school funds among school districts, poor families lack a viable political strategy for correcting the inequality.[48]

The above rules of the game—rewarding "excellence" and financing schools locally—illustrate the complementarity between the political and economic power of the upper class. In each case, adherence to the rule has the effect of generating unequal consequences via a mechanism that operates largely outside the political system. As long as one adheres to the "reward excellence" principle, the responsibility for unequal results in schooling appears to lie outside the upper class, often in some fault of the poor—such as their class culture, which is viewed as lying beyond the reach of political action or criticism. Likewise, as long as the local financing of schools is maintained, the achievement of equality of resources among children of different social classes requires the class integration of school districts, an objective for which there are no effective political instruments as long as we allow a market in residential properties and an unequal distribution of income.

Thus, the consequences of an unequal distribution of political power among classes appear to complement the results of class culture in maintaining an educational system that has been capable of

[46]Some dimensions of this problem are discussed in S. Weiss, "Existing Disparities in Public School Finance and Proposals for Reform" (Research Report to the Federal Reserve Bank of Boston, no. 46, February 1970).

[47]Recall that Owen, whose data appear in Table 2.3, found that the relationship of various measures of teacher quality to the family income level of the area served by the schools was considerably higher between cities than within cities.

[48]In 1969, federal funds constituted only 7 percent of the total financing of public elementary and secondary schooling. Moreover, current distribution formulas governing state and federal expenditures are only mildly egalitarian in their impact. See K. A. Simon and W. V. Grant, *Digest of Educational Statistics, 1969* (Washington, D.C.: Department of Health, Education, and Welfare, 1969).

transmitting status from generation to generation, and capable in addition of political survival in the formally democratic and egalitarian environment of the contemporary United States.

The role of the schools in reproducing and legitimizing the social division of labor has recently been challenged by popular egalitarian movements. At the same time, the educational system is showing signs of internal structural weakness.[49] These two developments suggest that fundamental change in the schooling process may soon be possible. Analysis of both the potential and the limits of educational change will be facilitated by drawing together and extending the strands of our argument.

THE LIMITS OF EDUCATIONAL REFORM

If the above attempt to identify the roots of inequality in American education is convincing, it has done more than reconcile apparent discrepancies between the democratic forms and unequal content of that education. For it is precisely the sources of educational inequality which we must understand in order to develop successful political strategies in the pursuit of educational equality.

I have argued that the structure of education reflects the social relations of production. For at least the past 150 years, expansion of education and changes in the forms of schooling have been responses to needs generated by the economic system. The sources of present inequality in American education were found in the mutual reinforcement of class subcultures and social-class biases in the operations of the school system itself. The analysis strongly suggests that educational inequalities are rooted in the basic institutions of our economy. Reconsideration of some of the basic mechanisms of educational inequality lends support to this proposition. First, the principle of rewarding academic excellence in educational promotion and selection serves not only to legitimize the process by which the social division of labor is reproduced. It is also a basic part of the process that socializes young people to work for external rewards and encourages them to develop motivational structures fit for the alienating work of the capitalist economy.[50] Selecting students from the bot-

---

[49]See S. Bowles, "Contradictions in U.S. Higher Education," mimeograph, 1971.

[50]Gintis, "Education, Technology, and Worker Productivity."

tom or the middle of the achievement scale for promotion to higher levels of schooling would go a long way toward equalizing education, but it would also jeopardize the schools' capacity to train productive and well-adjusted workers.[51] Second, the way in which local financing of schools operates to maintain educational inequality is also rooted in the capitalist economy, in this case in the existence of an unequal distribution of income, free markets in residential property, and the narrow limits of state power. It seems unwise to emphasize this aspect of the long-run problem of equality in education, however, for the inequalities in school resources resulting from the localization of finance may not be of crucial importance in maintaining inequalities in the effects of education. Moreover, a significant undermining of the principle of local finance may already be underway in response to pressures from the poorer states and school districts.

Of greater importance in the perpetuation of educational inequality are differential class subcultures. These class-based differences in personality, values, and expectations, I have argued, represent an adaptation to the different requirements of adequate work performance at various levels in the hierarchical social relations of production. Class subcultures, then, stem from the everyday experiences of workers in the structure of production characteristic of capitalist societies.

It should be clear by this point that educational equality cannot be achieved through changes in the school system alone. Nonetheless, attempts at educational reform may move us closer to that objective if, in their failure, they lay bare the unequal nature of our school system and destroy the illusion of unimpeded mobility through education. Successful educational reforms—reducing racial or class disparities in schooling, for example—may also serve the cause of equality of education, for it seems likely that equalizing access to schooling will challenge the system either to make good its promise of rewarding educational attainment or to find ways of coping with a mass disillusionment with the great panacea.[52]

---

[51]Consider what would happen to the internal discipline of schools if the students' objective were to end up at the bottom of the grade distribution!

[52]The failure of the educational programs of the War on Poverty to raise significantly the incomes of the poor is documented in T. I. Ribich, *Education and*

Yet, if the record of the last 150 years of educational reforms is any guide, we should not expect radical change in education to result from the efforts of those confining their attention to the schools. The political victories of past reform movements have apparently resulted in little if any effective equalization. My interpretation of the educational consequences of class culture and class power suggests that these educational reform movements failed because they sought to eliminate educational inequalities without challenging the basic institutions of capitalism.

Efforts to equalize education through changes in government policy will at best scratch the surface of inequality. For much of the inequality in American education has its origin outside the limited sphere of state power, in the hierarchy of work relations and the associated differences in class culture. As long as jobs are defined so that some have power over many and others have power over none—as long as the social division of labor persists—educational inequality will be built into society in the United States.

Poverty (Washington, D.C.: The Brookings Institution, 1968). In the case of blacks, dramatic increases in the level of schooling relation to whites have scarcely affected the incomes of blacks relative to whites. See R. Weiss, "The Effects of Education on the Earnings of Blacks and Whites," *Review of Economics and Statistics* 52, no. 2 (May 1970): 150–59. It is no wonder that Booker T. Washington's plea that blacks should educate themselves before demanding equality has lost most of its once widespread support.

B. EQUAL OPPORTUNITY IN THE LABOR MARKET

.3. *Economic Theories of Racism**

MICHAEL REICH

IN THE early 1960s it seemed to many that the elimination of racism in the United States was proceeding without requiring a radical restructuring of the entire society. There was a growing civil rights movement, and hundreds of thousands of blacks were moving to northern cities where discrimination was supposedly less severe than in the South. Government reports pointed to the rapid improvement in the quantity of black schooling as blacks moved out of the South: in 1966 the gap between the median years of schooling of black males aged 25–29 and white males in the same age group had shrunk to one-quarter the size of the gap that had existed in 1960.[1]

But by 1970 the optimism of earlier decades had vanished. Despite new civil rights laws, elaborate White House conferences, special ghetto manpower programs, the War on Poverty, and stepped-up tokenist hiring, racism and the economic exploitation of blacks has not lessened. During the past twenty-five years there has been virtually no permanent improvement in the relative economic position of blacks in America. Median black incomes have been fluctuating at a level between 47 percent and 62 percent of median white incomes, the ratio rising during economic expansions and

---

*This essay is based on work in progress on my Ph.D. thesis; I am indebted to Samuel Bowles for critical guidance at every stage.

[1]U.S. Bureau of Labor Statistics, *The Social and Economic Status of Negroes in the United States, 1969*, no. 375, p. 50.

falling to previous low levels during recessions.[2] Segregation in schools and neighborhoods has been steadily increasing in almost all cities, and the atmosphere of distrust between blacks and whites has been intensifying. Racism, instead of disappearing, seems to be on the increase.

Racism has been as persistent in the United States in the twentieth century as it was in previous centuries. The industrialization of the economy led to the transformation of the black worker's economic role from one of agricultural sharecropper and household servant to one of urban industrial operative and service worker, but it did not result in substantial relative improvement for blacks. Quantitative comparisons using U.S. Census data of occupational distributions by race show that the occupational status of black males relative to white males is virtually the same today as it was in 1910, the earliest year for which racial data is available.[3]

Besides systematically subjugating blacks so that their median income is 55 percent that of whites, racism is of profound importance for the distribution of income among white landowners, capitalists, and workers. For example, racism clearly benefits owners of housing in the ghetto, where blacks have no choice but to pay higher rents than for comparable housing elsewhere in the city. But more important, racism is a key mechanism for the stabilization of capitalism and the legitimization of inequality. We shall return to the question

[2]The data refer to male incomes, and are published annually by the U.S. Census Bureau in its P-60 Series, *Income of Families and Persons*. Using data for the years 1948 to 1964, Rasmussen found that, after controlling for the effects of the business cycle, the average increase in the racial ratio of median incomes was only .3 percent per year, or 5 percent over the 16 years. See David Rasmussen, "A Note on the Relative Income of Nonwhite Men, 1948–64," *Quarterly Journal of Economics*, 84, no. 1 (1970): 168–172. Thurow, using a slightly different technique, estimated that no relative increase in black incomes would occur after unemployment was reduced to 3 percent. See L. Thurow, *Poverty and Discrimination*, (Washington, D.C.: Brookings Institution, 1969), pp. 58–61. Batchelder found stability in the ratio over time despite migration from the South to the North; within regions in the North, the ratio declined. Alan Batchelder, "Decline in the Relative Income of Negro Men," *Quarterly Journal of Economics*, 78 (November 1964): 525–548.

[3]Since income data by race are not available before 1940, a relative index must be based on racial occupational data. Hiestand has computed such an index: he finds at most a 5 percent increase in blacks' status between 1910 and 1960; most of this improvement occurred during the labor shortages of the 1940s. See D. Hiestand, *Economic Growth and Employment Opportunities for Minorities*, (New York: Columbia University Press, 1964), p. 53.

of who benefits from racism later, but first let us review some of the economic means used to subjugate blacks.

Beginning in the first grade, blacks go to schools of inferior quality and obtain little of the basic training and skills needed in the labor market. Finding school of little relevance, more in need of immediate income, and less able to finance their way through school, the average black student still drops out at a lower grade. In 1965 only 7.4 percent of black males aged 25–34 were college graduates, compared to 17.9 percent of whites in the same age bracket.

But exploitation really begins in earnest when the black youth enters the labor market. A black worker with the same number of years of schooling and the same scores on achievement tests as a white worker receives much less income. The black worker cannot get as good a job because the better-paying jobs are located too far from the ghetto, or because he was turned down by racist personnel agencies and employers, or because a union denied admittance, or perhaps because of an arrest record. Going to school after a certain point does not seem to increase a black person's job possibilities very much. The more educated a black person is, the greater is the disparity between his income and that of a white with the same schooling. The result: in 1966 black college graduates earned less than white high school dropouts. And the higher the average wage or salary of an occupation, the lower the percentage of workers in that occupation who are black.

The rate of unemployment among blacks is twice as high as among whites. Layoffs and recessions hit blacks with twice the impact they hit whites, since blacks are the "last hired, first fired." The ratio of average black to white incomes follows the business cycle closely, buffering white workers from some of the impact of the recession.

Blacks pay higher rents for inferior housing, higher prices in ghetto stores, higher insurance premiums, higher interest rates in banks and lending companies, travel longer distances at greater expense to their jobs, suffer from inferior garbage collection and less access to public recreational facilities, and are assessed at higher property tax rates when they own housing. Beyond this, blacks are further harassed by police, the courts, and the prisons.

When conventional economists attempt to analyze racism they usually begin by trying to separate various forms of racial discrimination. For example, they define "pure wage discrimination" as the racial differential in wages paid to equivalent workers, that is, those with similar years and quality of schooling, skill training, previous employment experience and seniority, age, health, job attitudes, and a host of other factors. They presume that they can analyze the sources of "pure wage discrimination" without simultaneously analyzing the extent to which discrimination also affects the factors they hold constant.

But such a technique distorts reality. The various forms of discrimination are not separable in real life. Employers' hiring and promotion practices, resource allocation in city schools, the structure of transportation systems, residential segregation and housing quality, availability of decent health care, behavior of policemen and judges, foremen's prejudices, images of blacks presented in the media and the schools, price gouging in ghetto stores—these and the other forms of social and economic discrimination interact strongly with each other in determining the occupational status and annual income, and the welfare, of black people. The processes are not simply additive, but are mutually reinforcing. Often, a decrease in one narrow form of discrimination is accompanied by an increase in another form. Since all aspects of racism interact, an analysis of racism should incorporate all its aspects in a unified manner.

No single quantitative index could adequately measure racism in all its social, cultural, psychological and economic dimensions. But, while racism is far more than a narrow economic phenomenon, it does have very definite economic consequences: blacks have far lower incomes than whites. The ratio of median black to median white incomes thus provides a rough but useful quantitative index of the economic consequences of racism for blacks. We shall use this index statistically to analyze the causes of racism's persistence in the United States. While this approach overemphasizes the economic aspects of racism, it is nevertheless an improvement over the narrower approach taken by conventional economists.

How is the historical persistence of racism in the United States to be explained? The most prominent analysis of discrimination among economists was formulated in 1957 by Gary Becker in his book *The Economics of Discrimination.*[4] Racism, according to Becker, is

[4]University of Chicago Press.

fundamentally a problem of tastes and attitudes. Whites are defined to have a "taste for discrimination" if they are willing to forfeit income in order to be associated with other whites instead of blacks. Since white employers and employees prefer not to associate with blacks, they require a monetary compensation for the psychic cost of such association. In Becker's principal model, white employers have a taste for discrimination; marginal productivity analysis is invoked to show that white employers lose (in monetary terms) while workers gain, from discrimination against blacks.

Becker does not try to explain the source of white tastes for discrimination. For him, these attitudes are determined outside the economic system. (Racism could presumably be ended simply by changing these attitudes, perhaps by appeal to whites on moral grounds.) According to Becker's analysis, employers would find that ending racism would be in their economic self-interest, but white workers would not. The persistence of racism is thus implicitly laid at the door of white workers. Becker suggests that long-run market forces will lead to the end of discrimination anyway: less discriminatory employers, with no "psychic costs" to enter in their accounts, will be able to operate at lower costs by hiring equivalent black workers at lower wages, thus bidding up the black wage rate and/or driving the more discriminatory employers out of business.[5]

The approach to racism argued here is entirely different. Racism is viewed as rooted in the economic system and not in "exogenously determined" attitudes. Historically, the American Empire was founded on the racist extermination of American Indians, was financed in large part by profits from slavery, and was extended by a string of interventions, beginning with the Mexican War of the 1840s, which have been at least partly justified by white supremacist ideology.

Today, by transferring white resentment toward blacks and away from capitalism, racism continues to serve the needs of the capitalist system. Although individual employers might gain by refusing to

[5]Some economists writing on discrimination reject Becker's "tastes" approach, but use the marginal productivity method of analysis. See, for example, Thurow, *Poverty and Discrimination*. The main substantive difference in their conclusions is that Thurow expects racism will be a little harder to uproot. See also A. Krueger, "The Economics of Discrimination," *Journal of Political Economy* 71 (1963): 481–86.

discriminate, hiring more blacks, and thus raising the black wage rate, it is not true that the capitalist class as a whole would profit if racism were eliminated and labor were more efficiently allocated without regard to skin color.

We will show below that the divisiveness of racism weakens workers' strength when bargaining with employers; the economic consequences of racism are not only lower incomes for blacks, but also higher incomes for the capitalist class coupled with lower incomes for white workers. Although capitalists may not have conspired consciously to create racism, and although capitalists may not be its principal perpetuators, nevertheless racism does support the continued well-being of the American capitalist system.

We have, then, two alternative approaches to the analysis of racism. The first suggests that capitalists lose and white workers gain from racism. The second predicts the opposite—capitalists gain while workers lose. The first says that racist "tastes for discrimination" are formed independently of the economic system; the second argues that racism is symbiotic with capitalistic economic institutions.

The two approaches reflect the theoretical paradigms of society from which each was developed. Becker follows the paradigm of neoclassical economics in taking "tastes" as exogenously determined and fixed, and then letting the market mechanism determine outcomes. The other approach follows the Marxist paradigm in arguing that racial attitudes and racist institutions must be seen as part of a larger social system, in placing emphasis on conflict between classes and the use of power to determine the outcomes of such conflicts. The test as to which explanation of racism is superior is, in some ways, an interesting test of the relative explanatory power of these competing social paradigms.

The very persistence of racism in the United States lends support to our approach. So do repeated instances of employers using blacks as strikebreakers, as in the massive steel strike of 1919, and employer-instigated exacerbation of racial antagonisms during that strike and many others.[6] Nevertheless, the particular virulence of

[6]See, for example, David Brody, *Steelworkers in America: the Nonunion Era* (Cambridge, Mass.: Harvard University Press, 1966); Herbert Gutman, "The Negro and the United Mineworkers," in *The Negro and the American Labor Movement*, ed. J. Jacobson (New York: Anchor Books, 1968); S. Spero and H. Harris, *The Black Worker* (New York: Atheneum, 1968), passim.

racism among many blue- and white-collar workers and their families seems to refute the radical approach and support Becker.

Which of the two models better explains reality? We have already mentioned that our approach predicts that capitalists gain and workers lose from racism, while the conventional approach propounded by Becker predicts precisely the opposite. In the latter approach racism has an equalizing effect on the white income distribution, while in the former racism has an un-equalizing effect. The statistical relationship between the extent of racism and the degree of inequality among whites provides a simple, yet clear test of the two approaches. This section describes that test and its results.

First, we shall need a measure of racism. The index to be used, for reasons already mentioned, is the ratio of black median family income to white median family income (abbreviated as B/W). A low numerical value for this ratio indicates a high degree of racism. We have calculated values of this racism index, using data from the 1960 Census, for each of the largest forty-eight Standard Metropolitan Statistical Areas (SMSAs). It turns out that there is a great deal of variation from SMSA to SMSA in the B/W index of racism, even within the North; southern SMSAs generally demonstrated a greater degree of racism. The statistical techniques used exploit this variation.

We shall also need measures of inequality among whites. Two convenient measures are (1) the percentage share of all white income which is received by the top 1 percent of white families, and (2) the Gini coefficient of white incomes, a measure that captures inequality within as well as between social classes.[7]

Both of these inequality measures vary considerably among the SMSAs; there is also a substantial amount of variation in these within the subsample of northern SMSAs. Therefore, it is interesting to examine whether the pattern of variation of the inequality and racism variables can be explained by causal hypotheses. This is our first source of empirical evidence.

A systematic relationship across SMSAs between racism and

---

[7]The Gini coefficient varies between zero and 1, with zero indicating perfect equality, and 1 indicating perfect inequality. For a more complete exposition, see H. Miller, *Income Distribution in the United States* (Washington, D.C.: Government Printing Office, 1966). Data for the computation of G_w and S_1 for 48 SMSAs were taken from the 1960 Census. A full description of the computational techniques used is available in my dissertation.

white inequality does exist and is highly significant: the correlation coefficient is $-.47$ (the negative sign indicates that where racism is greater, income inequality *among whites* is also greater).[8] This result is consistent with our model and inconsistent with the predictions of Becker's model.

This evidence, however, should not be accepted too quickly. The correlations reported may not reflect actual causality, since other independent forces may be simultaneously influencing both variables in the same way. As is the case with many other statistical analyses, the model must be expanded to control for such other factors. We know from previous inter-SMSA income-distribution studies that the most important additional factors that should be introduced into our model are: (1) the industrial and occupational structure of the SMSAs, (2) the region in which the SMSAs are located, (3) the average income of the SMSAs, and (4) the proportion of the SMSA population that is black. These factors were introduced into the model by the technique of multiple regression analysis. We estimated separate equations using the Gini index and the top one percent share as measures of white inequality.

All SMSAs ($n = 48$):

$$G_w = 0.492 - 0.097(B/W) - 0.134\,PM - 0.066\,WC - 0.012\,MWY$$
$$ (3.29) \qquad\quad (5.50) \qquad\;\; (1.89) \qquad\;\; (3.49)$$
$$R^2 = 0.685$$

elasticity: $-.19$ $-.11$ $-.09$ $-.21$

$$S_1 = 0.094 - 0.059(B/W) - 0.043\,PM + 0.029\,WC + 0.001\,MWY$$
$$ (4.32) \qquad\quad (3.80) \qquad\;\; (1.81) \qquad\;\; (0.72)$$
$$R^2 = 0.511$$

elasticity: $-.55$ $-.19$ $.19$ $.10$

$$G_W = 0.480 - 0.076(B/W) - 0.130\,PM - 0.073\,WC - 0.012\,MWY$$
$$ (1.79) \qquad\quad (4.74) \qquad\;\; (1.99) \qquad\;\; (2.92)$$
$$R^2 = 0.690$$

$$+\ 0.038\,PNW$$
$$(0.74)$$

[8]The correlation coefficient reported in the text is between G_w and B/W. The equivalent correlation between S_1 and B/W is $R = -.55$. A similar calculation by S. Bowles, across states instead of SMSAs, resulted in an $R = -.58$.

Non-southern SMSAs ($n = 36$):

$$G_W = 0.400 - 0.098(B/W) - 0.088\,PM + 0.078\,WC - 0.002\,MWY$$
$$\qquad\quad (2.10) \qquad\quad (3.00) \qquad\quad (2.10) \qquad\quad (0.46)$$
$$R^2 = 0.319$$

$$S_1 = 0.067 - 0.062(B/W) - 0.028\,PM + 0.034\,WC + 0.0043\,MWY$$
$$\qquad\quad (2.80) \qquad\quad (2.00) \qquad\quad (2.00) \qquad\quad (1.90)$$
$$R^2 = 0.355$$

Where
G_W = Gini coefficient of income for white families
S_1 = Share of all white income received by top 1 percent of white families
B/W = Ratio of black median family income to white median family income
PM = Percent of SMSA employment in manufacturing
WC = Percent of SMSA employment in white-collar occupations
MWY = Median white family income in SMSA
PNW = Percent of nonwhite SMSA population

Figures in parentheses represent absolute *t*-values of coefficients.

All the equations showed strikingly uniform statistical results: racism was a significantly un-equalizing force on the white income distribution, even when other factors were held constant. A 1 percent increase in the ratio of black-to-white median incomes (that is, a 1 percent decrease in racism) was associated with a .2 percent decrease in white inequality, as measured by the Gini coefficient. The corresponding effect on the top 1 percent share of white income was two and a half times as large, indicating that most of the inequality among whites generated by racism was associated with increased income for the richest 1 percent of white families. Further statistical investigation reveals that increases in racism had an insignificant effect on the share received by the poorest whites, and resulted in a decrease in the income share of the whites in the middling income brackets.[9] This is true even when the southern SMSAs are excluded.

Within our model, we can specify a number of mechanisms that further explain the statistical finding that racism increases inequality among whites. We shall consider two mechanisms here: (1) total wages of white labor are reduced by racial antagonisms, in part

[9]A more rigorous presentation of these variables and the statistical results is available in my dissertation.

because union growth and labor militancy are inhibited; and (2) the supply of public services, especially in education, available to low- and middle-income whites is reduced as a result of racial antagonisms.

Wages of white labor are lessened by racism because the fear of a cheaper and underemployed black labor supply in the area is invoked by employers when labor presents its wage demands. Racial antagonisms on the shop floor deflect attention from labor grievances related to working conditions, permitting employers to cut costs. Racial divisions among labor prevent the development of united worker organizations both within the work place and in the labor movement as a whole. As a result, union strength and union militancy will be less, the greater the extent of racism. A historical example of this process is the already mentioned use of racial and ethnic divisions to destroy the solidarity of the 1919 steel strikers. By contrast, during the 1890s, black-white class solidarity greatly aided mineworkers in building militant unions among workers in Alabama, West Virginia, and other coal-field areas.[10]

The above argument and examples contradict the common belief that an exclusionary racial policy strengthens, rather than weakens the bargaining power of unions. Racial exclusion increases bargaining power only when entry into an occupation or industry can be effectively limited. Industrial-type unions are much less able to restrict entry than craft unions or organizations such as the American Medical Association. This is not to deny that much of organized labor is egregiously racist or that *some* skilled craft unionists may benefit from racism.[11] But it is important to distinguish actual discrimination practice from the objective economic self-interest of union members.

The second mechanism concerns the allocation of expenditures for public services. The most important of these services is education. Racial antagonisms dilute both the desire and the ability of poor white parents to improve educational opportunities for their children. Antagonisms between blacks and poor whites drive wedges between

[10]See Brody, *Steelworkers in America*; Gutman, "Negro and the United Mineworkers"; and Spero and Harris, *Black Worker*.

[11]See, for example, H. Hill, "The Racial Practices of Organized Labor: the Contemporary Record," in *The Negro and the American Labor Movement*.

the two groups and reduce their ability to join in a united political movement pressing for improved and more equal education. Moreover, many poor whites recognize that, however inferior their own schools, black schools are even worse. This provides some degree of satisfaction and identification with the status quo, reducing the desire of poor whites to press politically for better schools in their neighborhoods. Ghettos tend to be located near poor white neighborhoods more often than near rich white neighborhoods; racism thus reduces the potential tax base of school districts containing poor whites. Also, pressures by teachers' groups to improve all poor schools is reduced by racial antagonisms between predominantly white teaching staffs and black children and parents.[12]

The statistical validity of the above mechanisms can be tested in a causal model. The effect of racism on unionism is tested by estimating an equation in which the percentage of the SMSA labor force which is unionized is the dependent variable, with racism and the structural variables (such as the SMSA industrial structure) as the independent variables. The schooling mechanism is tested by estimating a similar equation in which the dependent variable is inequality in years of schooling completed among white males aged 25–29 years old.[13]

All SMSAs (n = 41 for unionism and n = 48 for schooling inequality):

$$\text{Unionism} = -0.637 + 0.646\,(B/W) + 0.863\,PM + 0.291\,WC + 0.086\,MWY$$
$$(2.20) \qquad (3.58) \qquad (0.90) \qquad (2.55)$$
$$R^2 = 0.544$$

$$\text{Edginw} = \quad 0.563 - 0.563\,(B/W) - 0.185\,PM - 0.117\,WC + 0.014\,MWY$$
$$(6.22) \qquad (1.86) \qquad (1.25) \qquad (1.30)$$
$$R^2 = 0.566$$

Non-southern SMSAs (n = 31 for unionism and n = 36 for schooling inequality):

[12]In a similar fashion, racial antagonisms reduce the political pressure on governmental agencies to provide other public services which would have a pro-poor distributional impact. The two principal items in this category are public health services and welfare payments in the Aid to Families with Dependent Children program.

[13]These dependent variables do not perfectly represent the phenomena described, but serve as reasonable proxy variables for these purposes.

$$\text{Unionism} = -0.028\,(B/W) + 0.450\,PM + 0.527\,WC \qquad R^2 = 0.214$$
$$\phantom{\text{Unionism} =} (0.04) \qquad\qquad (1.69) \qquad\quad (1.69)$$

$$\text{Edginw} = \quad 0.33 - 0.504\,(B/W) - 0.063\,PM - 0.104\,WC \qquad R^2 = 0.497$$
$$\phantom{\text{Edginw} = 0.33} (4.07) \qquad\qquad (0.88) \qquad\quad (1.24)$$

Where Unionism = Percent of blue-collar employees in SMSA working in establishments with a majority of workers covered by collective bargaining agreements;

Edginw = Gini coefficient of years of schooling completed for white males, aged 25–29.

Once again, the results of this statistical test appear to confirm the hypothesis of the radical model. The racism variable is statistically significant in both education equations and its sign predicts that a greater degree of racism results in greater amount of schooling inequality among whites. The effect of racism on unionization rates is less clear: although the coefficient of racism is positive and significant (implying a higher degree of unionization where there is less racism) for all the SMSAs, together, the estimate for non-southern SMSAs yields a coefficient of racism not significantly different from zero. The racism variable in the "all SMSAs" equation may therefore be picking up *regional* differences in unionization.

All in all, the empirical evidence suggests that racism is in the economic interests of capitalists and other rich whites, and against the economic interests of poor whites and white workers. Nevertheless, a full assessment of the importance of racism for capitalism would probably conclude that the primary significance of racism is not strictly economic. The simple economics of racism does not explain why many workers seem to be so vehemently racist when racism is not in their economic self-interest. In extra-economic ways, racism helps to legitimize inequality, alienation, and powerlessness—legitimization necessary for the stability of the capitalist system as a whole. For example, many whites believe that welfare payments to blacks are a far more important factor in their taxes than is military spending. Through racism, poor whites come to believe that their poverty is caused by blacks who are willing to take away their jobs, and at lower wages, thus concealing the fact that a substantial amount of income inequality is inevitable in a capitalist society. Racism thus transfers the locus of whites' resentment toward blacks and away from capitalism.

Racism also provides some psychological benefits to poor and working-class whites. For example, the opportunity to participate in another's oppression compensates for one's own misery. The parallel here is to the subjugation of women in the family: after a day of alienating labor, the tired husband can compensate by oppressing his wife. Furthermore, not being at the bottom of the heap is some solace for an unsatisfying life; this argument was successfully used by the southern oligarchy against poor whites allied with blacks in the interracial Populist movement of the late nineteenth century.

Thus, racism is likely to take firm root in a society that breeds an individualistic and competitive ethos. In general, blacks provide a convenient and visible scapegoat for problems that actually derive from the institutions of capitalism. As long as building a real alternative to capitalism does not seem feasible to most whites, we can expect that identifiable and vulnerable scapegoats will prove functional to the status quo. These extra-economic factors thus neatly dovetail with the economic aspects of racism in their mutual service to the perpetuation of capitalism.

.4. Job Discrimination and Education: Rates of Return to Education of Mexican-Americans and Euro-Americans in Santa Clara County, California

PHILIP M. BLAIR

THIS ARTICLE examines income, education, and the likelihood of ethnic discrimination in the labor market. The study site is Santa Clara County, an important industrial metropolitan area in northern California, with a 1970 population of approximately one million. The study uses U.S. Census data collected in 1966 by the Santa Clara Planning Department in a door-to-door survey of 267,000 households in the county.[1] The tools of the analysis are incomes and private and social marginal internal rates of return to investment in education.

Human capital, like physical capital, is a factor of production. An important part of human capital is the amount of schooling a person takes before entering the labor force. The marginal rate of return to schooling expenditure is generally considered the best available measure of the profitability of investment in education.[2] To date,

[1]Santa Clara County Planning Department. *1966 Special Census Manual: Part I, Organization and Operations, Santa Clara County Special Census of April 1, 1966,* 1968. *Part II, Detailed Exhibits, Santa Clara County Special Census of April 1, 1966,* 1968. *Note:* Santa Clara County is coterminous with the San Jose Standard Metropolitan Statistical Area of the federal Census.

[2]Rates of return have certain methodological advantages and disadvantages over "present values of lifetime net income stream." Both are alternate measures of the profitability of educational investment. Some of these advantages and disadvantages

rates of return to investment in schooling have been estimated in approximately thirty studies in as many countries or regions.[3] Rates have not previously been computed in a concentrated labor market as small as a single county or metropolitan area, however. Nor have they previously been estimated specifically for Mexican-Americans as a separately identified group.[4]

Our sample of the Santa Clara County population, for which we estimate the rates of return reported here, consists of 8,490 Mexican-American and 102,600 Euro-American[5] (as well as 860 Afro-Ameri-

---

are reviewed in Philip Blair, "Rates of Return to Majority and Minority Groups in Santa Clara County, California" (Ph.D. diss., Stanford University, 1971). On balance, rates of return seem to be the better indicator of profitability than present income value. Rates of return can be directly compared with rates to physical capital, whereas, in general, present values cannot. On the other hand, solving the discount formula for the rate occasionally yields multiple solutions (depending on the number of "sign changes" in the income stream), the economic meaningfulness of which must then be assessed by the researcher. Present income values, in contrast, have *unique* values for a given lifetime stream, once a discount rate is assumed.

[3]For the United States as a whole, Gary Becker (*Human Capital* [New York: National Bureau of Economic Research, 1964]) has made estimates of rates of return to schooling based partly on 1940 and 1950 Census data and partly on other survey data. Giora Hanoch, in both "Personal Earnings and Investment in Schooling" (Ph.D. diss., University of Chicago, 1965) and "An Economic Analysis of Earnings and Schooling," *Journal of Human Resources* 2, no. 3 (Summer 1967): 310–329, estimated rates for "whites" and "nonwhites" in the North and South, using the 1:1000 sample of the 1960 Census, without making adjustments for unemployed, taxes, growth, mortality, academic ability, or estimating actual schooling costs.

Outside the United States, the nearly thirty rate of return studies made to date have been summarized by Martin Carnoy in "The Political Economy of Education," mimeographed (Stanford University, 1970). As a few examples, rate of return estimates have been made in India (Nalla Gouden, 1967), Great Britain (Blaug, 1967), Mexico, Venezuela, Colombia, and Chile (Carnoy, 1967). Present value estimates have been made for northern Nigeria (S. Bowles, "The Efficient Allocation of Resources in Education: A Planning Model With Applications to Northern Nigeria" [Ph.D. diss., Harvard University, 1965]). See also G. Psacharapoulos, "The Economic Returns to Higher Education in Twenty-Five Countries," mimeographed (London School of Economics, Higher Education Unit, 1970).

[4]Mexican-Americans are statistically lumped with "whites" in the federal Census. However, the Census separately presents certain results for "WPSS—White Persons of Spanish Surname," a less accurate representation of Mexican-Americans. In any case, rates of return to educational investment have not previously been estimated for either "Mexican-Americans" or "WPSS."

[5]We define "Euro-Americans," as whites minus Mexican-Americans, as classified in the 1966 Santa Clara County census. This is the same as the term "Anglos," commonly found elsewhere. We also occasionally use the term "Chicanos." When we do, we mean it synonymously with "Mexican-Americans."

can[6]) employed nonstudent male heads of households in which the household head was the only employed member of the household.[7] Mean incomes and the rates of return are estimated both for majority- and minority-group members who reside in the county as a whole and majority- and minority-group members who reside in that subregion of the county designated as the "Mexican-American ghetto," that is, those census tracts (districts) having a Mexican-American population exceeding 30 percent of the total. Stratifying the sample into these two places of residence permits us to distinguish any purely ethnic effects on incomes and the rates from those effects associated with ghetto residence regardless of ethnic origin.

The study considers the question: Does the Mexican-American minority population in Santa Clara County receive the same incomes and/or marginal rates of return as the Euro-American majority residing there? If not, how do the minority incomes and rates of return differ from those of the majority?[8] The specific concerns are

[6]Because blacks constitute only 1 percent of the Santa Clara County population (vs. 10 percent Mexican-Americans), our results for blacks are less reliable than they are for Mexican-Americans and Euro-Americans. The results for blacks are thus de-emphasized in this study. Neighboring counties have a larger proportion of black population than Santa Clara County and would thus be better places for specifically studying returns to schooling of blacks. We use the term "black," "Afro-American," and "Negro" synonymously in this study.

[7]An additional 48,000 Santa Clara County households having *two* nonstudent breadwinners (mostly working married couples) instead of *one* breadwinner were also analyzed. The results for the two-breadwinner households are not reported in this article, however, since one-breadwinner data more closely relate the schooling to the income of one individual and are, therefore, statistically more meaningful than results for two-breadwinner households. For the two-breadwinner results, see Blair, "Rates of Return to Majority and Minority Groups in Santa Clara County."

[8]One could argue that to estimate a rate of return in a region as small as a metropolitan area or single county of one million persons, any possible biasing effects of migration into or out of the area on return rate should be taken into account. Specifically, do today's students now living in the area, who might use rates of return (consciously or unconsciously) in deciding if it "pays" for them to take additional schooling, have essentially the same characteristics as the sample of employed-in-1966 people for whom the rates were estimated? Large in-migration into Santa Clara County has taken place. Much of the employment has been in high-quality defense and electronics which pay relatively high salaries for given levels of schooling. The good climate is an additional attraction, so the high pay is "real" and not merely compensatory for an undesirable location. At given schooling levels, then, the highest "quality" people (highest academic ability, quality of their education, etc.) migrated in.

By neglecting (as we have done) any difference between the income-productivity

summarized in the following three questions: (1) Do the actual patterns in incomes and the marginal rates of return appear to suggest ethnic discrimination? (2) If so, does this discrimination seem to be located primarily on the education or on the employment side of the system? (3) Are the observed patterns consistent with the known large minority "dropout" phenomenon?[9]

This last question tests the assumption that students experience a "sheepskin effect" on rate of return as a result of completing diploma levels of schooling. It is generally believed that marginal return rates are normally higher at the completion of schooling levels that yield a diploma than they are for "dropping out" after completing schooling levels that do not yield a diploma. Obtaining a graduation certificate is expected to have a pecuniary value of its own beyond the number of additional years of schooling it represents.[10]

The study shows that Mexican-Americans in the Santa Clara County are worse off than Euro-Americans of the same age and with the same amount of schooling in the nominal incomes they earn and in their probability of employment. Furthermore, Mexican-Americans receive a lower rate of return than Euro-Americans to investing in finishing high school and college, but get a much higher rate of return to investing in dropout levels of high school and college. These rates are not significantly affected by differential rates of employment or by rather large fluctuations in public expenditures per pupil on schooling. Thus, these findings seem to imply that the lower incomes and the pattern of rates of return are primarily the result of

characteristics of the immigrants who were part of the 1966 county census sample of the labor force and the students now being educated in Santa Clara County schools, our reported return rates probably include some positive differential return to "quality," beyond that to schooling level attained. Thus, neglecting the effects on rates of return of migration into or out of the county *may have overstated* somewhat the "true" marginal return rates due only to school attainment level. The overstatement in the reported rates is probably true for both majority and minority groups, though, since the same migration considerations apply to both.

[9]See, for example, *San Francisco Chronicle*, 31 August, 1970.

[10]W. Lee Hansen et al., "Schooling and Earnings of Low Achievers," *American Economic Review* (June 1970): 409–418, however, showed that the "sheepskin effect," although common, is not universal. For low-achievement students specifically, he found that a certain number of years of additional job experience or a certain number of points scored on the Armed Forces Qualification Test brought greater income return than did additional formal schooling, even when the formal schooling led to a high school diploma.

discrimination in pay for similar skills, rather than primarily caused by inequality in schooling expenditures or employment rates.

THE RESULTS

Incomes

Columns *A* and *B* of Table 4.1 show mean incomes of Euro-American and Mexican-American employed nonstudent male heads of one-breadwinner households that are located county-wide, as a function of the schooling of the head. Table 4.1 is a summary for all ages of detailed schooling-age-income profiles not shown here. Columns *D* and *E* give the same information for households located in the Mexican-American ghetto of the county. We can see from column *C* that, on the (unweighted) average, the incomes of Mexican-Americans living in Santa Clara County are less by $1,713 than those of Euro-Americans of the same schooling level. This difference represents about 20 percent of the mean Euro-American income of these household heads ($9,000). The ethnic income gap at constant schooling can be interpreted as either a "tax" on minority status or a "rent" to majority status; in either case, it is a gross indication that ethnic discrimination exists. From a comparison of the income differences in column *C* with those in column *F*, we see that the average ethnic income gap at constant schooling level is about 50 percent smaller in the ghetto (where it is $880) than it is county-wide ($1,713).

An alternative measure of the Mexican-American's economic disadvantage in relation to the majority is the number of additional years of school-attainment level needed by Mexican-Americans, beyond the schooling needed by Euro-Americans, to earn a specified income. This average "ethnic schooling penalty" against Mexican-Americans amounts to about two and one-half years of additional schooling for all ages county-wide. At younger ages, both the majority and minority income-versus-schooling curves have less steep slopes than for all ages, while the vertical income gap at given schooling is about the same. Hence the "schooling penalty" for young Mexican-Americans is even greater than it is for all ages.

Table 4.2 consolidates various measures of Mexican-Americans' economic disadvantage relative to Euro-Americans in our sample.

Table 4.1.　Mean Incomes and Income Differences for Employed Nonstudent Male Heads of One-Breadwinner Households in Santa Clara County and Its Mexican-American Ghetto, All Ages, 1966
(In Dollars)

Schooling Attainment Level, Years	In Santa Clara County			In Mexican-American Ghetto		
	Mean Income and (Sample Size)		Ethnic Difference At Given Schooling Level $A - B = C$	Mean Income and (Sample Size)		Ethnic Difference At Given Schooling Level $D - E = F$
	Euro-American A	Mexican-American B		Euro-American D	Mexican American E	
K–6	6,877 (919)	5,614 (914)	1,263	5,179 (155)	5,200 (347)	519
7–8	7,736 (3,818)	6,361 (978)	1,375	6,629 (370)	5,732 (314)	897
9	8,130 (1,641)	6,423 (404)	1,707	6,789 (147)	5,904 (131)	885
10–11	8,382 (6,580)	6,730 (1,095)	1,652	6,971 (502)	6,223 (338)	748
12	$9,333 (23,995)	7,537 (1,405)	1,796	7,629 (971)	6,489 (290)	1,140
13–15	10,595 (17,507)	8,991 (520)	1,604	7,933 (416)	6,784 (72)	1,149
16+	13,976 (25,199)	11,386 (273)	2,590	9,738 (231)	8,916 (18)	822
Column average	9,290	7,577	1,713	7,258	6,464	880[a]
Column range	7,099	5,772	—	4,019	3,716	—
Difference between column ranges —			1,327			303
Column *SD*	2,210	2,030	180	1,154	1,110	44

SOURCE: Blair, "Rates of Return to Majority and Minority Groups in Santa Clara County."
[a] Differs slightly from $7,258 - 6,464 = 794$.

**Table 4.2.   Indicators of Mexican-American Disadvantage Relative to
Euro-American Employed Nonstudent Male Household Heads, in Mean,
Range, and Standard Deviation of Income in Santa Clara County and Its
Mexican-American Ghetto, All Ages 1966**
(In Dollars)

Type of Mexican-American disadvantage relative to Euro-Americans	One-Breadwinner Households		Two-Breadwinner Households	
	County-wide	In Mexican-American Ghetto	County-wide	In Mexican-American Ghetto
Average deficiency in Mexican-American income	1,713	880	1,954	1,985
Average deficiency in range of Mexican-American income	1,327	303	352	1,991
Deficiency in Mexican-American standard deviation of income	180	44	100	409

SOURCE: One-breadwinner households: Table 1, columns C and F; two-breadwinner households; Blair, "Rates of Return to Majority and Minority Groups in Santa Clara County," Table 6.

Although schooling-age-income profiles, income differences at constant schooling, and rates of return were also computed for black household heads, the sample of blacks in the county was not large enough to yield significant results.

Schooling Costs

To estimate county-wide marginal rates of return to investment in schooling, we need to know average county-wide institutional schooling cost per pupil, by ethnic membership of the pupil and grade level. We estimate these schooling costs for the academic year 1967–68[11] by using a process of pupil-weighting of institutional

[11]The sample of persons surveyed in the 1966 county census was actually educated decades earlier, in 1950–51, on the average. At that earlier date, institutional schooling costs were only about 40 percent of what they were in 1967–68 (constant dollars). The bias introduced into return rates by using the higher 1967–68 schooling costs (as we have done), therefore, would tend to cause our reported return rates to be somewhat understated for both Mexican- and Euro-Americans.

schooling costs in the different school districts. The computation was made from the ethnic proportions in the populations living in the sixty-eight school districts that make up the county, and school district-wide costs per pupil by grade, from county and state department of education records for that year.

We also made separate estimates of the average institutional schooling costs per pupil attending schools located in the Mexican-American ghetto subregion of the county. Table 4.3 gives these estimated average institutional schooling costs per pupil, in both the county-wide and ghetto schools, by grade level and ethnic membership of the student.

Table 4.3. Estimated Average Annual Current[a] Institutional Schooling Cost per Pupil in Santa Clara County and Its Mexican-American Ghetto, 1967–68

(In Dollars per Average Daily Attendance)

Schooling Attainment Level, Years	Euro-American Pupils		Mexican-American Pupils		Afro-American Pupils	
	County A	Ghetto[d] B	County[b] C	Ghetto[d] D	County[c] E	Ghetto[d] F
K–6	581	535	547	503	575	529
7–8	649	597	610	562	643	592
7	721	664	678	624	714	657
10–11	721	664	678	624	714	657
12	721	664	678	624	714	657
13–14	1,160	1,068	1,090	1,001	1,148	1,055
15	1,873	1,725	1,762	1,624	1,854	1,708
16+	1,873	1,725	1,762	1,624	1,854	1,708

SOURCE: Column *A* value × average reduction factor (Blair, "Rates of Return to Majority and Minority Groups in Santa Clara County").
[a] Excluding capital expenditures, which are generally less than 5 percent of current costs.
[b] .94 × column *A* values.
[c] .99 × column *A* values.
[d] .92 × county-wide values for same ethnic group.

In the institutional schooling-cost estimates, we find that the average institutional schooling expenditure per Mexican-American pupil living in the county as a whole is about 6 percent less than the average county-wide institutional schooling expenditure per Euro-American pupil.

In addition, the average institutional schooling expenditure per pupil of any ethnic group attending a school located in the Mexican-American ghetto is about 8 percent less than the average institutional schooling expenditure per pupil of any ethnic group attending schools located in the county as a whole. Thus, a Mexican-American pupil living *within the Mexican-American ghetto area* of the county suffers both the 6 percent and 8 percent average deficiencies in institutuional schooling expenditure per pupil relative to the county population as a whole (which is 86 percent "Euro"), one figure superimposed on the other.

Institutional schooling expenditures actually differ not only from school district to school district within the county, but also from school to school within a school district, and even between classrooms within a given school. Our estimates in Table 4.3 of the differences between *average* per-pupil institutional schooling expenditure on majority and minority pupils, then, are probably somewhat understated. In any case, as shown below, any error in judging "true" county-wide average institutional schooling cost per pupil has only a minimal effect on our reported return rates.[12]

Rates of Return

The marginal internal rate of return (R) to taking a given increment of schooling is estimated by solving the discount formula

$$\sum_{i=1}^{n} \Delta y_i /(1 + R)^i = 0$$

for the (constant) nominal annual percentage rate R that equates the discounted stream of schooling *costs* (negative ΔY_i) to the discounted stream over lifetime of additional income *returns* (positive ΔY_i) associated with the additional schooling. The age index i on the sum-

[12]I am indebted to Henry Levin for comments concerning the relative unreliability of the average institutional schooling costs we have used (computed, as they were, from school-district average costs) and their effect on return rates. We find that institutional schooling cost does not affect rate of return much anyway. Becker, *Human Capital*, showed that institutional schooling cost is a much smaller fraction of total social schooling cost than is income foregone: the latter commonly amounts to at least three-fourths of total social schooling cost.

mation begins at $i = 1$, the time of the student's decision to continue additional schooling or enter the labor force. The upper age index, $i = n$, corresponds to retirement age; in our study we assume retirement to be at age 65.

Although institutional schooling costs are a much smaller component of total social schooling cost than income foregone, both of these cost components are included in our estimate of total social schooling cost. Total *private* schooling costs, on the other hand, include income foregone plus privately paid tuition and privately paid school-supply costs, but exclude institutional schooling costs.[13] The same net income benefits (*before* taxes) are used as the estimate of return in both our private and social return rate calculations.

The estimates of the county-wide social and private, and the ghetto social and private marginal internal rates of return are shown in Table 4.4 as functions of ethnic membership and pairs of proximate schooling levels.

In general, the absolute values of the marginal rates of return in our sample are small (10 to 12 percent in the county, and lower in the ghetto). They are smaller than marginal rates estimated in other studies for larger regions or for the United States as a whole.[14] The low rates are probably at least in part the result of the relative homogeneity of our sample (within ethnic group). It contains fewer extraneous factors, such as regional or sectoral differences in the population, so the results ought more nearly to approximate the return to schooling alone. Disregarding the "consumption" aspects of education, then, the apparently low real rates of return found in this study seem to support the idea that people are generally overinvesting in education.

Second, the marginal rates to university completion (16+/14th) for both Euro- and Mexican-Americans, county-wide, are slightly higher than the marginal rates to secondary school completion (12th/10½). This increase in marginal return rate to school completion apparently contradicts the commonly held notion that mar-

---

[13]In both our private and social return rate estimates, only 75 percent of total annual income was assumed to be foregone during schooling, to allow for the possibility of summer employment.

[14]See note 3 above, and Blair, "Rates of Return to Majority and Minority Groups in Santa Clara County."

Table 4.4. Marginal Internal Rates of Return to Schooling of Employed Nonstudent Male Heads of One-Breadwinner Households in Santa Clara County and Its Mexican-American Ghetto, All Ages, 1966
(In Percent)

Higher Schooling Level Instead of Lower Schooling Level, in Years	In Santa Clara County						In Mexican-American Ghetto			
	Private Rate			Social Rate			Private Rate		Social Rate	
	Euro-American	Mexican-American	Afro-American	Euro-American	Mexican-American	Afro-American	Euro-American	Mexican-American	Euro-American	Mexican-American
7th/3rd	(36.0)[a]	13.3	n.a	(29.3)	7.9	n.a	(9.4)	17.6	(5.2)	9.6
9th/7th	6.3	b	neg.	5.1	b	neg.	(11.9)	1.1	(7.6)	1.0
10th/9th	4.1	20.4	(−11.6)	3.4	15.2	(−11.6)	8.6	11.1	6.6	10.0
12th/10th	9.8	8.1	11.3	8.7	7.1	10.5	7.5	b	6.6	b
14th/12th	7.6	11.1	11.3	7.1	10.5	10.7	4.4	−1.0	3.7	−1.2
16+/14th	9.9	8.7	12.4	9.2	8.0	11.8	6.7	8.9	6.2	8.4
Column average	12.3	12.3	11.7	10.5	9.8	11.0	8.1	9.2	6.0	6.7

SOURCE: Blair, "Rates of Return to Majority and Minority Groups in Santa Clara County."
[a] Parentheses mean that the indicated figures are the least reliable in their columns.
[b] No economically meaningful solution.
neg. = negative and undetermined.

ginal return rates to school completion inevitably "fall off" at increasing schooling for any ethnic group, because the increased educational investment is supposed to be subject to continually diminishing marginal return.

Instead, our county-wide rates of return to completing high school and college appear to support the reasoning in Carnoy's dynamic model of education as an elite-forming and elite-serving process,[15] in which a country or region's marginal rate of return to university completion may either exceed or be less than its marginal rate of return to secondary and primary school completion, depending on its current stage of "development." When the university-completion marginal rate exceeds the secondary-completion marginal rate (as it does in our sample) it means, according to that model, that non-elite students have long since permeated the primary school system and have dominated the enrollment in the secondary system for some (shorter) length of time; but they have not yet replaced elites as the dominant enrollment in the university system.

The rates reported in Table 4.4 have not been adjusted for unemployment, taxes, or mortality. These adjustments would *reduce* all rates below their reported values. On the other hand, addition of a "psychic income" pecuniary equivalent to the consumption value of education and the inclusion of an economic growth factor would tend to adjust the return rates *upward*. The adjustment for unemployment has a negligible effect on rates of return, since income foregone (cost) is lowered as well as the net benefits to schooling. Taxes and mortality also result in negligible downward adjustments of the rates.[16]

In estimating school costs, we show that Mexican-American students attend schools which, on the average, have lower costs per pupil than Euro-American schools. If costs per pupil are a good measure of the quality of schooling, including the lower costs per pupil of Mexican-American schools in our social rate of return estimates would raise the real rate of return to Mexican-American investment. If this "quality" adjustment equalized Mexican- and Euro-American rates, we could say that lower incomes for Mexican-Americans are primarily the result of receiving lower-quality schooling (as measured by costs per pupil). Thus, "descrimination" could

[15]See Carnoy, "The Political Economy of Education."

[16]Blair, "Rates of Return to Majority and Minority Groups in Santa Clara County."

be attributed to discrimination in the training market rather than the labor market. In fact, however, even assuming that Mexican-American institutional schooling costs are 20 percent below Euro-American costs per pupil produced little change in the rates of return to Mexican-Americans.[17] Although costs per pupil may represent only part of the discrimination in schooling and may not pick up the fact that teachers devote less time to transferring skills to Mexican-Americans (even though they are paid the same as for teaching Euro-Americans), apparently much of the discrimination in income is the result not of poorer training, but of actual differences in income paid because of ethnic identity. Furthermore, the small effect of adjusting incomes for unemployment leads us to conclude that the difference between Mexican-American and Euro-American rates of return to completing high school and college is caused by income discrimination, not by higher unemployment of Mexican-Americans.

These adjustments are the only ones made in the study, so we do not know what the full effect on rates of return of making all possible adjustments would be. Nevertheless, if we neglect "psychic income" as being essentially unmeasurable, we can plausibly assume that the over-all net effect of making all reasonable adjustments to the rates of return would probably reduce them. After considering the probable net effects of all adjustments, then, we still conclude that, on the average, the unadjusted rates of return exhibited in Table 4.4 are not much higher than rates of return to low-risk securities.

Of course, in a discrimination study such as this one, the relative *patterns* in the majority and minority's marginal rates of return at various schooling levels and places of residence are of more interest than their absolute values. These relative patterns are examined next.

Ethnic Effect on Return Rates

We are interested in determining whether the Mexican-American (minority) group's marginal rates of return to schooling are significantly different from the Euro-American (majority) group's return rates, and, if so, whether such ethnic difference could plausibly be attributed either to schooling-type or employment-type discrimination.

---

[17]Ibid.

The pattern of county-wide (social and private) marginal internal rates in Table 4.4 shows clear evidence of the predictable "positive certificate effect" in the Euro-American group's rates. And, although the Mexican-American rates are not consistently smaller in absolute value than those of the majority group, there is a noticeable "*opposite* certificate effect*" in the Mexican-American marginal rates county-wide. Mexican-Americans in Santa Clara County receive smaller marginal return rates than Euro-Americans to schooling at diploma completion levels; they get larger marginal return rates that Euros at the noncompletion, or "dropout," schooling levels.[18]

This ethnic difference in the "completion" and "noncompletion" marginal rate of return patterns additionally suggests that Mexican-Americans in the county are discriminated against in the labor market; they reap a lower economic reward to investing in a high school or college diploma but dropping out yields a higher rate of return.[19] The distortion in economic return, the "opposite certificate effect," suggests that Mexican-American students may sense their inferior future potential marginal rates to graduating from high school or college and their superior marginal rates to "dropping out," and so adjust their schooling differently from students of the majority group.

Table 4.5 consolidates the several indicators of the economic disadvantage felt by the Mexican-Americans in our sample. It repeats the "one-breadwinner" half of Table 4.2, and adds ethnic differences (Euro minus Mexican-American) in social marginal return rates—differences derived from Table 4.4.

The first component of Mexican-American disadvantage is a lower income *level* at the same age and schooling level attainment of employed, nonstudent, male heads of one-breadwinner county-wide households. The average difference is $1,713 lower (19 percent) than Euro-American income. This county-wide ethnic income gap is almost 100 percent greater than in the Mexican-American ghetto, where it is $880.

---

[18]Carnoy found evidence of a similar "opposite certificate effect" when comparing rates of return for urban and rural dwellers in Puerto Rico; see Martin Carnoy, "Rates of Return to Education and the Growth of Human Resources in Puerto Rico," *Comparative Education Review* (February 1972).

[19]See note 9 above.

Table 4.5.   Over-All Summary of Mexican-American Disadvantage Relative to Euro-American Employed Nonstudent Male Heads of One-Breadwinner Households in Santa Clara County and Its Mexican-American Ghetto, All Ages, 1966

Type of Mexican-American Disadvantage Relative to Euro-Americans		Residence County-Wide		Residence in Mexican-American Ghetto	
Average deficiency in Mexican-American income		$1,713		$880	
Average deficiency in range of Mexican-American income		1,327		303	
Deficiency in Mexican-American standard deviation of income		180		44	
Opposite Certificate Effect: Euro-American Social Marginal Return Rate	At diploma completion levels	at 12/10½: +1.6% (pos.)	at 16+/14: +1.2% (pos.)	at 12/10½: n.a.	at 16/14: −2.2% (neg.)
Minus Mexican-American Social Marginal Return Rate	At diploma noncompletion levels	at 10½/9: −11.8% (neg.)	at 14/12: −3.4% (neg.)	at 10½/9: −3.4% (neg.)	at 14/12: +4.9% (pos.)

SOURCE: Tables 4.2 and 4.4.

The second ethnic distortion is a deficiency in the Mexican-American income *range*, about 19 percent of the majority's income range. This is a $1,327 short fall, county-wide. The ethnic deficiency in income range is also more pronounced in the county as a whole than in the Mexican-American ghetto area, where it is $303.

The third distortion is the ethnically opposite "certificate effect" in the county-wide marginal rates of return observed above. County-wide, Euro-American minus Mexican-American marginal rates are *positive* at both the high school (12) and college (16+) diploma completion levels, and *negative* at nondiploma levels (10½ and 14).[20]

[20]This study permits us to assess some of the strengths and weaknesses of marginal return rate as a tool for sensing discrimination. The marginal return rates observed in our sample (Table 4.4) failed to reveal the consistent differences in income seen in Table 4.1 between the Euro-American majority and the Mexican-American minority

Within the Mexican-American ghetto, on the other hand, no clear pattern emerges in the Euro-American minus Mexican-American marginal return rates.

Other Income Factors

Factors other than school-attainment level can affect a group's income and, consequently, its rates to investment in schooling. How much, then, of the apparent opposite certificate effect in the majority and minority's rates in our sample is real, and how much is merely an artifact of not having made enough "corrections" for other factors that could affect income?

The academic ability of the student and the quality of the schooling received would, if corrected for, probably attenuate the certificate effects in both the majority and minority's return rates. That is, the "peaks and valleys" in Table 4.4, if corrected for income-determining factors other than quality of schooling, ethnicity, and residence, would be "flattened out" to a certain extent. This flattening would be caused by: (1) only the more academically able of the Mexican-American students probably even entered high school, whereas practically all the "Anglos" of the same age did (correcting for ability would lower Mexican-Americans' rate of return to 10.5 years of school);

---

group at given school attainment level and residence. This insensitivity of rates of return to income level is true even when the ethnic income differences are as large as 20 percent. When the income of one of the groups is consistently lower at given school attainment levels than the income of the other group (as is the case in our sample), then the first group's income-foregone (i.e., its costs) is also lower than the second's (see Becker, *Human Capital*). Rates of return are raised by the lower income-foregone.

On the useful side, however, we have seen how using marginal rates as our instrument (Table 4.4) "amplified," and thus plainly revealed the majority's and minority's "certificate effects" that were less obvious in the incomes themselves (Table 4.1). This desirable ability of marginal return rate to capture a certificate effect if there is one comes from the fact that when the increase in a particular group's income caused by that group's taking a particular schooling increment is relatively large, then that income-foregone cost (figured at the lower of the two proximate schooling levels) is relatively small. These two factors combine to yield a relatively *large* marginal return rate to that particular increment of schooling. And, by the same token, if certificate effects obtain and if the marginal income gain resulting from the taking of a particular step of schooling is relatively *small*, then the income-foregone cost (again computed at the lower of the two proximate schooling levels) is in this case relatively *large*, which yields a relatively *small* marginal return rate to taking that additional schooling.

and (2) minority schooling is known to be of generally inferior *quality* to majority schooling, even when there are equal costs per pupil.

Data on such characteristics as academic ability of persons in the sample and quality of their schooling were not available at the time of the study. Neither were data on workers' labor productivity by ethnic membership (another possible partial explainer of income difference). These corrections (for academic ability, schooling quality, and labor productivity) were therefore not made. Future research may determine how much of the "zigzag" seen in the Euro- and Mexican-American county-wide marginal rates of Table 4.4 is caused by ethnic income discrimination alone, and how much of it can be explained by ethnic difference in academic ability, schooling quality, and worker productivity in the sample. In any case, ethnic differences in these other income factors are manifestations of an over-all discrimination in a society. We should avoid the temptation to "overpurify" the findings by attempting to "separate out" allegedly "independent" income-explaining variables.

Ghetto-Residence Effect on Return Rates

The certificate effects in both the majority's and minority's marginal return rates are less noticeable in the Mexican-American ghetto subregion of Santa Clara County (where the return rates are also less reliable) than in the county as a whole (See Table 4.4). Unlike the county as a whole, the marginal rates in the ghetto *fall* slightly for the majority from high school completion to college completion.

When we compare *absolute values* of the ghetto and county-wide rates for a given ethnic group, we see that ghetto residents (majority as well as minority) generally do worse in rate of return than county-wide residents of the same ethnic group. Although we speak of this as a "ghetto-residence *effect*" on income and rates of return, we are really referring only to *correlation* between place of residence and economic welfare, and not to causality between them. While it is true that people who live in the ghetto earn less money for the same schooling than those who live in the county as a whole, it is more likely that the reverse causality is true: people of given schooling live in a "ghetto" *because* they are poor, other things being equal.

IMPLICATIONS

The main purpose of this study is twofold: (1) to compare Mexican-American and European-American incomes and marginal rates of return to schooling in an industrial metropolitan area to see if any unique "ethnicity effect" appears on the incomes and rates; and (2) to compare these incomes and rates in the whole sample with those prevailing in the high-concentration Mexican-American ghetto subregion of that area, to see if any additional separate "ghetto residence effect" occurs.

Judging by the Santa Clara County private rates of return to schooling estimated in this study (See Table 4.4), getting a high school diploma (8.1 percent private marginal return rate to Mexican-Americans) or a college degree (8.7 percent private marginal rate to them) simply does not "pay off" for Mexican-Americans as it does for members of the Euro-American majority group (rates are 9.8 percent for high school completion and 9.9 percent for completing a college degree).

Dropping out of high school after finishing the tenth or eleventh grade, on the other hand (20.4 percent high school dropout private marginal return rate to Mexican-Americans), or dropping out of college after the thirteenth, fourteenth, or fifteenth years and short of graduation (giving Mexican-Americans an 11.1 percent college dropout private rate) is, as an investment, considerably more rewarding to the Mexican-American than staying in either high school or university until completion. In the sample we examined, then, dropping out of school before graduating may be the economically rational thing for Mexican-American students to do.

Students of the Euro-American majority group, on the other hand, get much *lower* private marginal return rates to schooling if they drop out of either high school or college than if they stay in: "Euros" get only a 4.1 percent private marginal return rate when they drop out of high school and 7.6 per cent return rate when they drop out of college. By staying in school until completion, on the other hand, they get 9.8 percent for completing high school and 9.9 percent for completing college. It *is* rewarding for Euro-American students to invest in their high school diplomas or college degrees: they get higher marginal return rates by doing so.

Minority persons probably realize that the rate they receive to investment in additional schooling is higher at dropout levels and lower at completion levels. The minority member may thus adjust his schooling differently from the majority. This explanation of the dropout phenomenon would put less emphasis on sociocultural determinants of school-taking behavior, such as childhood conditioning, parents' SES, students' motivations and aspirations, educational quality, and academic ability (at the same time recognizing their partial role). It would, instead, place greater stress on the observed fact of real ethnic money-wage discrimination in the employment market for equal age and school-attainment qualifications.

We do not wish to imply that Mexican-American students *should* drop out of school just to get better marginal return rates to their investment in schooling. Moreover, even the 8.1 percent private marginal rate to Mexican-Americans completing a high school diploma and 8.7 percent private marginal rate to their completing a college degree are higher than 5 percent bank interest. Nevertheless, these marginal private return rates for Mexican-Americans who graduate from high school or college are modest at best and may not have sufficient "holding power," in light of family and social pressures on the Mexican-American to earn. Thus, exhortations to Mexican-Americans to complete their schooling, as well-meaning as they may be, do not appear to agree with the reward patterns we have seen in this study.

As the Mexican-Americans' traditional source of manual employment in agriculture and food processing in the Santa Clara Valley declines, and as these persons are thrown into greater competition with "Anglos" for the increasing proportion of high-skill nonmanual jobs,[21] Mexican-Americans' future economic well-being and improvement are not assured.

Increased institutional schooling expenditure per pupil on Mexican-American pupils (with improved *quality* of schooling assumed) would probably improve Mexican-Americans' marginal rates of return to diploma completion only slightly.[22] Neither would a fuller rate of

---

[21]See Walter Fogel, "Education and Income of Mexican-Americans in the Southwest" (Mexican-American Study Project, Advance Report 1, Division of Research, Graduate School of Business Administration, UCLA, 1965).

[22]See Eric Hanushek, "The Production of Education, Teacher Quality, and Efficiency," in *Do Teachers Make a Difference?* (Washington, D.C.: U.S. Office of Education, 1970), pp. 79-99.

employment of the Mexican-American labor force have much impact on their marginal return rates to schooling.

Apparently, only efforts to ensure that employers and unions pay employed Mexican-Americans of given school attainment and age the same money wages as their Euro-American counterparts and provide equal access to the same kind of work will close the ethnic income gap and equalize rates of return to investment in schooling.

.5. *Rational Income Decisions of Blacks and Everybody Else**

STEPHAN MICHELSON

MUCH OF the variation in individual earnings can be explained by individual labor market characteristics: sex, race, age, education, region, experience, ability, etc. These characteristics fall into two categories: those which are not subject to deliberate change (sex, race, age, blindness, or other physical disability) and those which can be deliberately affected (education, training, region, participation). The former variables will be denoted by Z; the latter by S. Ex post facto, it is often assumed that a person's characteristics are fixed. Initially, of course, only some characteristics are set at their final levels, and the individual may choose which others to obtain. The term "strategy" will denote the choice of S characteristics which a person desires and for which he strives, though an a priori strategy is not always observed as a set of ex post characteristics.

Income studies have assumed implicitly that in choosing among n strategies people follow the rule, Choose S_i to maximize $E(Y)$, where $Y = Y(S_i, Z)$. Only the form of the income function $Y(S, Z)$ and the variables S and Z have varied from study to study, not the implicit decision rule. In this study another decision rule will be discussed and

*I am grateful to Samuel Bowles, Rashi Fein, Susan Gilbert, Henry M. Levin, and Rosemary Moyer for their comments, and to Arthur Blake and Walter Davis for inspiration.

applied to blacks in the United States. This model has the virtue that it can utilize data which are inappropriately employed in traditional income-generating approaches. In addition, it may be more relevant than traditional approaches in explaining choices made by minority-group members who face discrimination.

VIEWS OF RATIONALITY

Herman Miller has noted that growth of the economy will, by itself, generate higher earnings for people with certain characteristics a decade from now than those with the same set of characteristics now receive.[1] He does not discuss the more relevant problem (from the point of view of following one strategy or another) of the *difference* in rate of growth of income under different strategies.

Pigou has pointed out that people are myopic in their choice of occupations.[2] A "personal optimism towards the facts on the part of the persons directly concerned" makes a correct assessment of the facts difficult.[3] However, it may be neither irrationality nor misinformation which leads an individual to choose a strategy which, on average, is bad. Marshall, for example, explained that there are reasonable responses to uncertain situations other than maximizing expected income.

But, on the other hand, if an occupation offers a few extremely large prizes, its attractiveness is increased out of all proportion to their aggregate values . . . young men of an adventurous disposition are more attracted by the prospects of great success than they are deterred by the fear of failure. . . .[4]

An "adventurous disposition" in modern terminology would be a "preference for risk," and would be honored as rational under individualistic welfare criteria. Even if it is found that in the long run people continually choose an S_i which on average leaves them with

[1]Herman P. Miller, *Income Distribution in the United States* (Washington, D.C.: Government Printing Office, 1966), pp. 133–183.

[2]A. C. Pigou, *The Economics of Welfare* (London, England: Macmillan Co., 1962), p. 492.

[3]Ibid., p. 491.

[4]Alfred Marshall, *Principles of Economics* (London, England: Macmillan Co., 1948), p. 554.

less income than would some other possible strategy, S_j, it may be the decisions were appropriately made (from facts in hand) on some basis other than maximizing expected income. It also may be, of course, that myopia or misinformation consistently prevent optimal decisions.

In a recent critique, Carol and Parry investigated the rationality of a person's staying in school when certain occupations requiring less education pay well.[5] They correctly attack the myth that from the point of view of maximizing expected income, it is always advisable to continue in school. They do not discuss, however, whether this rule correctly describes the process of rational choice. By discounting future earnings by occupation, using median schooling per occupation and opportunity costs of schooling, Carol and Parry arrived at values of discounted net lifetime earnings for sixty-seven occupations. Under different assumptions regarding which costs of education are borne by whom and about time lost in the military, the rankings change. That is, a family which must bear the cost of a son's education faces a different ranking of favorable occupations than a family which does not carry such costs. It may, on the average, be better for the first family to invest its money in the capital market and for the son to enter an occupation which requires less formal schooling.

Though the point of the article is well made—that it is not always rational to continue in school—the view of rationality used is extremely limited. Education may be a better hedge against inflation, for example, than a savings account and a better hedge against uncertainty than the stock market. Mean earnings per occupation, the measure used in their calculations, may not be equilibrium observations. Fringe benefits, as Carol and Parry admit, were not considered, nor were data separated by race or region. However, there is another important data problem when utilizing the rule "maximize expected income" in an empirical study of behavior. Observed mean values are not the *expected* values facing the decision maker even in the absence of differential growth rates. Therefore, mean values are not the correct values to observe even if one does accept maximization of expected income as a decision rule.

[5]Arthur Carol and Samuel Parry, "The Economic Rationale of Occupational Choice," *Industrial and Labor Relations Review* 21, no. 2 (January 1968): 183–196.

EXPECTED EARNINGS:
A CORRECT DEFINITION

One of the problems of interpreting the expected earnings of any strategy is correctly identifying the relevant data. An example of occupational choice will make this clear. Many more people study to be musicians than do become musicians. With the same years of training, one person may be applauded at his debut, another greeted with silence. The failure may become a lesser musician, a music teacher, or something else—say, an economist. The expected earnings of a person embarking on a performer's career should be a weighted average of the earnings of musicians, music teachers, and economists.

For another example, consider professional athletes. Rosenblatt says that "a large proportion of Negroes than whites apparently aspire to careers in sports."[6] There is some evidence that blacks may be excluded from sports. Rosenblatt correctly argues that to determine whether there is discrimination in sports, the *average* players, not the superstars, should be considered. Concentrating on baseball, Rosenblatt finds, "The higher the batting average, the larger the proportion of Negroes in that performance category."[7] He concludes that the average black is excluded from the sport.

Suppose an estimate is made of the expected earnings of a black entering professional sports. It might be found, by observing professional athletes, that this is one of the most lucrative careers for blacks. Indeed, the mean earnings of black athletes *may* be higher than the mean earnings of white athletes. Let us assume that they are. Suppose the chance of being employed as an athlete is better for whites than for blacks with comparable skills. Suppose, in addition, that better alternative employment is available for whites who fail than for blacks who fail.

Despite the observation that the average black athlete earns more than the average white athlete, the *expected earnings* of whites entering professional athletics could be substantially higher than those of blacks. Average earnings of persons *in* an occupation do not rep-

---

[6]Aaron Rosenblatt, "Negroes in Baseball: The Failure of Success," *Trans-action* 4, no. 9 (September 1967): 51–53.   [7]Ibid., p. 52.

resent expected earnings of people *entering* the occupation. This is not a problem of the form of estimation, of the time change of earnings, or even of the observation of disequilibrium points. It is a result of observing only successes, despite the fact that a new entrant may not be a success. Marshall observed,

Next we have to take account of the influences exerted on real rate of earnings in an occupation by the uncertainty of success and the inconstancy of employment in it.

We should obviously start by taking the earnings of an occupation as the average between those of the successful and unsuccessful members of it; but care is required to get the true average. For if the average earnings of those who are successful are £2000 a year, and of those who are unsuccessful are £400 a year, the average of the whole will be £1200 a year if the former group is as large as the latter; but if, as is perhaps the case with barristers, the unsuccessful are ten times as numerous as the successful, the true average is but £550. And further, many of those who have failed most completely, are likely to have left the occupation altogether, and thus to escape being counted.[8]

Of course, not only failures leave an occupation. People move up the ladder as well as down, and choice of initial occupation may be part of a strategy for occupational (and monetary) advance. Some law school graduates become and remain lawyers; some become lawyers to move into politics or corporate management; and some first become clerks, then lawyers. The expected earnings in any future year for a person presently in law school, then, cannot be determined from observations on only lawyers. Nor can the expected lifetime earnings of present clerks be calculated from observations only on clerks.[9]

A general formula for the expected earnings (at some future time) of a new entrant to an occupation is:

$$E(Y) = \sum_i (Y) P(i),$$

where $E(Y)$ is expected earnings, Y_i is average income in occupa-

[8]Marshall, *Principles of Economics*, p. 554.

[9]Indeed, in a licensed profession such as law, the expected earnings of a student must take into account the risk of not obtaining a license to practice (failing the bar examination).

tion i, and $P(i)$ is the probability of being in occupation i,

$$O \leq P(i) \leq 1, \text{ and } \sum_i P(i) = 1.$$

Occupations are only a conspicuous example of the possible problem. Can the earnings of rural residents, of southern blacks, of central-city whites, of Indians on reservations be predicted without considering the likelihood of their changing locations? Can the effect of additional years of school or training be estimated by "holding region and size of place constant," if additional years of school or training induce changes in location? Is expected income from college well estimated by the observed income of only college graduates?

EXPECTED EARNINGS:
AN EXAMPLE

It is possible to make some crude calculations on expected earnings in 1962 based on occupational entry at a previous time. These calculations are derived from the survey of occupational change which was taken in conjunction with the "1962 Survey of Current Population," as reported by Blau and Duncan.[10] These data are somewhat inappropriate for the following reasons:

1. They provide first occupation and 1962 occupation for all male respondents, ages 25–64. Some of the people who will change occupations have not yet done so. Thus, the data understate the extent of occupational change.

2. The occupational change as given includes the change over time of the occupational structure. Since people of all ages are shown together, there is no way to separate effects of structural change from typical success-failure changes of occupation.

3. We would require information on the point in a person's career at which he changes occupation to determine his average annual income, but this information is unobtainable from the data.

4. The data give median income, whereas mean earnings are desired.

5. Other earnings-generating factors are not taken into account.

[10] Peter M. Blau and Otis Dudley Duncan, *The American Occupational Structure* (New York: John Wiley & Sons, 1967).

A more complete model would calculate probabilities of changing occupation for each educational level by region, by age, etc.[11]

6. The data are not separated by race. Since some racial minority groups tend to be in occupations that pay less, the spread of expected incomes for a person with known Z characteristics (e.g., race) will be smaller than that indicated here. Presumably blacks are less upwardly mobile in any occupation than are whites; thus mobility measures vary with percent of white workers.

Expected earnings were calculated for seventeen occupations from data showing mobility from first job to job held in 1962. These calculations with median earnings (also given by Blau and Duncan) appear in Table 5.1. Several comments are appropriate.

Because median earnings were used, the spread in the original data is less than would be the spread of mean earnings. Use of median

Table 5.1.   **Actual and Expected Earnings by Occupation**

Occupation	Median Earnings	Expected Earnings
Self-employed professionals	$12,048	$9,432
Salaried professionals	6,842	6,807
Managers	7,238	6,276
Salesmen, except retail	6,008	5,964
Proprietors	5,548	5,570
Clerical	5,173	5,668
Retail salesmen	3,044	5,566
Craftsmen, manufacturing	5,800	5,387
Craftsmen, other	5,482	5,262
Craftsmen, construction	5,265	5,156
Operatives, manufacturing	4,636	4,938
Operatives, other	4,206	4,906
Services	3,233	4,600
Laborers, manufacturing	2,189	4,497
Laborers, other	2,189	4,610
Farmers	1,992	3,582
Farm laborers	488	3,700

Source: Median earnings from Table 2.1, weights from Table 2.4 in Peter M. Blau and Otis Dudley Duncan, *The American Occupational Structure* (New York: John Wiley & Sons, 1967).

[11]For example, 2.5 percent of those in the sample who started as self-employed professionals were laborers in 1962. Certainly this does not represent the occupational path of those with four or more years of college.

earnings also reduces the amount of possible divergence in the expected earnings, which are merely weighted sums of the occupational medians. As long as there is occupational mobility, the expected earnings of entrants into the highest-paid occupation will be less than the mean earnings of those who stay in that occupation. Similarly, the expected earnings of those in the lowest-paid occupation will be higher than the mean of those who stay, since some will move upward. To the extent that there is mobility in any characteristic, the distribution of the expected earnings resulting from the choice of that characteristic will have a different dispersion from the distribution of actual earnings.[12]

After consideration of occupational mobility, there are some important differences in the ranking of occupations by earnings. Salaried professionals do better than managers if the hazards of being a manager are considered, whereas eventual managers apparently earn more than eventual salaried professionals.[13] Similarly, beginning retail salesmen can expect earnings higher than craftsmen and about equivalent to proprietors, but the median earnings of eventual craftsmen and proprietors are more than 60 percent higher than those of eventual retail salesmen. Expected income for farm laborers is greater than that for farmers—reverse of the order of the medians—*because* farmers stay on the farm while farm laborers do not. Of the initial farmers 35 percent were eventual farmers or farm laborers, compared with 26.3 percent of initial farm laborers.

Although in many cases there is little difference between median and expected earnings, in other cases the difference is large. Laborers can expect to earn over twice the median laborer income, and farm laborers can expect over 7.5 times the farm laborer median income. Self-employed professionals, of course, must expect less income upon entering than after becoming well established. Proprietors, although faced with good chance of failure, can expect approximately what they observe in incomes because there is also a high chance of advancing to manager. The initial proprietor has a chance of becoming an eventual laborer (3 percent); indeed, he has a higher chance than

[12]The true dispersion is not always smaller. The range of opportunity open to high school graduates includes income of college graduates.

[13]The term "eventual" is used here only to indicate people who are observed in the occupation indicated. "Eventual," of course, does not necessarily mean "successful" or "permanent."

from any of the other first seven occupations and a higher chance of becoming an eventual farmer than from any other occupation except initial farmers and farm laborers.

In principle this approach can be applied to every S variable. For analysis of the *expected* income from any *strategy* (choice of S_i, whether S_i is obtained or not), corrections such as those outlined above should be made. However, it is possible to assume that rational behavior is not based on the expectation of S_i, but on the extraordinary utility attached to the attainment of S_i, however unlikely that attainment may be. Only certain S_i are amenable to such analysis, of course, specifically those which are most desirable to any particular society. The next section outlines an analysis of people of "adventurous disposition."

A GENERAL APPROACH TO RATIONAL CHOICE

Consider a person about to decide among n strategies to desired S. He will choose that strategy which maximizes a utility function weighting and evaluating relevant information pertaining to the S_i, given his Z characteristics. Since his utility function is not known and only real-world evidence of it can be observed, functions which maximize something other than utility must be tested.[14] The goal, of course, is to determine a function which is only different from the utility function by a monotonic transform. In the traditional approach, as has been stated, $E(Y)$ is maximized, where $E(Y)$ is a function of S and Z.

(1) Max $E(Y)$ where $E(Y_i) = G(S_i, Z)$ and $i = 1, n$.

This would be a good rule if it is assumed that a person maximizes utility of expected income,

(2) Max $U[E(Y)]$,

and that a higher expected income yields a higher utility. In a risk situation, however, more than just expected income must be considered. A utility function which evaluates all possible incomes can be postulated and maximized:

---

[14]The attempt here is merely to formulate a reasonable behavioral theory, not to identify that behavior with any abstract notion of "utility." See I.M.D. Little, *A Critique of Welfare Economics*, 2nd ed. (New York: Oxford University Press, 1957).

(3) Max $E[U(Y)]$

where Y is the *distribution* of income for a given strategy.

In order to utilize Equation (1) as a proxy for Equation (3), the utility mapping must be such that Max $E(Y)$ occurs uniquely at the same S_i as Max $E[U(Y)]$.

One might err badly by using mean incomes for certain characteristics where expected incomes are significantly different, considering the probability of changing characteristics.[15] But he could also err badly by assuming that Equation (1) is a good decision proxy for Max $E[U(Y)]$, in a world of chance. One can at least investigate the properties of decisions based on other rules. For example, choose that strategy j which maximizes the probability of achieving high income. This could be combined with minimal constraints, such as $E(Y_j) > O$, $E(Y_j)$ within one standard deviation of $E(Y_i)$ as determined from Equation (1), etc.[16]

To keep the argument straightforward and simple, consider two unimodal distributions A and B with positive means. The mean of distribution A is greater than the mean of distribution B, but B extends to higher ranges than A, as shown in Figure 5.1. If the curves represent income distributions resulting from two strategies, then the "maximize expected income" criterion demands choice of A. The probability of getting an income higher than M, however, is greater with strategy B. Thus, a plausible alternative explanation for some people following a strategy which, on the average, seems not to "pay"

[15]It is quite conceivable, for example, that Hanoch's lifetime earnings patterns, as derived from the 1960 Census by multiple regression, describe no one's expected earnings path. Giora Hanoch, "Personal Earnings and Investment in Schooling" (Ph.D. diss., University of Chicago, 1966). In generating earnings for males, he held constant family size, number of children, size of place, and time in place; and stratified by region, age, and race in a multiple regression of earnings on schooling. Use of these variables may be justified as necessary to specify the correct plane of observations of the major variables and to calculate correctly mean earnings, given a set of characteristics. But the next step, that of assigning mean values to most variables to calculate values of Y as other variables vary, could easily derive figures with little relationship to a person's *expected earnings*. This is especially true where the variables are binary and mean values are, for any individual, impossible values.

[16]People who aim for high incomes will enter occupations in which high incomes occur, even if on average they achieve low incomes. Another extreme rule would be loss avoidance: maximize *minimum* possible income. People who follow this rule overeducate in the Carol and Parry sense, and do not become proprietors.

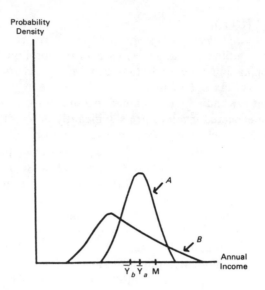

Figure 5.1. Income Distributions Resulting from Two Strategies

is that they are using a different rational decision criterion from that of maximization of expected income.

The decision function implied by the choice of distribution *B* in Figure 5.1. is:

(4) Max $P(Y \geq M)$ where $P(Y \geq M) = F(S_i, Z)$.

The statistical advantage of this formulation is that observed data need not be subject to the criticisms (set out above) on the use of means as expected observations. The question no longer is one of the probability of staying in a given circumstance (location, occupation, etc.). The question is, *if* one can maintain certain characteristics, what is the probability of achieving *high* income?

STRATEGY: CHOICE BY BLACKS

In particular, this model represents a reasonable kind of question for a member of an oppressed group in a society to ask. Minority group income distributions are characterized by a general lack of

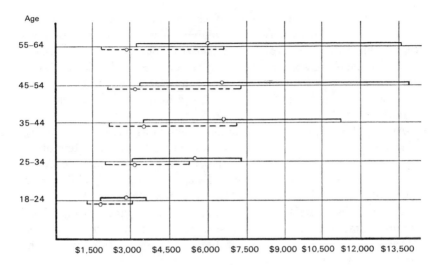

Mean earnings of persons:

o = mean earnings of age group
┌────┐ = range of white earnings by years of school
└────┘ = range of nonwhite earnings by years by years of school
(range defined from average earnings of males with 0–7 years of school in the South to males with 5 or more years of college outside of the South).

SOURCE: *U.S. Census of the Population: 1960*, Occupation by Earnings and Education: Final Report PC(2)–7B.

Figure 5.2. Range of Mean Earnings in 1959, Whites and Nonwhites.

high incomes.[17] Figure 5.2 shows the range of average earnings for nonwhites and whites by age. The range is drawn by taking the average earnings for people in the South with few or no years of school at one end and in the non-South with five years or more of college at the other. The range of average earnings, over years of school, is seen to be much greater for whites than for nonwhites. This would be more true for whites vis-à-vis blacks.[18] As distribu-

---

[17]Alternatively, because oppressed group members find low incomes the norm, getting above a low income may be of paramount importance. Blacks entering teaching, for example, lose the chance for a high income, but gain security from extremely low income.

[18]The percent of nonwhites who are non-Negro increases as higher levels of schooling are considered. Thus, average earnings reflect changing race and region composition, exaggerating the average effect of schooling on blacks.

tion of individual earnings are not shown, one does not see which educational strategies may make higher earnings *possible* for non-whites. High earnings are not only possible but can be *expected* by whites in choosing appropriate S characteristics. A black, not being able to *expect* a high income under any strategy, might choose strategies on the basis of Equation 2, the best chances of a high income.[19]

An oppressed group can be roughly defined as one which, because the construction of society limits its opportunities, finds few of its members with high incomes relative to observed incomes in dominant groups. The utility functions of such a group might differ from those of the dominant group. High income ("making it"), a rare event, may be a prestigious event. One can imagine having a high income some year in one's life as a prize worth many sacrifices. "Making it" may be expensive, in lifetime income terms, but worthwhile in utility terms.

There are, then, three possible ways of viewing decision making by blacks as different from that by whites. In the first place, any strategy leads less certainly to its expected goal, because success still is often in the hands of the dominant group.[20] Similar utility valuations of chances of income may lead whites and nonwhites to choose differently because the chances differ. Second, the expected benefit from any strategy is less for nonwhites. Finally, the utility valuations themselves may differ and differ such that the chance of a high income— not just a marginal few dollars, but "making it"—is highly valued in the utility functions of blacks.

Consider athletes once again. The mean earnings of successful black athletes may be incorrectly used as expected earnings of a new athlete. But under the assumption that average black players are not retained, the mean does correctly reflect the upper range of possible earnings. The probability of having income M or higher, in baseball, can be estimated, although the probability of remaining in the sport

---

[19]It must be stressed that I have no external evidence that this is so. This exercise merely explores the implications of this choice criterion; I cannot prove that it is more accurately descriptive than other criteria. The following, if true, would at least be consistent with this choice criterion: At given low income levels, do blacks tend to gamble more and insure less than whites?

[20]Empirically, this simply means that income-generating functions do not fit non-white data as well as they fit white data.

cannot be calculated. If the black utility function weights the range of possible incomes highly but essentially ignores the probability of achieving that income, then Equation 4 will define rational black behavior better than Equation I. Pigou's "optimism" may explain this unrealistic weighting in utility functions.[21]

This argument can be generalized so that only successes need be considered. Under a decision-making function which looks only at the upper income end and disregards the possibility of not succeeding in gaining sought-after characteristics, then probabilities of "making it," given S, are all that need be observed. If only the most favorable income-generating characteristics are considered, then one can observe the probabilities of high income for *anyone,* whether he has these characteristics or not. It is correct, in this situation, not to evaluate variables at population means but to choose the most favorable other characteristics which a person might acquire, varying one of major concern.

BLACK CHOICE OF SCHOOLING

As has been mentioned, a possible move a black can make is from the South to the North. For maximum earning possibilities, he should have made that move long ago. He should be a head of a household and live in an urban area.[22] Thus, looking at whites and blacks in the non-South, not recently moved, and presently heads of households, one can study the possibility of achieving specified incomes as years of schooling vary.

Probability estimates were derived from multiple regressions on sets of dummy variables. Four samples of urban males were selected by two stratifications: whites (except with Spanish surname) and

[21]Strotz has investigated the welfare effects of budget decisions with fixed income, where the decision maker is myopic with respect to future utility. The same myopia in terms of generating, as opposed to distributing, future incomes is deserving of equally careful analysis. Robert Strotz, "Myopia and Inconsistency in Dynamic Utility Maximization," *Review of Economic Studies* 23, no. 3 (March 1956): 164–180.

[22]Extensive income-generating experiments with the 1/1000 sample of the 1960 Census lead to these conclusions. This work is reported in my "Income of Racial Minorities" (Ph.D. diss., Stanford University, 1968). Results from other income generating studies are similar: Hanoch, "Personal Earnings and Investment in Schooling"; Leonard Weiss, "Concentration and Labor Earnings," *American Economic Review* 56, no. 1 (March 1966): 96–117.

Table 5.2.   Probability of Achieving Specified Incomes[a]

Age and Income Level	Black				White			
	Years of School				Years of School			
	0–7	8–11	12–15	16+	0–7	8–11	12–15	16+
Age 24–27								
$3,500	.34	.44	.54	.61	.55	.69	.77	.80
4,500	.15	.21	.30	.43	.33	.50	.61	.70
6,000	.00	.05	.08	.24	.02	.15	.28	.52
Age 32–35								
$3,500	.49	.59	.69	.76	.71	.85	.93	.96
4,500	.27	.32	.42	.55	.56	.72	.84	.93
6,000	.01	.06	.09	.24	.28	.41	.54	.78
Age 40–45								
$3,500	.54	.68	.72	.90	.76	.87	.92	.99
4,500	.29	.37	.50	.69	.61	.75	.84	.96
6,000	.10	.13	.19	.42	.31	.44	.60	.82
Age 52–57								
$3,500	.46	.59	.64	.82	.70	.82	.86	.94
4,500	.28	.35	.49	.67	.56	.70	.79	.92
6,000	.08	.11	.17	.40	.29	.42	.58	.80

[a] For males in the non-South, not moved from a noncontiguous state within the past five years.

minorities (nonwhites plus white with Spanish surname), age 24–39 and 40–64. Within each subsample four age categories were delineated, as well as region (South or non-South), whether moved from a noncontiguous state in the last five years, and household status (head, primary, other). In addition, a variable in the minority subsamples separated blacks and American Indians from other minorities. Weeks worked were not held at a mean, but estimated from the other characteristics and varied with them in the calculations.[23]

The probabilities of obtaining three specified income levels (or higher) are shown in Table 5.2 for males with desirable characteris-

[23]More detail can be found in Michelson, "Income of Racial Minorities." Note that personal income, not earnings, is the dependent variable. Each income level was estimated separately, by assigning a 1 to the dependent variable if the person had income greater than or equal to that specified, a 0 if his income was lower. The probability of being in each of the five weeks-worked categories was also estimated. Then $P(Y \geq M) = \Sigma_i P(Y \geq M \mid W_i)P(W_i)$, $i = 1, 5$, gave the estimates given here. The highest income level considered was $6,000.

tics (in the non-South and not recently moved) at four levels of schooling. As can be seen, the probabilities increase with schooling, increase then fall by age, and are higher for whites than for comparable blacks.

BLACK INCENTIVES

Judging the possibility of "making it" with different schooling characteristics, the black male must be impressed with the better opportunities available with more education. This effect may considerably outweigh the chance of not completing college. It may outweigh the fact that even with a college degree, the economic world is risky enough that his likely gain is little more than his sure costs. Ex post facto observations that lifetime income patterns are not related to schooling, on average, for nonwhites may be explained by considering that nonwhites did not make schooling decisions so as to maximize income.[24]

These probabilities are subject to several interpretations, but none leads to conclusions other than that the black has a consistent incentive to strive for high education. Schooling benefits his chances of high income less than it does for whites, in terms of increase over all schooling levels. For example, in the age group 32–35, blacks have a .27 probability of attaining $4,500 or more and whites a comparable .28 at the $6,000 level, with little or no schooling. But the blacks' .27 doubles to .55 by the end of college; the whites' .28 nearly triples to .78.

Another way to look at the change in probabilities is to ask by how much a strategy decreases uncertainty of rising above a certain income level. This approach is better applied to low income levels, where one can posit as a decision rule the attempt to guarantee at least a minimum income. The search for an assured floor may lead in quite different directions from the search for a possible high income. However, incentives to acquire education are the same from this approach as from considering the effect directly on probabilities. There

[24]I refer, of course, to Hanoch's attempts to develop lifetime earnings patterns for different schooling levels. The fact that income-generating equations fit blacks poorly may be due to demand considerations, but why blacks continue to seek an education in the face of these demands still must be answered.

is a great effect from college education, smaller but positive effects from other levels, in reducing uncertainty of the specified income as seen from the next lower schooling level. Table 5.3 contains these calculations.

Table 5.3.   Incremental Effect of Additional Years of School in Terms of Reducing Uncertainty of Income[a]

Age and Income Level	Black Years of School			White Years of School		
	8–11	12–15	16+	8–11	12–15	16+
Age 24–27						
$3,500	15	18	15	31	26	13
4,500	7	11	19	25	22	23
6,000	5	8	17	13	15	33
Age 32–35						
$3,500	20	24	23	48	53	43
4,500	7	15	22	36	43	56
6,000	5	3	16	18	22	52
Age 40–45						
$3,500	30	12	64	38	38	88
4,500	11	21	38	36	36	75
6,000	3	7	28	19	25	55
Age 52–57						
$3,500	24	12	53	40	22	50
4,500	10	22	35	32	30	62
6,000	3	7	28	18	28	52

[a] Percent of $(1 - P(Y))$ at previous educational level which is gained by moving to level specified in the column head.

Thus it may be rational for a black to acquire an education although his expected return is negative. It may be rational to aspire to high education although the chances of accomplishment are slim. It may simply be the best strategy available to him.

When less than the best characteristics are considered, the probability of changing them also must be considered. The preceding figures were estimated on the basis of a black's having moved out of the South more than five years before, if he lived originally in the South. The eventual advantages to a southern black from moving North are estimated in Table 5.4. Southern black males are com-

**Table 5.4.   Eventual Advantage of Moving North
for Southern Blacks** [a]

Age and Income Level	Years of School			
	0–7	8–11	12–15	16+
Age 32–35				
$3,500	33	38	45	51
4,500	21	22	25	30
6,000	4	4	4	5
Age 40–45				
$3,500	36	45	48	73
4,500	21	23	28	38
6,000	8	8	9	12

[a] The percentage difference in income probability, North vs. South $\dfrac{p(Y_n) - p(Y_s)}{1 - p(Y_s)}$ where $p(\ )$ is the probability of attaining at least the specified income, n is North, s is South (not recently moved in both cases).

pared with northern black males, both not having moved from a noncontiguous state in the five years preceding the census. Advantages for northern males *recently moved* are less, but in most cases the improvement over staying in the South is immediate.[25]

As seen in Table 5.4, a southern black considering his income at the specified ages usually will find it more advantageous to move North than to continue in school—should that be the issue—in terms of increasing his chances for relatively good income levels. This is not true when *high* incomes are considered, however. Except for the obvious high-income areas, sports and entertainment,[26] college education is the best strategy for higher incomes for black or white

[25]The black who moves North has a slightly higher risk of unemployment in the first few years, as measured by the probability of having $1,000 or lower income, than one who stays in the South. His chances of $6,000 or more may also be smaller at first. His chances of obtaining median income or higher are better in the North, despite the handicap of a recent move.

[26]When the occupation "artist or performer" was entered in an income-generating equation already specified by years of school, blacks and Indians age 40–59 showed earnings almost $3,000 higher than would be expected. Whites had an income almost $2,000 *lower* than expected. Both results, significant at the 1 percent level, are presented in Michelson, "Income of Racial Minorities."

(though still considerably better for white), even at the sacrifice of northward migration.

CONCLUSION

The theoretical and statistical manipulations above have one main purpose: to show that behavior thought to be irrational[27] or un-analyzable[28] is, and can be seen to be, rational and even reasonable. To analyze all behavior in the same way is to ignore the realities of immutable and different Z characteristics, such as race, and the harsher reality that economic response varies according to these characteristics.[29]

There are a number of other Z characteristics that bring about a differential response from the economy and that might therefore reasonably be expected to change one's rational behavior patterns. For example, lower-class mannerisms are greeted with disfavor by people with economic power. The American dream is that one's social-class background is not important in achieving economic success, and to the extent that people accept this dream, their whole pattern of rational behavior is molded by it. Disillusion with the dream could cause not just behavior changes, but changes in the *pattern* of response to various stimuli; that is, changes in rationality.

Current social phenomena can be explained as a shift in the mode of rational response to a not particularly changed economic condition. Thus "street people" as a mild example, Weathermen as a more extreme example, and Black Panthers and Young Lords as obvious examples are probably not acting so as to maximize anything *expected*. They may, however, be acting (as each sees it) so as to maximize the possibility of establishing the counter-culture, the revolution, the sane society. The probability of succeeding is not part of the decision function. This is certainly true on an individual level, and probably true also at a group level. Anyone who sees himself

[27]See James S. Coleman et al., *Equality of Educational Opportunity* (Washington, D.C.; U.S. Office of Education, 1966).

[28]See Hanoch, "Personal Earnings and Investment in Schooling."

[29]Economists tend to analyze black and white income generating processes separately just because they recognize that they respond differently to the market, and the market responds differently to them. Yet such analyses still assume that the same functional form should describe both groups, and even the same variables.

engaged in a struggle in which ethical values are involved ("fighting the good fight") does not proceed so much by a calculation of the probability of winning as by the necessity of persevering. A person's realization that he is in fact engaged in moral (and sometimes mortal) combat is personally devastating because he must then change more than just his behavior, but his entire rational process. Labeling that new process "irrational" because behavior stemming from it is not that which would be induced by maximization of expected income is an intellectual blindness contained in, but not unique to, the economics profession.[30]

This article has proceeded as if income were the desideratum, and only rational behavior toward gaining it required analysis. Needless to say, the goal of rational behavior need not be what we expect it to be. Thus, what we have accomplished here is to place in some perspective the value of analyses of income as a function of Z and S characteristics: Such analyses measure the average response of the economy to the combinations of characteristics. They measure neither the response of the economy to a change in such characteristics, nor the response of people to the economy. They neither indicate nor guide rational behavior of blacks—and possibly of everyone else.

---

[30]Gary S. Becker, defining "rational behavior" in a manner which includes the model presented above, shows how several forms of *irrational* behavior (behavior not consistently applying *any* maximizing rule) may still lead to results expected from traditional analysis (such as downward sloping demand curves). He does not explore the case presented here, in which traditional analysis does *not* predict the observations. His point is nonetheless valid that school-going and other behavior consistent with the rational process presented here *may* still be simply irrational. See "Irrational Behavior and Economic Theory," *Journal of Political Economy* 70, no. 1 (February 1962): 1–13.

C. EQUAL OPPORTUNITY
IN EDUCATION

.6. *The Case for Equal Educational Opportunity**

THOMAS I. RIBICH

THE ECONOMICS of education, though little more than a decade old as a scholarly pursuit, has proceeded through several stages of study and several varieties of "conventional wisdom." First were the optimistic days of manpower projections and simple rate-of-return calculations that reinforced the sentiment of most intellectuals and reformers that educational spending was indeed deserving of great expansion. Then came the gloomy investigations of the late 1960s indicating that the available means for improving educational quality and lengthening school careers had strikingly little power. Presently, scholarly work and predominant opinions are multifaceted and, to some degree, a reaction to the painful results of the second-stage studies. There is a persistent search (partially rewarded) for school variables that do have power, a widespread belief that we may be handling education all wrong, a proliferation of suggestions (with tentative experimentation) on how major reorganization of schooling might proceed—and all of this overlaid with an atmosphere of agnosticism concerning statistics and progress reports. Another feature of current thought is the reassertion of equality of opportunity as a policy goal. It is the political-economic implications of that goal, and its interrelations with what we have discovered about the economics of education, that forms the broad focus of this article.

*The completion of this essay was made possible by a grant from the National Science Foundation.

123

Much of the analysis involves casting old arguments in a new light and attempting to pin down more securely the meaning and significance of equality of educational opportunity. One of the major analytic goals will be to identify as unambiguously as possible those aspects of the question that, to me, seem inherently ambiguous, or at least still in desperate need of more rigorous solutions. The essay is more "talky" than most "modern economics," partly because of ambiguities to be wrestled with, partly because the topic is one that lends itself to the approach of "economics as a moral science" (to use Kenneth Boulding's phrase), and partly because it is an attempt to cover a large panoply of issues in order to arrive at a broad synthesis in addition to an analysis of some specific arguments. It makes no claim, however, to being exhaustive—only a little more complete and "synthetic" than economic essays on this question that have appeared earlier.

WHAT IS IT?

A major problem in discussing equality of educational opportunity is settling on a definition of the term. It makes a great difference in the analysis whether one accepts a relatively mild, traditional meaning or a more ambitious definition concentrating on "outcomes" rather than "inputs." Those who currently write and discuss equal educational opportunity tend to start with the presumption that it is outcomes that count. But the older idea of opportunity still has some popular appeal and cannot be dismissed lightly.

To oversimplify greatly, equality of opportunity in the traditional sense implies that the same type of educational facilities should be made available on equal terms to all social-economic classes. It is the chance to benefit that matters; what individuals and groups do with that opportunity is their business, not society's. No clear-cut presumption states that outcomes will be equal among all identifiable social groups, but a loosely held belief indicates that if money or social class were not a formal barrier to entry into various types and stages of education, under classes (on average) would get about as much out of the educational system as those in upper classes, and any gap remaining would not be a severe or legitimate source of complaint.

Those who emphasize outcomes, on the other hand, stress the fact that equal resource inputs, or equal availability, defined in any operational way, may very well lead to unequal outcomes that are both severe and unjustified. Outcomes can be defined in either an academic or socioeconomic sense, and discussion of that will occur a little later, but the most important common characteristics of nearly all versions of the outcomes viewpoint is that opportunity be defined in terms of one's chances for acquiring a certain status, whether academic, social, or economic. Though no one seems to have put it exactly this way, the new and predominant school of thought on this question regards equal educational opportunity as an educational system in which a child born into low socioeconomic circumstances will have as high a probability of attaining high academic (or occupational) credentials as a child born into high socioeconomic circumstances.

A DEFENSE OF EQUAL INPUTS

Can anything be said in defense of the older idea of equal opportunity? One possible apology is the notion that one should be able to make distinctions between various degrees and types of social equality, and equal educational opportunity was simply one of the more modest and limited forms of equality. There was no presumption that class distinction would be erased overnight with the imposition of equal educational opportunity. Before, as now, one should be able to make distinctions between a completely egalitarian society, a society with frictionless class mobility, and a society that simply offers the same opportunities within the educational system. Certainly such distinctions do not outrun the nuances of language or the subtleties that can be built into the law. And if such distinctions are indeed claimed to be false, then one must also dismiss as nonsense episodes such as the Supreme Court decision on desegregation, revolving around what was and was not equal in terms of schooling.

Another defense is that those who talked about equal educational opportunity in the traditional sense did have in mind real progress toward an egalitarian society, and equal educational opportunity seemed a convenient early step to get consensus on, once the facts were understood and the issue put forcefully. Among those who have abandoned the more traditional sense of the term, a large number have probably simply come to view the step of equal resource inputs as too modest a step, either because more seems possible politically or because new evidence suggests that equal resource inputs, defined in any reasonable way, merely brings us less far down the road to egalitanianism than was thought earlier.

But all that these two arguments say is that there *may* not be anything fundamentally wrong with a definition in terms of inputs. Still, is there anything right about it? Semantic and legal distinctions and the evolution of "progressive" ideology are interesting matters, but is there nothing that social science has to offer to buttress the traditional form of goal? Something should indicate that "social welfare" (or economic welfare) is uniquely served by the attainment of the specific goal under consideration. As it happens, there are such arguments for the traditional notion of equal opportunity. They can be found among some of the more standard neoclassical writings; but they are not often well expressed or prominent, and nearly always they are developed in an abstract form not closely related to debates among those in the educational establishment.

AN ECONOMIC DEFENSE

The case for equal opportunity of the traditional sort is perhaps most easily made by reference to a private-market approach to educational investments. Perhaps the earliest, and almost certainly the most epigramatic, statement of the issue is in A. C. Pigou's *Economics of Welfare* (1948) when he noted that "In a perfectly adjusted community . . . as between men of different degrees of the same capacity—the duke's son and the cook's son alike—more would be invested in the abler than in the less able." More recent statements can be found in modern neoclassical writers such as Gary Becker and Milton Friedman. The basis for the statement is very much wrapped up with the rate-of-return approach of much of the economics profession during the last decade. The argument begins with the explicit or implicit assertation that the main reason why the affluent spend more on education than the poor is that they have the accumulated savings for undertaking the investment, or at least have accumulated sufficient saleable assets to back up any loan they might undertake. The poor, on the other hand, *must* borrow in order to finance the investment; they have little or no accumulated wealth to reassure a lender, and the human capital they are investing is in itself a poor form of collateral. The reason for the cost is that loan default cannot be collected easily: you cannot repossess a human being as you can a car or a refrigerator, or sell him off as you might an unprofitable machine or factory.

Several aspects of this viewpoint are interesting. First of all is the clear-cut advantage in having equality of opportunity present in this sense. If there are no capital-market barriers, then those who end up investing are clearly the ones who make the best use of the expenditure. The logic is almost irresistible: surely a talented but poor youth, rather than an affluent slow-witted one, should acquire a given educational opportunity, and talent can be portrayed as a high rate of return. Therefore, the net gain is higher without the capital-market imperfection.

Starting from this insight, all that seems required in order to achieve equality of opportunity is to make the capital market "perfect"—to permit the poor to borrow money at the same rate as the rich—so that a specified educational investment in a poor individual is just as likely to be undertaken as the same type of investment in an affluent youth. Now that prescription has a loud note of unreality about it when considering the primary and secondary years of education. There, uniform agreement asserts that education should be a public enterprise, free of charge, with perhaps consideration of simply giving subsidies to parents and letting them select the school of their choice. No one really seems prepared to leave the educational investment decision for children entirely in the hands of parents, or to argue that externalities and social benefits of education at those ages are merely incidental. But it does have distinct relevence for postsecondary education, especially of the straight vocational sort, and the idea has certainly been one of the major inspirations behind the current enthusiasm for loans as a partial replacement for scholarships. It also can serve as a norm we might try to approximate, or simulate, when attempting to encourage equality of opportunity at lower levels of education, putting aside for a moment the other issues involved there.

What the free-market model is essentially saying is that the removal of capital-market barriers to borrowing will result in the same amount of educational investment in rich and poor of given "ability." The free market has the convenience of completely decentralizing, and making completely private, the decision about ability and the type of education that is suitable. To see how this can be simulated in the nonmarket setting of public elementary and secondary education, consider the simple (and somewhat naïve) approach that assumes that ability is fairly measured by IQ, and the amount of education received is measured by cost per pupil and years of schooling. Suppose also (with Pigou and many others) that students with greater "ability" generally make "better use" of quality education and extra years of schooling. Hence, those with higher IQs would be given more education, and more and relatively better resource inputs during their education. It can be argued that that is what a "perfect free market" solution would approximate, since those with greater ability would be willing to borrow more than those with less ability because their higher ability combines better with educational inputs and their rate of return would be higher.

More specifically, what should be asked is what makes a "perfect market" solution, or a public education approximation to such a solution, *economically* desirable. The answer comes straight from standard efficiency arguments that are at the heart of most economic reasoning. The specific principle involved goes back at least as far as Adam Smith, who noted that a free market will produce a situation where "all rates of return are equal." Making the principle more specific, educational investments, undertaken with approximately full knowledge and with perfect capital markets, will produce a situation where, for this type of investment, all rates of return are equal for all available investment opportunities. Educational investment, *for each individual*, in terms of both quality improvements and more years of schooling, will be extended, to the point where the rate of return is equal to the free-market rate of interest, which in turn will be the same for everyone if capital markets are made perfect. That follows because no one can be expected to invest beyond the point where the return of his investment is below the rate at which he can borrow or lend money, and all would be inclined to invest until further extension drops the return on additional educational investment to the market rate of interest—the inevitable decline caused by the ordinary workings of diminishing returns from adding resource inputs and the fact that, as education proceeds further into adolescence or adult life, fewer years remain to reap the benefits of the education acquired.

What this means, then, is that all educational investments undertaken will be worthwhile in that they will yield a return that is better than can be had elsewhere. An individual making an educational investment will always come off better; there is no general reason why anyone should suffer by way of his investment. An educational investment opportunity that is declined is one where the individual will not be made better off as a result of the investment since the rate of return in the market is more attractive. In short, a perfect capital market, or an approximation to it, would seem to fulfill the conditions of theoretical welfare economics for obtaining the economic optimum where no room exists for further clear-cut improvement— no one can be made better off without making someone else worse off. One may not be happy with the distribution of income that results from pursuing such a course of action, but a perfect capital-market solution may be thought of as at least more egalitarian than a situation where market imperfections and class status are permitted large influence; and if further equalizing of incomes is thought necessary, then direct transfers of income—taxing the affluent and giving the money to the nonaffluent—seems a course of action preferable to indulging in educational investments that pay rates of return below the market rate of interest and (by inference) the rate of return on other types of "physical" investments such as machines and factories.

To put the case succinctly, equality of opportunity defined in terms of equal inputs for those of equal ability is what can be expected from a perfect capital market and extending investments beyond what a perfect capital market generates would diminish the total flow of income and would be a less efficient way to redistribute income than direct transfers. Equal opportunity, in the "old" sense of the term, is consistent with—and, indeed, a necessary condition for—the achievement of an "economic welfare" optimum; and pursuing a more ambitious form of equal opportunity runs the risk of being inconsistent with economic optimality, or at least requires a more complex and economically unorthodox line of reasoning for its justification.

By this stage, many a reader will be bursting with objections to the slick simplicity of the preceding analysis, not to mention feeling some discomfort about the general conclusion. The foregoing can, however, be regarded as simply a model, a starting point, an abstraction—a crude Platonic ideal, if you will—to derive at least some economic implications that are firm. The next step is to challenge that abstraction, to see if the complications that deserve attention destroy, or at least make ambiguous, the conclusions deduced from the model.

A CLOSER LOOK AT THE ASSUMPTIONS

Let us begin with the items that were explicitly put aside: the matter of parental responsibility and the existence of externalities. There seems to be no great trouble in integrating these more explicitly into the model while leaving the basic conclusions intact. That parents may decide selfishly to skimp on the education of their children could be viewed as simply the decision of the family—who might be regarded as the atomistic, and indivisable, consumer-decision unit. But our social unwillingness to take a chance with parental stinginess and shortsightedness is surely a fundamental and sensible reason for school attendence requirements and public financial support of education. Still, as noted earlier, with the selection of individuals to be educated to different levels and the quality of the resource inputs, we can still attempt to keep in mind what would happen under perfect capital markets and adequate foresight on the part of individuals. An attempt can be made to invest as much in young individuals as they themselves would invest *if* they really knew the benefits of education and *if* they could borrow in a perfect capital market on the same basis as an adult.

Externalities can be handled by simply adding the appropriate additional amount to the education of all to account for the benefits that flow to persons other than those who are the direct recipients of the education. That, by necessity, must be handled by public support —under the presumption that, by and large, individuals do not consider external benefits flowing to society at large in reckoning the amount they are willing to pay for education. If we are dealing with higher education where the individual is paying for that part of his education that benefits him directly, externalities can be handled by some sort of partial subsidy arrangement added on top of the private expenditures. These two assumptions, swept partially under the rug, hence create no insurmountable difficulties when faced directly.

The more serious complications have been barely hinted at so far. One interesting problem, more or less neglected in economic discussions of equal opportunity, is the issue of "psychic returns" from education. Economists and others have been careful to stress the obvious point that education offers more benefits than financial gain, but no one seems to have followed through the implications of that point for equality of opportunity. First, it should be noted that psychic, or consumption, returns to education surely affect individual decisions about educational investments. It is the *total* rate of return, financial and psychic together, that is the real determinant of whether or not an individual would be willing to undertake a given educational investment. It is plausible that a rich and a poor individual of given "ability" will earn the same rate of financial return on a given educational investment, and it may also be the case that the two individuals will derive precisely the same psychic enjoyment from acquiring their education, but it does not follow that they will perceive the same total rate of return in the sense that they would be willing to pay the same amount for the same educational experience. The consumption elements of education—the plain psychic pleasures of greater knowledge and ability, the presumed joy of learning, etc.— should be regarded as "consumer" items in the full sense of the term, including the near certainty that they are income and wealth "elastic" to at least some degree. (To phrase the last nontechnically, someone with greater wealth and a higher lifetime income will probably purchase more of this consumption good, just as they would other consumption goods.) And while it is reasonable that a rich and a poor individual of the same ability will make the same income *gain* as a result of an educational experience, this hardly means they will end up with the same total income. The initial wealth endowment of the rich individual, and the income that it generates, will almost surely incline him to be willing to pay more for a given educational opportunity and to invest generally in higher quality education.

This argument could be interpreted to suggest that it is only the "frills" of education, or the "dilettantish" aspects, that the rich individual would acquire above and beyond that purchased by the poor individual; but that would surely be an overly narrow interpretation of psychic returns. It might also be argued that social mobility is what really interests us, that rich and poor individuals of the same ability should take the same amount of education for the income earning motive and would therefore arrive at the same earned income and the same approximate location on the occupational status ladder. But that does not quite follow, even if one puts aside the possibility that family connections can unbalance job competition and that the acquisition of interesting knowledge not having market value may still have value regarding social status. Jobs also have psychic returns associated with them, and higher-earning jobs generally have higher psychic returns in terms of occupational status and the status of simply earning more money. A wealthy individual, or his parents, might be willing to experience a substantial financial loss in order to win entrance into a high-paying position; the poor individual may not be willing to pay much at all, even though he would enjoy the high-status job as much.

But while this argument indicates that a perfect capital market will not produce equality of opportunity in terms of the amount and quality of education acquired, or in terms of chances for acquiring given social, occupational, or earned-income status, it might still be possible to achieve these goals by rationing education strictly according to ability. A perfect capital market, as was demonstrated, does not quite do that; but a system of public financing of education could manage to enforce such an arrangement. It might be argued, however, that this departure from a perfect capital-market approximation would not be optimal (and perhaps not even stable): wealthy individuals would be willing to buy the entry into educational opportunities that more talented poor individuals won by demonstrating superior ability—and the poor would be willing to sell. In other words, it would seem possible to make some individuals better off without making anyone worse off by allowing the original ability rationing to be undermined by such market transactions. But if equality of opportunity is valued by society for its own sake, that would not necessarily follow. Even if society as a whole had no other vested interest in seeing that the more talented individual acquired the education in question, regarding equality of educational opportunity as a social imperative would lead to disallowing such buying away of ability-demonstrated admissions of scarce educational opportunities.

At this stage it should be noted that the argument has a direct implication for the financing of equal educational opportunity: unless psychic returns are insignificant, strictly private financing of education will not achieve the most modest version of that goal even under the most ideal of capital markets. The fairly lengthy (though obscure) tradition that has associated equal opportunity with truly free markets, suggesting at times that the road to equal opportunity lies in the direction of getting the government out of the education business, seems to have at least one serious flaw.

A few additional issues deserve consideration. Some of these are woven through recent discussions on the topic of equal opportunity, but they are presented here with somewhat different nuances.

The most obvious point that deserves close consideration is that rich and poor individuals do not have the same average abilities, at least not as ability is customarily measured. Forgetting about the possibility that a rich man's son *may* have a better endowment of genes, there is still the uncontestable fact that he has a better break in terms of home environment. It could be argued, perhaps, that ability as measured by IQ tests taken shortly before entry into formal education is the really relevant ability—it measures the "raw material" that the school has to deal with—and, further, that equal educational opportunity refers to what formal schooling manages to do with that raw material. That, however, seems a pretty severe semantic strain. It is probably more sensible to say that ability refers to "innate potential," that is, the maximum level of eventual attainment an individual can achieve given optimum "cultivation" from birth. It is likewise sensible to say that the educational system should not be limited to that part of education that takes place in classrooms during certain ages, but rather, all things that contribute to learning, including the important matter of home environment. So if the observed average "ability" difference—as measured on standardized tests—between children from rich and poor families is presumed due to differences in home environment, it can be reasoned quite directly that equality of opportunity is not being acheived by simply matching ability (as usually measured) with inputs in the formal educational system.

The foregoing argument could be stated with more subtlety and richness of detail. Home environment could be extended to include neighborhood environment and general social milieu; race and class discrimination could be named as aggravating factors of considerable importance; and the intricacies of social-psychological interrelations among students in the same classroom and between students and teachers could be mentioned. But none of that would change the analysis substantially. It would only make stronger the case against working with the formal and limited notions of ability and the educational system.

One other factor deserves special emphasis, however: the practical difficulty of specifying what equal resource inputs really are. No less the point we have just discussed, this difficulty has undermined the idea that there is reasonableness in the traditional notion of equality of opportunity. The point can be made with two simple examples. First, even though the per-pupil costs of the education of poor children are precisely the same as that of rich children, poor children may still be getting inferior resources because the same teacher salary in "slum and suburb" will result in appreciably better teachers in the suburb because of the more "congenial" work atmosphere there. Second, even if rich and poor student are in the same classroom, the middle-class teacher is more favorably disposed to the well-mannered son of the affluent parent, so that the ability of the son of the poor parent does not get an even chance of blossoming fully.

All in all, the older input-oriented notion of equality of opportunity, after close inspection, seems to have little to stand on. The economic efficiency rationale proposed earlier is undercut when broader and more subtle considerations are brought to bear. More importantly, we seem to do violence to ordinary language meanings if we attempt to claim that measurable equality in formal schooling inputs *really* fulfills the ideal connoted by the term equality of educational opportunity.

A CRITIQUE OF THE OUTCOMES GOAL

If the more traditional notion is deservedly defunct, or simply unappealing, it does not follow automatically that we move to a straight outcomes definition of the equal-opportunity goal. One necessary condition, it would seem, is that the lower-achieving socioeconomic group be somehow "excused" for the meager home background they provide their children, and/or that the higher-achieving group be "undeserving" of the advantage they are able to impart to their progeny. It can be argued, not unpersuasively, that a good bit of the striving that men do is for the sake of their children, and that such a motive has general social approval. If a man fails, his children have a lesser chance of succeeding; the reverse is true if he is successful. We refrain from inheritance taxes that are completely confiscatory because we generally approve the motive of intergenerational transmission of success, and it seems a strong flirtation with inconsistency to say that those individuals who experience economic success should not be able to transmit it in the special form of an educational head start (pardon the expression) for their children, supplementary schooling at home, and formal schooling of extraordinary quality. To assert the equal-outcomes goal with complete fervor would, therefore, involve either an assertion that it is somehow unfair to transmit accomplishment of sons and daughters in this one special fashion, or a broader attack on the whole notion of inheritance.

An exploration of the general problem of inheritance is beyond the scope of this essay. But it is perhaps not unreasonable to argue against the special form of inheritance under consideration on the basis that one's earned-income level and occupational status really are something special, and clearly distinguished from the mere provision for the satisfaction of material wants. The same exception can be made for the closely related, but not identical, matter of educational accomplishment. Mobility and equality along these dimensions can be viewed as so important to general social health and a just society that they override, in this instance, the conflicting principle of inheritance. That kind of distinction can be made, but it seems to require something more. If we are talking about an identifiable social group who, in fair competition, has won success or developed a culture especially conducive to the academic and economic success of its children, the case for equality of outcomes seems to lose its edge. Presently, no one seems to be arguing that the unusually high academic attainment of Jewish and Oriental children is socially unjust, or that white Gentiles should be given compensatory education to make up for their cultural handicap. Clearly it is not just the problem of bringing the majority up to the lofty standards of the high-achieving group that explains the absence of complaint in this case—at an earlier time, when college and university education was the prerogative of the privileged few, justice was seen to be served by greatly expanding the availability of higher education. It is not a matter of majority or minority, but rather the matter of *privilege* that makes the difference. And "privilege" brings the clear suggestion of unfair, or unfairly won, advantage.

In the case of Jewish and Oriental children, we are in fact inclined to cheer their more-than-equal attainment because it was won in the face of *counter-privilege*—the competition was not quite fair, but the underdog won. When the underdog—who is so because of circumstances largely beyond his control—succumbs to his disadvantage and fails to attain equality, then inequality or outcomes seems a matter of serious and clear-cut ethical concern.

Similarly, if a social or cultural group develops that provides reinforcement for low attainment when there was no denial of privilege, we tend to be complacent about their less-than-equal outcomes, be they Mennonites or flower children. Thus, the complaint of unequal outcomes has unambiguous moral force only when the low-attainment group are the sons and daughters of those who have been to some extent victimized, and the meager advantages they can pass on to their children is hence a matter of "unfair" circumstance.

If the socioeconomic position of the parents does not reflect unfair circumstance but their own disinclination to strive, then the failure of sons and daughters to achieve because of home background can be thought of as just desserts for the parents, if not necessarily for the children. One could try to press hard on that last qualification, but the issue seems sufficiently ambiguous that it could be handled adequately by the famous John F. Kennedy rejoinder that life simply tends to be unfair.

What makes this issue especially complex is the difficulty in trying to unravel the degree to which the socioeconomic position of the parents is the result of their socioeconomic striving, their own frailties, or the working of a socioeconomic system that unfairly thwarted or eased their way upward. This difficult determination, plus disagreement about how much "right" a parent has to influence his child's income and occupational future, may very well be the chief reasons why reasonable men can still disagree about the extent to which the norm of equal outcomes should be pursued.

The economic efficiency case for equal outcomes is no more clear-cut than the ethical case, and perhaps less so. At least two important economic points should be made. First, because a child from a poor family has the same inborn potential as the child from a rich family does *not* clearly imply that it is economically efficient to apply sufficient human-resource investment so that the poor child attains the same final academic outcome as the child from the affluent family. Educational inputs by parents do not have exactly the same economic implications as educational inputs in more formal settings, even though both may logically be regarded as part of the educational system. The relatively high quality of the educational input from a rich family is to a large degree an unavoidable by-product of the affluence of the family. Moreover, the time spent by parents with children is presumably voluntary, and there is no clear, a priori reason to think it is suboptimal, that either too much or too little time is spent by either rich or poor parents, taking into account the fact that the parents' time also has value in terms of income that could be earned and in satisfaction of their own leisure. Now, policies aimed at achieving equal outcomes do not tend to focus on reforming parental practices. Institutional substitutes are at issue here. And, once again, a priori reasoning fails to provide any clear guide: there is no convincing reason why providing an institutional substitute to make up for what poor children lack vis-à-vis rich children passes any of the standard tests of welfare economics. It is not at all unlikely that the total return on that special effort will fail to be as large as the costs. The return will, almost by definition, be the same as it is for the child of a rich family (given a strong interpretation of equal outcomes), but no extra costs are required in the rich child's case. How much extra cost is required to obtain for poor children the same average outcomes in an institutional setting is strictly an empirical question; and the cost could well be enormous in relation to benefits enjoyed by the directly affected parties and for society as a whole.

Exactly what the costs would be is not entirely clear: no situation exists where, under circumstances that could conceivably be replicated on a large scale, enough resources were devoted to the education of very low-status individuals to bring their average level of accomplishment up to that of individuals raised in affluent homes. Nevertheless, on the basis of the "second-stage" studies mentioned in the introduction of this paper, the belief has grown that the costs of attaining that target would be substantial indeed, and would likely exceed by a good deal the benefits received by those directly affected by the education.

The second economic problem is closely related to the first, if somewhat more complex. Note, first, that the attainment of equal educational outcomes need not imply any additional total spending on education. Resources could simply be shifted from the affluent to the poor until the equal-outcomes goal was attained. With no increase in total educational spending, we might conceivably do no worse than break even in very strict economic-efficiency terms—no net increase in resource costs occur, and the economic loss experienced by the affluent may be counterbalanced by the gain experienced by the poor. But while there is no economic necessity for an increase in total spending, such an outcome in the face of an attempt to spend more on the poor is nearly impossible to envision. The affluent are not likely to sit still for a decline in the quality or quantity of their children's education. Moreover, increasing educational investments for the poor while keeping such investment on the affluent unchanged implies that the affluent will experience a diminution in their expected income as competition in high-skill occupations grows more intense. To attain expected income levels, and to avoid a sharp decline in relative status, the affluent can be expected to accelerate improvement in educational quality (and quantity) for their children in any of several ways. Thus, moves toward equality will be counteracted to some extent, will be more expensive than it first might seem, and could lead to "overspending" on education.

CONCLUSION

The problems involved in an equal-outcomes approach hardly mean that we can settle back to an input definition of equal educational opportunity, for the difficulties there are no less serious. These problems do imply, however, that substantial progress beyond equal "inputs" and toward equal "outputs" will probably involve some economic costs, and complete equality of outcomes may be so expensive that we may well choose to fall short of achieving complete equality of outcomes, at least in the near term. Exactly how far, and how fast, we progress toward the equal output goal should, and probably will, depend both upon how costly such progress turns out to be and upon the degree to which we value such progress.

More could be added to this rather simple moral, and several of the other inferences in this essay could be usefully extended with the help of some of the many interesting concepts and measurements in the economics of education that have been generated recently. That, however, would involve considerable interloping on the other essays in this volume.

.7. The Political Economy of Public School Finance*

STEPHAN MICHELSON

TRADITIONAL SOCIETIES transmit a fund of knowledge to succeeding generations. Most of these societies transmit both general and vocational information, and allocate labor, without the institution that is presumed to perform both of these functions in modern societies: public schools. A number of explanations account for the lack of this institution in earlier societies. Among the more obvious are that the scope of today's science prevents any individual from acquiring all of society's knowledge, that the combinations of skills required changes from generation to generation, and that technology requires the ability to adapt to change more than any particular (static) skill. Thus, today's society requires institutions within which knowledge is stored (libraries), expanded (research), utilized (development), and transmitted (schools and training programs). Younger members of society are engaged in finding out how to utilize these resources, and in learning the rudiments of advanced technology. More importantly, perhaps, they learn communication skills, since the decision about what work to pursue is no longer traditional, but based on market forces.

This would be an acceptable description of the functioning of public schools in society were there not compelling reasons to question at

*The historical portion of this essay in private circulation elicited helpful comments from Richard C. Edwards, Samuel Bowles, and others at the Center for Educational Policy Research. Additional help from Lottie K. Beaman, Polly Harold, Minnie Lawlars, Christopher S. Jencks, and Norton Grubb is greatly appreciated.

least its completeness. This model contains no mechanism that channels individual rational behavior into desired societal behavior. In an alternative explanation, the major difference between modern and traditional societies is that status and power are not legally inherited, and are not based on traditional relations (e.g., the attachment of a tribe for its chief), but are based on production relations, and are inherited only insofar as children replicate the productive characteristics of their parents.[1] The most important transfer of position from generation to generation occurs by having the children complete a set of requirements held as *objectively* desirable and used independently of class background to select the candidate best suited for a particular position.

This second interpretation would summarize succinctly that schools function so as to preserve class structure. That is, by and large they exemplify a set of rules that operates in society to select people into various relationships defined relative to the productive capacity of the nation. Schools induce different characteristics in different people, these characteristics being used later to select people to different economic positions. Additionally, schools may be called upon to establish the propriety of these rules, to promote the acceptance of the rules, hence the outcomes, among succeeding generations. The rules must be applied *fairly*, but the "right" people must benefit from them. Overt manipulation of outcomes occurs when the fairness doctrine is abandoned—and this we castigate as "favoritism." Schools function to manipulate outcomes covertly by changing the rules of the game over time.

If the school system does in fact operate to confer game-playing abilities differentially and in a biased fashion, then we should be able to identify how it does so. We should find, for example, that more resources are allocated to those people destined to "win" the economic game. In the extreme we should be able to differentiate among kinds of resources: those which produce workers, those managers, and perhaps those which produce rulers.

[1]Needless to say, wealth can be inherited. Position may also seem to be, such as Fords heading the Ford Motor Company. But this inheritance is of corporate power, and that power is used to place people from "the right family" in titular (and often real) leadership positions, but almost always only if they have a minimum of actual qualification. For example, the DuPont family recently experienced the overthrow of inherited position for lack of administrative ability.

We could also trace historically the development of the school system, and make a historical argument that schools function this way because they were established to function this way. Some argument along these lines appears below. The two arguments merge in that the *manner* in which ruling-class children are favored differs from area to area, depending on the history of each area, and particularly on the history of each area's school system. Thus, a thorough analysis of school-resource allocation involves immense statistical and historical efforts that are beyond my capacity to amass at the present time. This essay illustrates techniques required, and the results that can be expected.

One could cogently question whether schools must in fact discriminate in order to favor certain classes of children. If the schools merely succeed in maintaining the rank order of skills acquired elsewhere—and these skills are then employed to select the leaders from the followers—wouldn't this be sufficient? And isn't it in accord with current research findings?[2] To this the answer is clearly "Yes." This perhaps makes it more surprising that one can find resource disparities both historically and currently, as I will illustrate. Like many systems, the system by which social stratification occurs in the United States is redundant. Many facets are not strictly necessary, many inequalities in processes might be rectified without markedly improving such outcomes as social class or income inequality. But, though not strictly necessary, neither are these processes haphazard, as the succeeding analyses will demonstrate.

HISTORICAL EVIDENCE

Development of the school system in the Massachusetts Bay Colony and the subsequent Commonwealth of Massachusetts is better documented than most school systems. Many states designed their systems on the Massachusetts model, just as that colony's original educational statutes followed the Elizabethan laws of the early seventeenth century, and these laws had their roots in the Reformation. Indeed, the Reformation character of public education continued

---

[2]See, for example, James S. Coleman et al., *Equality of Educational Opportunity* (Washington, D.C.: U.S. Office of Education, 1966); or see the most thorough reanalysis of this document, F. Mosteller and D. P. Moynihan, eds., *On Equality of Educational Opportunity* (New York: Random House, 1971).

into the early nineteenth century. "The Bible was put into the hands of the people to be for each one an individual guide and help and at least an education sufficient to read and understand it was a necessary corollary."[3] The Massachusetts General Court, issuing the first law in the Colonies requiring the establishment of schools, made clear the ideological basis of the action: "It being one chief point of that old deluder, Satan, to keep men from the knowledge of the scriptures . . . ."[4] Massachusetts law required that townships of fifty households or more establish an elementary school that would focus on biblical training, and townships of one hundred households or more establish a grammar school to prepare children for university entrance. This "Old Deluder" law of 1647 had been preceded by a 1642 statute in which the court instructed town leaders "to take account from time to time of their parents and masters of their children concerning their calling and employment of their children, especially of their ability to read and understand the principles of religion and the capital laws of the country."[5]

Thus the religious basis of education, education for morality, co-existed with the need for a citizenry able to read, understand, and act according to law. At least one interpreter saw this latter function as predominant:

They [the General Court] knew that an industrious child was a squared stone fit to be builded into the edifice they were rearing, so they would have the children put to work. They called illiteracy barbarism, and therefore, not for the Church's sake nor for the child's sake, but for the sake of the commonwealth, they insisted on universal education.[6]

Whether moral or more Machiavellian reasons underlay the law, it was certainly not designed to liberate the children from the bonds of society, but to bind the children to the society. More importantly, no

[3]George Leroy Jackson, *The Development of School Support in Colonial Massachusetts* (New York: Teachers College, Columbia University, 1909), p. 7.

[4]*Records of the Governor and Company of the Massachusetts Bay*, ed. Nathaniel B. Shurtleff (Commonwealth of Massachusetts, 1854), vol. 2, p. 203; in Modern English as in Jackson, *Development of School Support in Colonial Massachusetts*. p. 16.

[5]Ibid, pp. 8–9.

[6]George H. Martin, *The Evolution of the Massachusetts Public School System* (New York: D. Appleton and Co., 1915), p. 9.

mention was made of the acquisition of skills, save those required for admission to the university.

The university at issue was Harvard University, which had been established by the court in 1636. Its entrance requirements were:

> Whosoever shall be able to read Tully or any other such like classical author at sight, and correctly and without assistance to speak and write Latin both in prose and verse, and to inflect exactly the paradigms of Greek nouns and verbs, has a right to expect to be admitted into the college, and no one may claim admission without these qualifications.[7]

At this time Harvard was essentially a divinity school. Its purpose was to maintain an elite class, though to do so by means of objective entrance examinations that the average student could not hope to pass. The privileged students, moreover, did not necessarily acquire skills in production or trade, or more basic skills which might be required to operate successfully in a labor market among upper-class progeny. No such market then existed, and the educational content served only to set "standards" for the populace, and identify the elite.[8]

Two threads run concurrently through the picture of early Massachusetts education. First, education of people who could not otherwise afford it was a sound investment, in terms of maintaining society. The school could replace the home as the prime transmitter of morals and culture, and if the people who controlled the government apparatus could control this ideology, government would function more smoothly.[9] The second thread seemed to contradict the first: schooling served to identify classes. In this regard, schooling functioned in its scarcity. Public schools attended by the masses perhaps served the first function, but, if so, they could not serve the second.

---

[7]Josiah Quincy, *The History of Harvard University*, ed. J. Owen (Cambridge, Mass., 1840), vol. 1, p. 515.

[8]"Of the five social classes identifiable in Massachusetts Bay, the most important was an 'upper' class composed of men of wealth and education..." George Lee Haskins, *Law and Authority in Early Massachusetts* (New York: Macmillan Co., 1960), p. 99.

[9]The decreasing religiosity and family ties of native-born progeny of the early puritans is well known. See Bernard Bailyn, *Education in the Forming of American Society* (New York: Vintage Books, 1960).

The resolution is that, from its beginnings, public education did serve both functions; it did so by creating two systems under one name. Primary schools were local and locally financed. Grammar schools to prepare students for entry into Harvard were required only in reasonably large towns. And only certain families could afford to send their children to such a school—"afford" in the sense of not needing the child's labor to help support the family. Thus, a low level of schooling was established for the many, a higher level for the few. Stratification occurred both between schools—from residential segregation and local control—and between levels of schooling. In the seventeenth and eighteenth centuries the difference in levels was obvious, since children who attended grammar schools usually went on to the university, then into government or the ministry.

The education system in Massachusetts developed with the colony's official participation—though this was regulatory and permissive only. In 1683 towns with five hundred or more families were required to support two grammar and two writing schools.[10] Schools had started as strictly local institutions, and though it died hard, complete local autonomy eventually died. In the earliest years of the eighteenth century the commonwealth had begun to supervise the running of schools, at first by establishing that they be inspected (by ministers—a holdover from the earlier religious schooling), and later by establishing public inspection authorities. The end of local autonomy meant that "The voting of school support was now the only power of importance remaining in the hands of the people."[11] Conceptions of the school were changing, and a move to "reform" the schools in the 1820s was part of the initiative for greater centralized political control. Massachusetts was one of the first states to establish a state board of education; Horace Mann became its first secretary in 1837.

[10]It should not be supposed that such schools were created just because they were required. The history of law is essentially the history of the thinking of the people who controlled state machinery. It is not the history of schools. For example, see Michael Katz, *The Irony of Early School Reform* (Cambridge, Mass.: Harvard University Press, 1968) on the failure of compulsory attendance laws.

[11]Elwood Cubberley, *Public School Administration*, rev. ed. (Boston: Houghton Mifflin Co., 1929), p. 153. In many states, of course, districts do exist independent of the town lines. In Hawaii, in contrast, there is but one, statewide school system, though with several subdivisions.

The Early Reform Era

School-reform rhetoric has been the basis of educational philosophy. In the early nineteenth century the economic value of education appeared in two ways. First, as Lester Ward put it later in the century, "From an economic point of view, an uneducated class is an expensive class."[12] This updated the "state benefit" theme from earlier times: the state benefits from education because it creates a working class out of an indolent class, a law-abiding class out of a lawless class.

A second economic benefit was the direct output created by the now educated (hence employed) person. As Horace Mann emphasized:

The greatest of all the arts in political economy is to change a consumer into a producer; and the next greatest is to increase the producer's producing power—an end to be directly attained by increasing his intelligence.[13]

The facts, however, belie the rhetoric. Michael Katz has analyzed the vote to abolish the public high school in Beverly, Massachusetts, in 1860. He has noted that skilled shoemakers in that town were being displaced by machines and unskilled labor. They had been offered *lower* wages. Their children did not get to attend Beverly High School, and their view of economic progress was that it destroyed satisfactory life styles. Katz analyzed the votes for and against the school. The "wealthy and prominent citizens" supported the school "as the harbinger of manufacturing and urban growth," and on the state-preservation arguments advanced above. The opponents to the school, however, consisted of an alliance between those citizens who had no children (and were not swayed to the position that they would benefit anyway, as citizens of a better state) and "the least affluent citizens [who] felt that the high school would not benefit their children."[14]

Already in the mid-nineteenth century, then, education was identified with industry. "The school became the means of instilling in the

---

[12]Rena L. Vassar, ed. *Social History of American Education,* vol. 2, *1860 to the Present* (New York: Rand McNally Co., 1965), p. 131. Quotation from Lester Ward, *Dynamic Sociology*, 1883.

[13]Vassar, *Social History of American Education* p. 236. Quotation from Horace Mann, "Education and Prosperity," 1848.

[14]Katz, *Irony of Early School Reform*, p. 85.

population the qualities necessary for success in industrial society."[15] This could easily be considered as improving the state by those people who controlled the state government, and those (such as landowner and businessmen) who most profited from economic growth. Such a goal for the state, hence for its education institutions, was not universally favored by the working class, its supposed beneficiaries. But what was the educational system to do that would produce "good" workers? What "qualities" led to industrial "success?"

The Outcomes of Schooling

Let us look at the structure and content of the schools themselves. Some relationship should exist between the schooling process and the intended outcome. (Another way to determine the function of schools would be to investigate those attributes of workers deemed important by employers. To the extent that schools are real-world oriented, they should help produce these attributes. I will consider only the first approach.)[16]

Elwood P. Cubberley described "Information" or "Knowledge" courses in 1929:

Facts, often of no particular importance in themselves, are taught, memorized, and tested for, to be forgotten as soon as the school-grade need for them has passed. Tool studies, as opposed to content studies and constructional activities, are greatly overemphasized, and are made ends in themselves. Years of a child's life often are spent in learning supposed uses of a tool for which there is no use outside of the schoolroom itself; weeks, months, and even years are spent in drilling on problems of a type no man in practical life ever solves, and which can be of no use to any one except a school teacher.[17]

Cubberley, of course, was arguing for "relevance," which to him meant differentiation of courses of study, and the use of testing to channel children into eventual occupations.[18] His description, how-

---

[15]Ibid., p. 43.

[16]For information on the second approach, see Herbert Gintis, "Education, Technology, and Worker Productivity," *American Economic Review* 61, no. 2 (May 1971): 266–79. Work is in progress on this subject by Richard C. Edwards.

[17]Cubberley, *Public School Administration*, p. 406.

[18]See Elwood Cubberley, *Changing Conceptions of Education* (Boston: Houghton, Mifflin Co., 1909), for an explicit statement to this effect.

ever, is of a system that had been channeling children into industry for close to a century. This might lead one to believe that the *content* of the course was not its crucial element. Indeed, textbooks in the late nineteenth century actually inveighed against creative thinking, as well as creative behavior. A current observer notes:

> Though scholarship was desirable, one might make too much of a good thing: the texts warned against reading and thinking too much and cautioned children about the vice of reading novels. A vein of anti-intellectualism lay close to the surface of the textbooks.[19]

Intellectualism was an elite characteristic, and therefore had to be preserved for the elite. For the masses, a "national character," an "American political concensus,"[20] in short, acceptance of one's place in (moral) society was the goal of education.

Thus, two elements of course content in public schools are indicated. First, the "real-world" content—as mundane as tool handling —did not relate to the actual industrial activities of the children. This was later decried by twentieth-century reformers, but indicates that perhaps this content was not the most important aspect of the "education" being received. Second, the moral content of the course was carried over from earlier "good citizen" functions of schooling. Good behavior was rewarded, bad behavior punished, and serious ills in society were not admitted. The child was taught to work (not *how* to work, just *to* work) and to behave.

Even before 1900 then, schools were functioning to produce workers, not from the cognitive content of the schooling—skill acquisition—but from the attitudes about the world. More important was the lesson in behavior learned from the structure of schooling itself. With explicit attention to deference to authority, proper decorum, suppression of individualism, and acceptance of social position, the schools could prepare workers for work better than the factories could.[21] But schools could obviously do even better; for example, they could teach relevant vocational skills, as Cubberley suggested. They could also do this more efficiently.

[19]David B. Tyack, *Turning Points in American Educational History* (Waltham, Mass: Blaisdell Publishing Co., 1967), p. 182.

[20]Ibid.

[21]Cohen and Lazerson quote the editor of the *Journal of Education* as boasting to this effect in 1900. "Education and the Industrial Order," *Socialist Revolution* (March 1970).

Later Reform: Efficiency

The early 1900s was the era of "scientific management," writings by Frederick W. Taylor, and the natural attempt to apply "Taylorism" to the schools. We could look briefly at the evidence about the resultant structure of the schools, and the message this communicated to the children. However, it should be clear at this point that the function of the school in promoting the acceptance of industrialization had already been in operation. In addition, the nature of production from the point of view of the worker was not so much affected by scientific management as it had been by industrialization and the resultant fragmentation of jobs and life styles, half a century earlier.[22] Scientific management did hasten the growth of low-level white-collar work. Its major effect may have been to create a higher class—a "respectable" class—to which children of the industrial workers could aspire. Education, the obvious path to this level, responded with increased differentiation of school courses.[23] It is in the context of the changing structure of the work force that increased emphasis on efficiency in the schools should be investigated. The myth that this emphasis perverted an earlier role of the schools, unconnected with producing labor for industry, should be dispelled.[24]

"Each year the child is coming to belong more and more to the state, and less and less to the parent" declared Elwood Cubberley in 1909.[25] The "state" now included the federal government, which had fiscally entered the field in 1862 with the passage of the Morrill Act promoting land-grant colleges. By 1911 a vocational education bill was in Congress, supported by the American Federation of Labor.[26]

[22]The employment of unskilled labor plus machines to replace skilled labor, and the change in work conditions and life style which ensued, was of course the major social phenomenon of the mid-nineteenth century. It is in this turmoil that Karl Marx lived, and this phenomenon he analyzed.

[23]This was the era also of vocational schools, the major struggle for which was over the concept of differentiated curriculum.

[24]For example, the feminization of the teacher force occurred in the 1840s in response to economic pressure caused by increased enrollments.

[25]Cubberley, *Changing Conceptions of Education*, p. 154.

[26]Vocational education was finally passed on the federal level as the Smith-Hughes Act, 1917. Norton Grubb has concluded that the convincing argument for passage was the curriculum differentiation aspect of vocational education. The label, not the skill, was the intended outcome of the differentiated high school curriculum, a dramatic step backward from democratic rhetoric. "The Impact of the Vocational Education Movement After 1910," typescript (Harvard University, 1971).

But the state had constitutional authority over education, and by 1929 only two states did not have a department of education.[27] Massachusetts had passed a compulsory attendance law in 1852, and by 1918 every state had some form of compulsory attendance law, though often poorly enforced.[28] Thus the child was indeed becoming more under the control of the state, and the state was creating institutions to administer this control.

The creation and popularization of measuring instruments aided the concept of scientific management of the schools. At the same time that "Thorndike and his students developed scales for measuring achievement in arithmetic (1908), handwriting (1910), spelling (1913), drawing (1913), reading (1914), and language ability (1916),"[29] the army tested its draftees to identify officer potential and those unfit for the service. The famous Army Alpha test seemed to serve this purpose, and testing quickly spread to the school system as a classification device.[30] Textbooks were made relevant to the functions that different school strata would perform. Throughout this "reform," Cubberley's pathetic vision of prewar democracy was not affected:

School systems with us are thoroughly democratic. An educational ladder *for all who can afford it and have the mental capacity to use it* extends from the kindergarten or primary school to and through the state university.[31]

Raymond Callahan expressed surprise at "the extreme vulnerability of schoolmen, especially school administrators" to business ideology.[32] Callahan's surprise at the immediate response of school officials to criticism from prestigious forums was itself a surprise. Given state control of education, one need only ask who controlled the state, and to what end? I cannot here detail that history. Suffice it to point out that business interests firmly controlled state power,

[27]Cubberley, *Public School Administration*, p. 36.

[28]Mississippi was the last state to adopt such a law, in 1918, reflecting the Southern reluctance to provide mass education. See Ibid.

[29]Lawrence Cremin, *The Transformation of the American School* (New York: Alfred A. Knopf, 1961), p. 186.

[30]Cremin shows that opposition to this use of tests was immediate and sophisticated, and also fruitless.

[31]Cubberley, *Changing Conceptions of Education*, p. 154; emphasis added.

[32]Raymond Callahan, *Education and the Cult of Efficiency* (Chicago: University of Chicago Press, 1962), Preface.

and probably still do.[33] That business interests controlled the schools through pressures on schoolmen is documented in Callahan's book. That schoolmen *were* businessmen was documented by George S. Counts in 1927.[34] However, it is both difficult and unnecessary to demonstrate the direct link between the segment of the population that gains from political decisions, and the making of these decisions. To demonstrate that schools are organized for the benefit of the few, the repression of the many, we need only look at how schools operate, and what the results of these operations are. It is interesting, and adds to the argument, if we can document how these results came about. But failing to find the process when the results are there is certainly not evidence that the process does not exist.

The Nature of Historical Evidence

The preceding dash through three centuries of educational history sets the stage for some current statistical analysis. Briefly, the argument is that the public educational system has traditionally had two purposes, and has performed two functions:

1. To socialize the masses into the market economy, and into acceptance of objective rules for class stratification; failure to rise would then be accepted as a *personal* failure, not a systemic failure.

2. To produce characteristics in children of the ruling class that would ensure their selection through the "objective" process into the next generation's ruling class. Initially the major characteristic was merely the certification of education itself. With increasing levels of general education the differentiating characteristics should be expected to be more subtle.

[33]See, for example, W. Domhoff, *Who Rules America?* (Englewood Cliffs, N.J.: Prentice Hall, 1967), or J. K. Galbraith, *The New Industrial State.* (Boston: Houghton Mifflin, 1967). Their views differ in particulars, but can agree on this generalization. See also Philip Stern, *The Great Treasury Raid* (New York: Random House, 1964) and John Gurley's review, "Federal Tax Policy," *National Tax Journal* 20, no. 3 (September 1967): 319–27, to see the predominance of business interests in the revenue side of federal fiscal affairs. See also G. Kolko, *Wealth and Power in America* (New York: Praeger, 1962) for a description of the benefits of business interests hidden within income statistics. Various issues of *Ramparts* magazine, *The Nation*, and other liberal journals also contain revelant documentation.

[34]G. S. Counts, *The Social Composition of Board of Education; School and Society in Chicago* (Chicago: University of Chicago, 1927), *Secondary Education and Industrialism* (Cambridge: Harvard University Press, 1929).

The purpose of public education is clearly control over the social-ization of the masses. Part of the preceding documentation has shown the rise of school control from local to larger levels. But the sensible next step in analysis is to question the *outcomes* of a control process, even if not documenting the process itself. One failure of Counts' approach is to assume that one set of people must vote dif-ferently from another set, when both sets are sitting in the same seats (school boards) and are not necessarily representative of the social and economic strata with which Counts identifies them. Katz's in-vestigation of a town-meeting vote is much more subtle, because these are citizens acting as citizens, not as "elected representatives." Indeed, Cubberley even suggests how to arrange school board elec-tions to undermine Counts' social-class identifications.[35]

Arguing against Counts' inferences, Roald F. Campbell, in a Stan-ford University dissertation, found (according to W. W. Charters) "no clear relationship between the stands taken by the officers of school legislation of social import and their social class positions in the community (as measured by their occupation and income).[36] Charters concluded, after a review of literature, that "Dominant class control has not been demonstrated . . . and on dominant class control rests a major share of the proof of the proposition that public schools support the values of the dominant class."[37] But more im-portant than the question of whether one can correctly identify members of social classes is the question in whose interests one votes when he has the opportunity. One may identify with a future social class, and may better assure that future by so voting.

Even more important, and a larger failure of Counts' approach, is the question of how many class issues come to a vote. Thus, issues such as starting schools at a fixed time each day, structuring them

[35]"One of the important results of the change from ward representation to elec-tion from the city at large, in any city of average decency and intelligence, is that the inevitable representation from these 'poor wards' is eliminated, and the board as a whole comes to partake of the best characteristics of the city as a whole." Cubberley, *Public School Administration*, p. 176.

[36]Quotation from W. W. Charters, "Social Class Analysis and the Control of Public Education," *Harvard Educational Review* 23, no. 4 (Fall 1953): 272, reporting on Campbell's dissertation, "The Social Implications of School Board Legislation," 1942.

[37]Ibid., p. 279.

one teacher to a classroom, one principal to a school, etc. are not voted on. The absentee authority—school boards and corporation directors—is legitimized by the public school structure, as is the hierarchy of authority within the school. These, however, may be the most vital messages communicated to children.[38]

The failure of Domhoff's approach to social decisions is in trying to identify the elusive process without considering the results. Domhoff makes much, say, of the interchange between business leaders and the Pentagon—yet to whom would any rational, well-meaning large government agency turn for advice on managing its affairs? The fact of interchange with those who presumably have relevant experience does not suffice to show that business interests are promulgated (again, by decision makers acting on behalf of their future class standing) unfairly. The case must first be made that this is so, that the decisions are indeed favorable to business. Then one would want to investigate how this came about.

In terms of schools, a reasonable place to start is "resource allocation." Are resources distributed unequally in favor of the already wealthy? If we determine that this is the case, then we should want to investigate how this is accomplished.[39] We will find, for example, that in some areas of the country (particularly New England) resource differentials occur largely between districts, with largely equal allocation within districts; and in other parts of the country (particularly the South) differentials occur more within than between districts. The partition of variation, as well as the amount of variation, can be seen as a historical phenomenon. A complete study, as has been indicated, would follow each area's development and show how variation in resources became institutionalized. In the next section unequal resource allocation between and within districts is demonstrated. There *is* a phenomenon that needs to be explained.

[38]See Robert Dreeben, *On What Is Learned in School* (Reading, Mass.: Addison-Wesley Publishing Co., 1968).

[39]Such studies are proceeding. For example, it is known that variation in property tax valuation is more important than variation in tax rate in determining variation in expenditures per pupil among school districts. See David Cohen et al., "The Effects of Revenue Sharing and Block Grants on Education" (Harvard Graduate School of Education, 1970). See also Steven Weiss, "Existing Disparities in Public School Finance and Proposals for Reform" (Research Report for the Federal Reserve Bank of Boston, 1970).

SCHOOL RESOURCE ALLOCATION

"Resources" produce outputs. Labor and capital, buildings and machines, are resources. Knowledge is a resource—the knowledge of running the machines, as well as how to punch in, how to accommodate oneself to the production environment, how to fill out invoices, etc. Money, the unit of account that compares resources and employs them, is not in the production sense a resource. It is as necessary as knowledge to any business, but it is the use of that money which is productive; money itself can produce nothing save a light for a cigar.

To the extent that the production analogy is useful in discussing education, resource allocation should be investigated from the point of view of real resources.[40] The study of educational resource allocation has little ancient history but there is a long tradition of studying school finance.[41] Both the federal government and the National Education Association collect school finance data nationally, though these data do not agree.[42] Since 1965 attempts have been made to study real resources instead of finances, but no agreement exists on

[40]See, for example, Stephan Michelson, "Equal Protection and Resource Allocation," *Inequality in Education,* no. 2 (December 1969): 9–16.

[41]Adam Smith discussed school finance in terms of the incentives created by different arrangements. See the works of Cubberley, cited above, for extensive discussion of school financial arrangements. Economists have been interested in finance questions for a good deal longer than they have been involved in production questions. See, for example, Charles Benson, *The Economics of Public Education* (Boston: Houghton Mifflin Co., 1961). Econometric analyses of school production preceded those of production by only a few years—lack of computer technology rather than philosophy probably having forestalled earlier financial studies. For the pioneering works in determinants of school finance see Harvey Brazer, *City Expenditures in the United States* (New York: National Bureau of Economic Research, 1959); Werner Z. Hirsch, "Determinants of Public Education Expenditures," *National Tax Journal* 13 (March 1960): 29–40; Seymour Sacks and William F. Hellmuth, *Financing Government in a Metropolitan Area* (New York: Free Press, 1960); Jerry Miner, *Social and Economic Factors in Spending for Public Education* (Syracuse: Syracuse University Press, 1963); H. Thomas James, James A. Kelly, and Walter I. Garms, *Determinants of Educational Expenditures in Large Cities of the United States* (Stanford: Stanford University Press, 1966).

[42]A presentation of the magnitude of the differences between these two sources and a discussion of the reasons for these differences—but with no attempt to reconcile them—appears in Kenneth M. Deitch, "An Econometric Analysis of the Demand for American Education in the 1960's with a Statement of the General Economic Case for Public Education" (Ph.D. diss. Harvard University, 1966).

what a real resource is, nor any continuous data source from which to investigate the question.[43] If one can draw a conclusion from the literature in this young field, it is that we have no agreed output measure by which to judge schools, and no estimates of what it is that produces any so-far-suggested output. Though I am not sure such data would be relevant, the study of the allocation of real school resources is largely impossible at the present time.[44]

The investigation in this essay, therefore, will concentrate on finances, and will relate to the older literature on school finance. There are really two issues: finance and control. The real resource-allocation issue, though currently popular, is subsidiary. It is the question of the conversion of finance into real resources, which to a large extent is a matter of control: who makes the decision. True, one might want to correct for *prices*: if any resources cost more in District A than in District B, then a given budget can purchase fewer resources, and less output in A. "Equity" might demand that A have a larger budget than B. But this paper is not detailed enough for that: I will ignore price differentials.

The investigations here will be based on school *revenues*. Many investigators attempt to separate school *expenditures* into current and capital, and analyze current expenditures only. Besides the complexity of this problem, it implies that capital items are not productive.[45] Virtually all capital and nonrecurring funding is spread over

[43]See Coleman et al., *Equality of Educational Opportunity*; Samuel Bowles, "Towards an Educational Production Function," *Education, Income, and Human Capital*, ed. W. L. Hansen (New York: National Bureau of Economic Research, 1970); Jesse Burkhead, *Input and Output in Large-City High Schools* (Syracuse: Sycracuse University Press, 1967). The allocation of apparent real resources was the subject of Patricia Sexton, *Education and Income* (New York: Viking Press, 1964). However, Sexton made no attempt to demonstrate that those items she found allocated with favoritism toward the high-income schools were in fact resources to the children.

[44]In an attempt to study real resource allocation in one city I weighted production inputs by their apparent productivity. See Michelson, "Equal Protection and School Resources." Though the weighting technique may be theoretically valid, surely the estimates are not. The point of that exercise was more to demonstrate the complexity of the issue than to actually derive real resource measures.

[45]The U.S. Government *Handbook of School Accounts* suggests that library volumes are current expenditures, except when stocking a new library. But when a ten-year program to build up a library's collection is instituted, it apparently is a matter of discretion whether to consider the increment "above normal" as capital or current. Such decisions should not be allowed to influence our findings.

time on the revenue side, through loan repayments, sinking funds, capital accumulation accounts, etc. Thus, revenue is not only easier to investigate, but it is also a conceptually better measure of expenditures in general than any one year's expenditure figures themselves.[46]

The historical introduction to this essay indicates that control of school processes and funds is the predominant issue. Although policy and finance could conceptually be separated, in practice they seldom are. In this essay I will concentrate on the more tractable issues of school finance. The sections that follow will demonstrate the lack of federal and state financial equalization. I will deal with the question of "where" disparities in per-pupil expenditures occur, and will demonstrate that they exist at every level: among states, within states, and within districts. There is no unique answer to the question, "At which level of finance are the disparities the greatest?" That depends on the development of school districts, which differs in different parts of the United States. But disparities are not random. They are evidence of favoritism. And favoritism is an indication of system control. Thus, examining financial disparities is a first step in the investigation of school control, and the broad question of how and in whose benefit the current school system operates.

Interstate School Finance

Public schools are supported by three levels of government: local, state and federal. The percentage of support coming from these three sources varies greatly. In 1969 state funds contributed 9 percent of the total in New Hampshire, and 67 percent in North Carolina, and individual districts could be found that were even more disparate. These extremes reflect the general trend for state (and federal) support to be relatively larger in the South than anywhere else.[47] Table 7.1. shows that New England is the lowest state-support area, and the Southeast the highest (though state support at 64 percent for Alaska and 75 percent for Hawaii—60 percent and 85 percent in 1969—is excluded from the Far West area).

The federal share is obviously small in comparison to the state and local shares. However the power of the federal government to equal-

---

[46]"Nonrevenue receipts" such as gifts and endowments are excluded here.

[47]Actually Hawaii, which has a peculiar system of one district and six subdistricts, is the extreme state-supported system. Delaware, a "mideast" state, is southern in its state support of education, 72 percent in 1969.

**Table 7.1.   Percentage Distribution of Sources of Funds for Public
Elementary and Secondary Education, 1965 and 1969**

Area[a]	Federal		State		Local	
	1965	1969	1965	1969	1965	1969
New England	4.3	5.9	22.8	26.4	73.0	67.7
Mideast	2.7	4.8	41.4	43.4	55.9	51.8
Great Lakes	2.9	4.8	28.2	34.0	68.9	61.2
Plains	4.4	6.7	25.1	34.5	70.5	58.8
Southeast	6.5	12.3	53.2	56.0	40.3	31.7
Southwest	5.5	11.5	44.7	47.1	49.9	41.4
Rocky Mountains	5.7	8.2	31.0	32.8	63.3	59.0
Far West	3.6	6.0	40.9	36.2	55.5	57.8
United States	4.2	7.1	38.3	40.9	57.5	52.0

SOURCE: *For 1965:* Prepared by the Advisory Council on Intergovernmental
Relations, presented by John Shannon in "The Role of the State in Equalizing
Educational Opportunity," in *The Challenge of Change in School Finance* (New
York: National Education Association, 1967).   *For 1969:* Calculated from data in
Digest of Educational Statistics—1969,   USOE-10024-69 (Washington,   D.C.:
Government Printing Office, 1970).
[a] Washington, D.C., excluded from Mideast for want of "state" category. Alaska
and Hawaii omitted from Far West because of their unusual circumstances.   These
units also omitted from total for United States.

ize expenditures is not necessarily determined by its size. A better
starting point is the degree of inequality remaining after these other
units have allocated their funds.[48] The extent to which the federal
government equalizes among states, and the degree to which it could
equalize, are easily measured with Gini coefficients.

As used here, a Gini coefficient measures the equality of per-pupil
expenditures among governmental units. A coefficient of zero indicates complete equality: each state spends the same amount per
pupil. A coefficient greater than zero indicates the extent to which the
poorest X percent of the population receives less than X percent of
the funds, ignoring intrastate disparities. It is an average figure as X
varies from 0 to 100. Of course the Gini coefficient among states does

[48] "After" is used extremely loosely here. The proper discussion of effects of
various levels of finance is within the context of a completely specified behavioral
model. In a future monograph, Norton Grubb and I will present inequality measures
corrected for estimated local responses to different state and federal financing formulas. David Stern at MIT is also working on this problem. The present essay
avoids that level of complexity.

not indicate how much variation there is within states. But rearrangements of state and local funds within a state would not greatly affect that state's federal allocation. Therefore we can investigate the impact of the federal government on two areas of inequality—interstate and intrastate—separately.

There are two major federal programs: Title I of the Elementary and Secondary Education Act of 1965, a compensatory program to channel funds to poor children, and Impact Aid (P.L. 874) with which the federal government reimburses school districts for the financial hardship imposed by nearby government (mostly military) installations, when the children from these installations attend public schools. There is no reason to see a "system" behind the disbursement of federal education funds, other than the ordinary political system. Title I funds flow disproportionately to southern states because of an allocation formula based on the state's average per-pupil expenditure, or the *national* average if the state average is below the national average. Impacted-area funds depend mostly on the placement of military and space installations, and although the impact funds are part of the prize for getting the installation, I doubt that they are in any sense the primary raison d'être for political maneuvering regarding these installations.

Table 7.2 contains the Gini coefficients calculated among the states for the fiscal year 1968–69. Funds raised locally were considered in the absence of all other funds. Then a Gini coefficient was calculated for local plus state funds, and last, for total funds. The federal funds were then hypothetically redistributed among states so as to produce the lowest Gini coefficient possible with that amount of funds, with all other funds raised assumed the same. This latter assumption is surely fallacious: to some extent federal funds substitute for local and state funds, and total revenue would not decline by one dollar for every

Table 7.2.   Interstate Gini Coefficients, 1968

Local	Local and State	Total	Hypothetical
.223	.146	.135	.086

Source: *Digest of Educational Statistics, 1969.*

dollar of federal funds lost.[49] But it is a place to begin in determining the equalizing impact of federal funds.

With the assumption of fixed state and local revenues, the federal government's effort at equalization can easily be calculated. The Gini coefficient without federal funds is .146, which declines to .135 with federal funds, but could have declined to .086 if these funds had been allocated so as to maximally decrease inequality.[50] By a linear apportionment of the distance from .146 to .086, I calculate that the federal government advanced only 21.1 percent along that scale. That is, federal funds were only 21 percent as equalizing as they could have been.

The hypothetical Gini coefficient, in addition to giving a base against which to judge the equalizing effect of funds, shows that the equalizing effect of a small amount of funds can be quite large. Though federal funds are about one-fifth as large as state funds, they *could have* produced three-fourths as much equalization as state funds *did*.[51] But federal funds *were* slightly equalizing, among states, in 1968. Whether federal funds were equalizing on the whole depends on whether they were also equalizing within states. Thus I will follow similar procedures in investigating intrastate flows of funds.

Trends in Interstate Equalization

Data are available on state revenues and enrollments for several years, suggesting that interstate inequality has been declining (see Table 7.3). However, the decline is *not* due solely to the increased federal contribution. The inequality in local revenues sets the pattern for the inequality in total revenue. They both increase slightly in 1960 compared with 1956, and decrease by 1968.[52] It is clear that federal funds exert a more equalizing influence over time, measured

[49]There is a substantial literature on this subject that I will not detail here. In most cases the estimates of substitution of funds are improperly made from single regression equations insufficiently specified, and have no theoretical validity.

[50]I remind the reader that whatever other failure of the federal government may be inferred from these figures, it is not necessarily a failure to uphold the laws, which are not financial equalization laws in intent.

[51]A hypothetical difference of .06 compared with the actual difference from local to local plus state of .08 in the Gini coefficients.

[52]In Table 7.3 we can see a slight increase in inequality of local funds in 1969, and a larger increase in inequality of total funds.

Table 7.3.   Sources of Interstate Inequalities

Area	1956	1960	1969
Local	.251	.265	.220
Local and state	.162	.180	.136
Local and federal	.229	.241	.184
Total	.151	.163	.121

by the impact on local funds, excluding state funds. But it is also clear that *most* of the reduction in Gini coefficients for total revenue over time occurs without the inclusion of federal funds.

It also seems clear from Table 7.3 that states, the major equalizer, have become no more of an equalizer over time. The distribution of school revenues among states was more equal in 1969 than in 1956 mostly because more local funds were raised by poor states than by those in rich states. It would be folly to draw too many inferences from data as highly aggregated as these. However, this conclusion should come as some surprise to those people who see large governmental units as acting increasingly "liberally," where the "liberal" doctrine is equated with equalizing expenditures per pupil. A complete analysis would investigate whether the distribution of the tax *base* had equalized over this period, or whether, in contrast, poor districts had increased their effort (tax *rate*) relative to rich districts. If the latter effect were found to predominate, then it would be clear that local effort, not federal and state largesse nor wealth equalization, was the predominant factor behind school finance equalization in the past fifteen years.

Intrastate School Finance

Southern school districts were formed largely after the Civil War, northern districts before the war.[53] But traditional class divisions as well as "separate but equal" schools in the South allowed a great deal of overtly unequal resource allocation within southern districts. New England, in contrast, having developed under a rhetoric of equality of action of governmental units, developed many more locally-financed school districts as a means of maintaining inequalities. Massachusetts, for example, has 351 school districts compared

[53]See, for example, Cubberley, *Public School Administration*.

with South Carolina's 93, or Maryland's 24. Rhode Island has 39 districts, but a school-age population less than one-fourth that of Maryland. New Hampshire, with an even smaller school-age population, has 234 districts.[54] I will use these five states to calculate the effects of various levels of funding.[55] I assume that generalizations from these examples must be taken with caution, but I will make such generalizations nonetheless.

I have calculated Gini coefficients among districts within the three states for the same categories of funding as between states.[56] These are presented in Table 7.4. For Massachusetts and South Carolina two sets of coefficients are given, and though this adds to confusion, an explanation of the differences is necessary for the purpose of drawing generalizations.

Table 7.4. Intrastate Gini Coefficients, 1968–69

State	Local	Local and State	Total	District Units
Rhode Island	.180	.092	.055	39
New Hampshire	.141	.111	.085	234
Massachusetts [a]	.131	.091	.088	225
Massachusetts [a]	.130	.090	.086	157
South Carolina	.207	.085	.069	93
South Carolina	.184	.074	.055	46 [b]
Maryland	.127	.065	.050	24 [b]

[a] 1967–68
[b] Counties, not districts.

The problem is that Gini coefficients calculated from different numbers of districts are not strictly comparable: the greater the number of units, the larger the coefficient, all other things equal.

[54] Population figures are number of children ages 5–17 in 1968, from U.S. Department of Commerce, *Statistical Abstract of the United States, 1970*, Table 25.

[55] South Carolina and Maryland are the only states outside of New England on which I currently have data. The three New England states were chosen for differing industrial mix, from Rhode Island's virtual total industrialization to New Hampshire's lack of industrialization.

[56] The cavalier use of the first person singular is the traditional euphemism for one's research assistant—in this case Norton Grubb—who in fact collected the data, wrote the computer programs, and smilingly performed other necessary chores.

This can be seen in the case of South Carolina, in which the same data is aggregated over counties, and the Gini coefficients recalculated. When the number of units is cut in half, the coefficient for total funds is reduced from .069 to .055, a 20 percent reduction. This degree of sensitivity to the number of units could make any comparisons within any column in Table 7.4—say, between Massachusetts and South Carolina—highly suspect. However, I believe the comparison will stand. The 225-district sample of Massachusetts districts excludes consolidated districts—that is, the smallest towns—for which U.S. Census data was unavailable. These are likely also to be the poorest districts, so that the Gini coefficient is biased downward. The 157-district sample is merely a smaller sample of those districts for which the most complete set of data is available. Unlike the South Carolina comparison, the two Gini coefficients do not cover the same geographic (hence, financial) area. Thus the coefficients are affected by selection. Nevertheless, unless there are offsetting effects of selection on the one hand, and number of units on the other hand, the Gini coefficients seem insensitive to sample size with this large a sample.[57] I accept this conclusion and posit that South Carolina and Massachusetts can be compared without adjusting for the number of units, though some adjustment should be made in the case of Maryland.[58]

Inequality of local expenditures alone does not seem to be determined by region. However, the degree of equalizing by the state is this: in the South, the state acts as much more of an equalizer among districts than in New England. This finding refers back to the fact that state funds are a larger percentage of total funds in the South. They are distributed, by and large, through "flat grants' which allocate to each district an amount dependent only on the number of children enrolled.[59] The Massachusetts plan, which *intends* to be equalizing, has less equalizing effect than the southern plans be-

[57]A vital fact here is that the 157 districts contain 85 percent of the pupils in Massachusetts public schools. Gini coefficients for 349 districts in 1969 are virtually identical to those in 1968, 225 districts.

[58]If intradistrict distributions are more equal than interdistrict distributions, fewer large districts would lead to greater equality.

[59]North and South Carolina, which have "foundation" plans, may equalize more among districts than southern states in general.

cause it is less massive (and because its original intent has been sub-verted by legislative meddling, on which more below). Rhode Is-land state funds are highly equalizing, but not as much as South Carolina's, whose district funds are approximately as unequal as Rhode Island's.

Federal funds are slightly more equalizing in the South than in Massachusetts. This is probably because Maryland and South Caro-lina receive proportionately more Title I funds than does Massachu-setts, using the national average expenditures in their allocation formulas. The result is that, as expected (though not as starkly as expected), inequality in school finance is greater *among* districts in New England than in the South.

A feature of the measure used here should be noted before leaving this level of investigation. Berke et al. correlate the amount of federal aid per district with the amount of local revenue. They find negative (i.e., compensatory) but "inconsequential" correlations, "thus in-dicating that federal aid assists districts with less revenue for edu-cation as much as districts with greater funds for their schools."[60] The Gini coefficient measure is based on proportions, the Berke measure on absolute amounts. Even if federal aid were positively cor-related with local financing—more federal money going to wealthier school districts—poorer districts *might* be increasing their relative standing. A random association according to Berke's measure *must* be equalizing according to my measure.[61] This failure of federal funds to be strongly oriented toward underfinanced districts, how-ever, does weaken its equalizing effect.

Berke et al. also look at the allocation of federal funds by income characteristics of the school districts. In Massachusetts they find a correlation of $-.30$ between federal revenue and median family in-come, indicating that federal funds tend to flow somewhat to the

[60]Joel S. Berke et al., *Federal Aid to Public Education: Who Benefits?* (Syracuse: Syracuse University Press, 1971), p. 45. My Massachusetts sample of 157 districts gives this correlation as $-.30$, weighted by pupils. Berke et al. show an unweighted Massachusetts correlation of $+.06$ (federal funds with local funds). I am led to question Berke's sample or his use of unweighted correlations.

[61]Example: School district A spends \$400 per child, B spends \$650, before federal aid. A spends 61.5 percent of B. If \$40 of federal aid goes to A, and \$50 to B, then A will increase to 62.9 percent of B. The two districts are more equal even though more federal funds flow to the higher expenditure district.

poorer districts.[62] A correlation of − 1.00 would have indicated a
perfect linear relationship between low median income and high
federal school revenue. One might want to interpret the difference
between −.30 and −1.00 as a measure of the extent to which federal
revenues are not compensatory, though unfortunately some of this
difference may stem from a perfectly compensatory but not perfectly
linear relationship. Berke et al. also give correlations between federal
and state funds, but since the state funds themselves are equalizing to
different extents in different states, the variation in correlations of
federal with state funds is not interpretable.

Intrastate Equalization Effort

Gini coefficients can be used more readily than correlations in
determining the "effort" of a level of government. This is most easily
calculated for the federal government portion of total revenue, where,
it may be assumed, no community-behavior relationships are reflected in the data.[63] Hypothetical Gini coefficients were calculated
for the amount of federal funds that did flow into these states. These
calculations are presented in Table 7.5.

Table 7.5.   Intrastate Equalizing Effect of Federal Funds

State	Local and State	Total	Hypothetical	Federal "Effort"	Federal Funding, Percent of Total
Rhode Island (39)	.092	.055	.015	48.0%	6.7
New Hampshire (224)	.111	.085	.048	41.3	4.9
Massachusetts (225)	.091	.088	.040	5.9	6.9
South Carolina (93)	.084	.069	.005	19.0	12.1
Maryland (24)	.058	.050	.011	17.0	6.7

NOTE: "Effort" is the percentage reduction from local plus state to hypothetical
achieved by the actual allocation of federal funds.

[62]My weighted correlation between federal revenue and *mean* income on 157
districts is −.34 for 1968.

[63]This is not strictly true, as the presence of full-time employees of several large
school districts in Washington, D.C., attests. These people function to see that the
maximum amount of federal funds possible flows to the school district. On the other
hand I recently aided citizens of Mashpee, Massachusetts, in pressuring the local
school committee—which functions for three cities, of which Mashpee is the smallest—to apply for its first Title I money after six years of eligibility.

The federal "effort," the equalization effect of federal funds relative to their potential, is completely uncorrelated with the magnitude of federal funds. It is uncorrelated also with the degree of inequality of local and state funds. In general, federal funds are not nearly as equalizing as they might be, though they may fulfill other desirable criteria.

Similar calculations for state funds "after" local and federal funds are considered appear in Table 7.6.

Table 7.6.   Intrastate Equalizing Effect of State Funds

State	Federal and Local	Total	Hypothetical	Percent State Effort	State Funds as Percent of Total
Rhode Island (39)	.076	.055	.000	27.6	33.6
New Hampshire (224)	.115	.085	.051	46.9	9.1
Massachusetts (225)	.116	.088	.018	28.6	22.4
South Carolina (93)	.121	.069	.000	43.0	63.6
Maryland (24)	.103	.050	.000	48.7	37.3

Once again the equalization impact of state funds is apparently not a function of their relative magnitude. As expected, it does seem that state effort is a function of area. The only New England state in which state effort is large is the rural state, New Hampshire. The state acts as the protector of class differentiation in the North, and fails to equalize. In the South, it is the local government that performs this function, and therefore we find more effort at state equalization—though less in South Carolina than I would have expected—than in the North.

The potential impact of state funds in all states except New Hampshire is striking. Behaviorally, allowing school districts to raise their own funds, it is unlikely that states could actually reduce interdistrict equalization to nil, as implied by zero hypothetical coefficients in three states. But, clearly, states have considerable unused equalization power at current financing levels. It is the manner of distribution of funds, not their amount, which is remiss.

Other Intrastate Information

Andre Danière and J. Alan Thomas have studied financial inequalities in Massachusetts and Michigan respectively.[64] Thomas finds that "the inequalities remaining after the allocation of state aid are far from negligible. . . . [E]ven after state aid had been allocated, the typical pupil in the bottom quintile was receiving an education whose cost—and presumably quality—was only 64 percent of that provided to the typical pupil in the top quintile." He notes that "virtually all districts in the state receive some aid, even the richest," and even though more aid is given to the poorer districts, the actual equalizing does not approach the potential equalizing effect of state aid.[65] Thomas makes no attempt to analyze the functioning of the state school-support law in detail, and he specifically recommends continuance of some state support to wealthy districts, though "some means must be found to permit low evaluation districts to improve their programs so that the present variations in opportunity may be narrowed."[66]

Danière finds the same situation: the floor and ceiling to the state aid formula prevent serious equalization. The floor is a dollar amount per pupil which flows to every school district—a flat grant plan.[67] But Danière is more explicit about the process by which the equalization aspect of the state formula fails. "In order to avoid commitments . . . legislatures have found it convenient to specify the ratios without direct reference to their components."[68] Danière is explicit on who gains and who loses in the politics of formula manipulations:

[64]Andre Danière, "Cost-Benefit Analysis of General Purpose State School-Aid Formulas in Massachusetts" (Report to the Massachusetts Advisory Council on Education, 1969); J. Alan Thomas, "School Finance and Educational Opportunity in Michigan" (Michigan Department of Education, 1968).

[65]Thomas, "School Finance," p. 196.

[66]Ibid., p. 197.

[67]For a general discussion of state support formulas see Charles S. Benson, *Economics of Public Education*, 2nd ed. (Boston: Houghton Mifflin Co., 1968). Or see John E. Coons, William H. Clune III, and Stephen D. Sugarman, *Private Wealth and Public Education* (Cambridge, Mass: Belknap Press, 1970). For a brief account of formulas and details by state, see Albert R. Munse, *State Programs for Public School Support* (Washington, D.C.: U.S. Office of Education, 1965).

[68]Danière, "Cost-Benefit Analysis," p. 32; underlined in original. The components are the amount due as each district's local contribution and the basic support level which the state deems necessary.

Altogether, therefore, and subject to measures of actual performance in applications, it appears that the net result of "opening up" community choice through a "percentage equalization" formula is (1) a loss of opportunity to children of poorer or less responsible communities, (2) a persistent distortion of the original intent to the detriment of poorer communities and to the benefit of the richer ones, and (3) a lack of clarity concerning the objectives and performance of the formula.[69]

Analyzing the Massachusetts formula within this general context of legislative subversion, Danière concludes:

Even in its basic form, therefore, the Massachusetts formula suffers from two fundamental weaknesses: one is the favored treatment accorded communities with high private school populations, the other is the use of a common base $\bar{b}$ of socially required expenditure for all children. As was made clear in the analysis, however, a formula's performance depends very much on the manner in which its elements are specified and calculated. On this account, the Massachusetts computation leaves much to be desired. Finally, even the best formula can be spoiled by the imposition of floors, ceilings and special exceptions; this is where the Commonwealth has broken all known records, thoroughly subverting whatever virtues the formula could have claimed in its original state.[70]

Coons, Clune, and Sugarman are almost as forthright as Danière, though they phrase their argument toward their Proposition I (there is no Proposition II)—the quality of public education may not be a function of wealth other than the wealth of the state as a whole—and their "power equalizing plan" is geared to achieving Proposition I. For example:

The Ohio legislature, by delegating the financial responsibility to local districts and by engaging only in tokenism from the state treasury, transmuted the proper private advantage of the rich into a public institution having the essential economic characteristics of a private system. The new plan will do little to change this.[71]

They find similar situations in Nevada:

Thus, while Nevada has made another step toward state support of the full

---

[69]Ibid., pp. 32–33; most of quotation underlined in original.

[70]Ibid., p. 45.

[71]Sugarman, *Private Wealth and Public Education*, p. 80.

cost of public education, the same inequalities from voluntary local taxing which historically have benefited rich districts will continue to affect its school finance picture.[72]

And Utah, and Arizona:

It is unfortunate that this state, which has a relatively small equalization task, has done so little. . . . Why are dollars given to rich districts when the poor districts are not yet equalized? The answer must lie in expedience, as it surely does not lie in fairness.[73]

And Illinois.

In constructing a standard of state financing, we might not hold to equality measures such as low Gini coefficients. For example, Proposition I of Coons, Clune, and Sugarman does not call for equal expenditures per pupil, but calls for a disassociation of the inequalities from inequalities in wealth. Under currently existing financial arrangements, however, the two goals are the same.[74] The history and actuality of state equalizing, as my investigations and those herein cited show, should not lead to sanguinity regarding legislative action toward financial equalizing with present arrangements.

Intradistrict Resource Allocation

Any transfer of policy control to the school level would surely have to be accompanied by equalization of finances. Equal revenues per pupil would have to be received by each school—perhaps with adjustments for special students or deprived students—and then converted into resources at the school level. Equalization of finance does not necessarily imply a lessening of central control, however. School administrations can better afford to lose that debate and retain control than to foster the belief that control is really at issue.[75] On the other hand, to the extent that local governmental units serve to segregate

[72]Ibid., p. 87.

[73]Ibid., p. 125.

[74]Mathematically, the correlation of wealth with expenditures per pupil will be zero if expenditures per pupil are everywhere equal. Thus complete equalization is sufficient to fulfill Proposition I, though not necessary.

[75]See Stephan Michelson, "Principal Power," *Inequality in Education*, no. 5 (June 1970): 7–10.

social classes, control at the school level is not of such great import. Thus, for example, Detroit attempted to sue the State of Michigan for maintaining interdistrict disparities.[76] Earlier Chicago had (unsuccessfully) sued Illinois on the same issue.[77] Their contentions were that *interdistrict* disparities in capacity to finance schools overwhelmed intradistrict misallocation, a contention quite likely true.

One would conclude, then, that control at the school level will be a much more unlikely reform in the South than in the North. Equalization *among* districts within a state will be a more important issue in the North (and West)—as already evidenced in lawsuits—than in the South.

Nevertheless, there is little I can say about control of the educational process beyond the bland statement that the wrong people have the control. By showing that intradistrict inequalities exist, and that they favor the white and wealthy, I can perhaps add to the case that schools reflect as well as reinforce the political structure of which they are a part.

At the same time we should note that intradistrict and intraschool resource allocation operates at a low level of politics in which class forces are perhaps overwhelmed, more likely nonexistent. As long as "ruling class" children do not attend local schools, the system need not favor those middle-class children who do. So, for example, Martin Katzman concludes that there is little relationship between ethnic origin or race and the allocation of per pupil expenditures in Boston elementary schools.[78] In fact, his strongest correlate with per pupil expenditures is a measure of voting participation, reflecting perhaps the prime goal of the school bureaucracy: stay in power and don't make waves. But Katzman does not emphasize a positive correlation between percent white and per pupil expenditures among Boston's subdistricts. It is not clear why he rejects this finding.

A complaint in San Francisco charges that "The Spanish-Speaking ('Latino') schools of the Mission have the lowest instructional ex-

[76]*Board of Education* v. *Michigan*, General Civil No. 103342, Circuit Court, Michigan, Wayne County. The case has been dropped.

[77]*McInnis* v. *Olgilvie*, 293 F Supp. 327 (1968) (as *McInnis* v. *Shapiro*). *Serrano* v. *Priest*, and other cases have shown interdistrict inequities in school finance.

[78]Martin T. Katzman, "Distribution and Production in a Big City Elementary School System" (Ph.D. diss., Yale University, 1967).

penditure per pupil in any part of San Francisco." The following figures are cited:[79]

Per Pupil	Latinos	Others
Instructional expenditure	$513	$592
Total expenditure	$588	$677

A Chicago complaint is similar:

The disparities among elementary schools in the Chicago School System operate systematically to discriminate against non-Caucasian students and students from families of low or moderate income or dependent economic status. Elementary schools with a predominant enrollment of non-Caucasian students generally receive smaller per-pupil expenditures and budget appropriations than schools with a predominant enrollment of Caucasian students.[80]

Complainants presented the following figures:[81]

Per Pupil	Predominantly White	Mixed	Predominantly Nonwhite
Instructional expenditures	$459	$405	$413
Total appropriations	552	485	491

Detroit has allocated school resources in favor of the wealthy and white in the past.[82] In a many-faceted case[83] involving the allocation of teachers by race as well as (and perhaps more importantly than) an underappropriation of funds to black children, the fiscal 1970 figures presented in Table 7.7 were given.

[79]*Mission Coalition v. San Francisco Unified School District*, U.S. District Court, San Francisco, Civil Action No. C-70-2627. Plaintiffs' assertion of facts, 9 December 1970, p. 2. Year of data not specified, but presumably fiscal 1970.

[80]*Brown, Cortex et al. v. Board of Education of the City of Chicago*, United States District Court, Northern District of Illinois, Civil Action No. 71C-694, Complaint, pp. 6–7.

[81]From "Results of a Study of Patterns of Discrimination in Budget Allocations to Elementary Schools in the Chicago School District" (Report prepared at the Urban Systems Laboratory, MIT, under the supervision of H. W. Bruck, March, 1971, and submitted as Exhibit 1 to the Complaint), pp. 3–4.

[82]See Sexton, *Education and Income*.

[83]*Bradley v. Milliken*, United States District Court, Eastern District of Michigan, Civil Action No. 35-257. Remanded, see 433 F. 2d 897 (6th Cir., 1970). Paul Smith, using data supplied by the Detroit School Department, made these calculations— on behalf of the plaintiffs—at the Harvard Center for Law and Education.

Table 7.7.   **Per Pupil Teacher Cost, by Racial Composition of School, Detroit, 1970**

Schools	Percent Black		
	0–10	10–90	90–100
Schools with K–6 Only[a]			
Per-pupil cost, certified teachers	$417	$354	$360
Per-pupil cost, all teachers	432	374	380
Per-pupil cost, total personnel	495	427	430
(Number of schools)	(27)	(34)	(91)
Schools with K–7, K–8, or K–9[a]			
Per-pupil cost, certified teachers	$401	$377	$349
Per-pupil cost, all teachers	415	391	368
Per-pupil cost, total personnel	478	450	427
(Number of schools)	(32)	(26)	(18)

[a] A few schools were eliminated because of incomplete or inaccurate data. All figures are averages per school weighted by school enrollment.

In Washington, D.C., the favored area is specified geographically: the area west of Rock Creek Park is substantially whiter and wealthier than any other area of the city. "Anacostia" is also geographically divided from the center of the District, and is known as a poor and black area. Plaintiffs and defendants jointly stipulated to the following figures:[84]

Per Pupil	West of Rock Creek Park	City-Wide	East of Anacostia River
Teacher costs, including kindergarten	$622	$497	$445
excluding kindergarten	654	532	477

[84] "Second Joint Memorandum of Plaintiffs and Defendants," April 12, 1971, in *Hobson v. Hansen*, United States District Court, District of Columbia, Civil Action No. 82–66. Data for fiscal 1971.

Except for Washington, D.C., in many respects a southern city, the data presented here come from districts outside the South. John Owen analyzed nine large cities, including southern cities, concluding:

The empirical evidence presented here is consistent with the hypothesis that instructional expenditures are distributed unequally, and that school systems spend less on non-White and poor children than on other children in large American cities.[85]

Owen does not investigate differences between southern and northern cities, however. Nor, in pointing out that many desegregation problems—and associated resource allocation problems—transcended school district boundaries, did the Civil Rights Commission attempt to differentiate the problems by their history (or area).[86]

Thus, a large part of my hypothesis that the nature of resource-allocation inequalities differs in different areas is still largely untested. It does seem to be true, however, that large inequalities occur within as well as between districts, and that these inequalities are derived from the political process which favors wealth and whiteness.

SUMMATION

The difference in funds spent in different public schools is not the entirety of differences in school funds. To be complete, we should look at private schools, both secular and religious. Nor is the difference in expenditures on school the entirety of funds spent on education; museums, art galleries, private lessons, etc. exemplify overt nonschool educational expenditures that should be counted in any total reckoning of expenditure disparities. And more subtle forms of differences in resource allocation include the nutritional content of food consumed, summer camp, the particular television programs watched in the home (and discussions thereon), and so on. Estimates of the "complete" disparities in educational resources, by social class and ethnic origin, would be interesting. But they are not necessary.

[85]John Owen, "The Distribution of Educational Resources in Large American Cities," *Journal of Human Resources* 7, no. 1 (Winter 1972): 26–38.

[86]U.S. Commission on Civil Rights, *Racial Isolation in the Public Schools* (Washington, D.C.: Government Printing Office, 1965).

The American myth is not that all children receive equal resources from all sources, but that they are treated "fairly" by the market and by governmental agencies. I have stressed that to the extent that a strong history or rhetoric exists of equal treatment by a governmental unit, a proliferation of units will occur. In these areas, resource disparities will be located *between* units. But even in such places there are political in-groups and political out-groups. Politics is the vehicle for favoritism. The preceding sections have shown that the political system equalizes the disparities created by local financing of schools only to a small degree. The states, the major source of equalization funds, in fact do little compared to their financial resources. The federal government similarly accomplishes little compared to its equalization ability—and the argument that federal funds are a small percentage of the total was shown not to be a major factor in the federal government's failure to equalize.[87]

The over-all conclusion must be that hopes of financial equalizing through the legislative process are slim. The one possibility is that financial equalizing will be "given" if control over school processes is not at issue. This is what can happen if the courts intervene to demand financial equality among districts and/or within districts. But financial equalizing and control come together in several schemes now under consideration: vouchers, community control, state takeover of "failing" schools, etc.

Could this happen? Yes, it could. And the reasons are found on the opening pages of this essay. First, schools are not likely to change in the ways in which they are fundamentally under local control. This argument stems from Counts' and successor investigations (such as Domhoff-type studies of the people involved in overt decision-making) that fail to locate the most important areas of school operations. As long as the notion of "school" remains unchanged, then control by upper social strata of school functions is a luxury, not a necessity. Granted, they will fight to retain it. But as an economic class they will have lost little in losing that fight.

[87]I should at least mention the political reality that Congress would be reluctant to appropriate the amount of funds it now does under a stricter equalization formula. Though not differentiating between state and federal funds, David Stern is deriving behavioral estimates and conducting simulations which may be useful in estimating the amount and formulation of funds which might be required, under local school district autonomy, to achieve equalization among districts. Preliminary results indicate that complete equalization is *impossible* at reasonably high per-pupil levels. This work will appear in his Ph.D. dissertation at MIT.

Second, the school system is a redundant system in the general schema of socialization. For example, as long as schools are the qualifiers for economic position, and as long as jobs, job qualifications, and the productive process in general reflect limited class interests, schools will have little option regarding the product they turn out.

Finally, and sadly, it is logically fallacious to assume that equalizing one of many qualifications for income (status, for example) will equalize the attainment of that status. What it must do is reduce the importance of that qualification to zero. When everyone is educated equally, some other characteristic—one distributed unequally *and unfairly*—will bear the burden of differentiating among people. This is true over and above findings that education was not a major determinant of economic success anyway.[88] Thus, in a class society the struggle to de-class one institution of socialization is to some extent self-defeating. But the struggle is no less worthy for its inevitable frustration. What this paper has attempted to show is that it is not a *legislative* struggle, even though there may be legislative victories (such as decentralization or community control). It is not a judicial struggle, even though there may be judicial victories (say, for financial equalization). It is essentially a historic struggle, and the course of history will be determined by many factors beyond legislatures and courts. If equalization in schooling occurs, it may well take these other forces to produce it.

[88]See, for example, Stephan Michelson, "Incomes of Racial Minorities," manuscript (Brookings Institution, Washington, D.C., 1968).

.8. *Is Compensatory Education Possible?*

MARTIN CARNOY

THE SOCIAL purpose of schooling can be defined in a number of ways. Schooling can be viewed primarily as a place to train workers for the labor market of the nation or community. In that context, formal schools would teach the basic knowledge necessary for further specialized training. They would also instill the discipline and the cooperative attitudes necessary for a trained labor force. Social roles of children attending school would be associated with the vocations for which the children were being trained. Early in their school careers students would be grouped according to ability and molded into social and economic roles that would fit their abilities to society's "needs."

Although this is not exactly the theoretical basis for European education, in practice it functions quite closely to this model. In European state-capitalist countries such as the Soviet Union, schooling is even more closely associated with future vocation than it is in the West. This definition of the social purpose of schooling essentially condemns students from low socioeconomic backgrounds to low-ability tracks and low-status occupations.

In a more progressive view of schooling, the learning available to children and the training received in school is theoretically the same for all children. At the primary and secondary levels, all children receive a "general" education; this does not prepare them for a particular vocation, but is intended to give them the basic knowledge required of all good citizens. Students are not expected to absorb the material presented equally well, but the school does not define *what* material is presented to different students. All receive the same diploma; only the grades and recommendations accompanying the diploma differ. Once this general course is finished, it is in theory the option of the individual—on the basis of *his* criteria and needs—to shape his future occupational and social role. The U.S. system of public education is based on this theoretical model.

Nevertheless, in practice this model has also resulted in most students from low-income homes performing worse (and therefore taking less schooling) than students from higher-income families. It has also resulted in European-type "tracking" into vocational and academic branches of the same school. Even when the school system is centrally financed and does not—as in the United States—depend on the local tax base (Puerto Rico uses the U.S. model with central financing), low socioeconomic status (SES) students attend, on the average, schools with lower-quality resources per pupil than high SES students. A very small percentage of those who start out behind in the first grade catch up; on the contrary, even with dropouts biasing the comparison of test scores over time between low-SES and high-SES students, evidence seems to show a *growing* gap as more schooling is taken.[1]

Thus, if schooling is to correct for differential "education" opportunities in the family and environment, it should be *compensatory*. The ultimate objective of this recent compensatory philosophy of education in the United States is to equalize the performance of all *groups* of children going to school: groups of students entering with, on the average, different endowments in the first grade, would leave high school with, on the average, equal endowments. The function of the schools would be to allocate resources in a way that would fulfill this compensatory objective.

The equalizing nature of compensatory schooling hinges on several important assumptions:

1. The instruments used to measure equalization—for example,

---

[1]James Guthrie et al., "School and Inequality: A Study of the Relationship Between Social Status, School Services, and Post-School Opportunity in the State of Michigan" (Report prepared for the National Urban Coalition, Washington, D.C., September 1969).

reading, verbal, or math test scores—reflect the hiring criteria of employers and the criteria for status set by society. In a society that practices racial, sex, or ethnic discrimination, however, reading-score equalization will not do much to equalize economic and social roles. Blacks or Mexican-Americans coming out of high school with scores equal to those of whites will not necessarily gain equal entrance to universities or equal pay on jobs.

2. Although social role perception, highly correlated with social origin, race, and sex, is reinforced by the school even after test scores are equalized, the choice of future roles among graduates is equal. The case of women's education (women's average test scores are equal to men's) is a good example of the inadequacy of this assumption. The perception of "desirable" vocations for lower- and higher-socioeconomic-class students may be very different at the end of high school despite equal test scores for the two groups. From this standpoint alone, the structure of the present schools is probably incapable of equalizing different social, ethnic, racial, or sex groups' life possibilities at the end of a given period of schooling. Schools tend to reflect and reinforce rather than counteract the prejudices and perceptions of the outside world.[2] As Gintis has pointed out, noncognitive knowledge learned in school may very well be more important in determining future economic performance than cognitive knowledge.[3]

3. The relationship between teachers and students in the school is such that improving the "quality" of the teacher will result in compensating low-performance pupils. Compensatory education models in the United States assume that this relation is capable of producing equal performance on the part of different groups of pupils. Nevertheless, teachers apparently use learning models that expect pupils to *behave* in certain ways while learning. Lower-SES children are expected to learn in approximately the same way as higher-SES children, although the two have been exposed to different home and peer environments. Similarly, black, Mexican-American, Indian,

---

[2]See, for example, Edgar Z. Friedenberg, *Coming of Age in America* (New York: Random House, 1965).

[3]Herb Gintis, "Production Functions in the Economics of Education and the Characteristics of Worker Productivity," mimeographed (Harvard University, Department of Economics, 1969).

and other ethnically different groups are expected to learn in the same way as white middle-class children do. Teachers from outside the cultures of these children may not even be aware of differential reward systems in the different cultures. The learning environment in the classroom leads the teachers to treat those children with whom they can communicate well much better (and reward them more often) than children with whom they are having difficulty. The hierarchical relationship in the school leaves the child no recourse but to take his rewards and punishment from the teacher. As this paper tries to show, this relationship between teachers and students is apparently such that large transfers of school resources to presently "disadvantaged" groups will not even equalize average reading scores of the "advantaged" and "disadvantaged."[4]

The purpose of this essay is to test only the last of these three points: does it appear possible within the structure of the present "progressive" U.S.-type educational schooling system to equalize achievement or reading scores between different social, ethnic, sex, and racial groups, given that these groups are currently performing at very different levels? To test this hypothesis, we will use a number of studies already made in the United States and Puerto Rico which show the relationship between student attributes, teacher "quality" (as measured by various teacher characteristics) and school output (as measured by student achievement or reading score).[5] Equalization of reading or verbal scores is neither a sufficient nor necessary condition for equalization of group opportunities after schooling. Other measures and other means may be much more relevant. Never-

[4]The period of school during which this equalization could be accomplished is taken here as six years. This choice is in part the result of data availability. However, from the standpoint of observed reality as well, almost all fundamental reading skills are part of the school curriculum only in primary school. Although remedial reading can be continued into high school, most subjects by the seventh year build heavily on reading ability.

[5]See Martin Carnoy, "Family Background, School Inputs and Students' Performance in School: The Case of Puerto Rico," mimeographed (Stanford University, 1971); Eric Hanushek, "The Production of Education, Teacher Quality, and Efficiency," in *Do Teachers Make a Difference?*, U.S. Office of Education (Washington, D.C.: Government Printing Office, 1970) OE-58042, pp. 79–99; Henry Levin, "A New Model of School Effectiveness," in idem, pp. 55–78; Stephen Michelson, "The Association of Teacher Resourceness with Children's Characteristics," in idem, pp. 120–168. Some of the studies also measure school output by other variables, such as math achievement, student attitudes, and the amount of school the student expects to take.

theless, the reading or verbal criterion is widely held up as an effectiveness measure by educators themselves,[6] and it is therefore used here as our single criterion measure.

The studies used do not base their methodology on any theory of learning; rather, they assume that there are classes of variables that affect school outcomes. These classes of variables include the student's socioeconomic background (his family characteristics), his initial "endowment" when he enters school, the characteristics of the teachers he has in school, and the quantity of nonteacher resources available to him in school. The studies estimate the relation between components of these classes of variables and student achievement. They allow us to estimate the effect on achievement of incremental changes in school resources—especially the quality of teachers—holding constant the influence of other variables such as socioeconomic class of students, their age, and in one study, their performance in first grade. The studies further calculate the relationships of school variables, such as teacher characteristics, to student achievement for each *different* socioeconomic, ethnic, or racial group of students. Therefore, we are able to see whether the contribution of increasing the quality of teachers is different for one group than for another.

The results of the studies are strikingly similar. They generally show a positive relationship between so-called higher "quality" characteristics of teachers and exam score. They also show significantly different teacher input–school output relationships for different ethnic groups and, in Puerto Rico, for different class groups. Finally, they show that even if increasing teacher quality results in higher achievement, a large relative increase in teacher quality for those groups now getting low average achievement scores will at best bring them only part of the way toward equality with presently high scoring groups.

THE EVIDENCE

The following series of tables—numbers 8.1 through 8.5—present regression estimates of different studies for the relationship be-

---

[6]In performance contracting, school rank, etc., exam score is the single effectiveness measure used.

Table 8.1.   Third-Grade Reading-Achievement Estimates, White Nonmanual, White Manual, and Mexican-American Manual Students, California Sample, 1969

| | Coefficients | | |
Variable	White Non-manual	White Manual	Mexican-American Manual
First grade test score	0.72	0.79	0.97
Sex female	—	2.81	2.84
Repeat	—	−6.38	−8.92
Father clerical	−5.1	—	—
Teacher test score (3rd grade)	—	0.09	—
Percent of time spent on discipline	—	−0.07	—
Teacher test score (2nd grade)	—	0.06	—
Years since most recent educational experience (3rd grade)	−0.79	−0.57	—
Years since most recent educational experience (2nd grade)	−0.66	−0.68	—
Years of experience with SES level (3rd grade)	0.10	—	—
Years of experience with SES level (2nd grade)	0.20	—	—
Skilled father	—	—	8.22
Semiskilled father	—	—	5.96

Source: Hanushek, "Production of Education, Teacher Quality, and Efficiency," pp. 91–94.

tween home background of students, school inputs, and exam performance of students on verbal achievement or reading exams. The studies cover comparisons between Mexican-Americans and Anglos in California, Puerto Rican students from different sectors (urban/rural) and different socioeconomic classes, and blacks and whites in the northeast part of the United States. The results shown in these tables are regression coefficients; that is, the figure by each designated independent variable signifies the change in exam score resulting from a change in one unit of that independent variable, all other independent variables held constant.

On the basis of these figures, it can be argued that the contribution of school inputs, even when a child's home background is held constant, is significant and has an important effect on a child's perfor-

Table 8.2. Estimated School Production Functions (Reduced Form), Sixth-Grade Male Students, Puerto Rico, 1967, Dependent Variable, Spanish Reading Score

Variable	Urban	Rural
Hours of school attended daily	1.038	2.755[a]
Parent conversation	13.280	2.105
Age	−5.630	0.447
Average social class in the school (4 = low, 0 = high)	−6.797[a]	0.428
Teacher academic preparation	0.888	0.888[a]
Percent teachers certified	1.056	−2.201
Teacher experience	0.328	0.370[a]
Percent teachers on permanent contract	−3.105	−2.437
Class size	−0.555[a]	−0.103
Percent teachers male	−5.859[a]	−0.281

SOURCE: Carnoy, "Family Backgrounds, School Inputs and Students' Performance in School," Table 5.

[a] 90 percent significance level.

Table 8.3. School Production Functions (Reduced Form), Sixth-Grade Urban Male Students, Puerto Rico, 1967, Dependent Variable, Spanish Reading Score

Variable	Lowest Socio-economic Class, Urban	Highest Socio-economic Class, Urban
Hours of school attended daily	5.214[a]	−0.114
Parent conversation	21.000[a]	12.770[a]
Age	1.407	0.412
Average social class	−0.790	−9.101[a]
Teacher academic preparation	2.614[a]	−1.547
Percent teacher certified	28.130[a]	2.670
Teacher experience	−0.960[a]	1.063[a]
Percent teachers on permanent contract	−7.624[a]	−3.376
Class size	−1.297[a]	−0.108
Percent teachers male	−18.330[a]	3.713

SOURCE: Carnoy, "Family Background, School Inputs and Students' Performance in School," Tables 13 and 14.

[a] 90 percent significance level.

Table 8.4.   Schooling Production Function Estimates (Reduced Form) for White and Black Sixth-Graders in Eastmet, 1965, Dependent Variable, Verbal Score

Independent Variables	Regression Coefficients	
	Whites	Blacks
Sex	0.846	0.277
Age: 12+	−6.806	−3.808
Family size	−0.613	−0.382
Possessions	1.344	1.159
Kindergarten	2.135	0.461
Mother *ID*	−0.532	−0.395
Father *ID*	−0.395	0.227
Father's education	0.385	0.322
Mother has job	−0.270	−0.002
Teacher test score	0.323	0.336
Teacher's undergraduate institution	7.718	−1.891
Teacher's experience	0.835	−0.237
Teacher's preference for another school	1.030	−0.540
Teacher turnover	−0.181	−0.133
Volumes per student	0.498	0.101
Constant	−8.030	12.497

SOURCE: Michelson, "Association of Teacher Resourcefulness with Children's Characteristics," pp. 147–148.

Table 8.5.   Teacher Effects on Verbal Achievement, Means and Standard Deviations

	Elasticity	Mean	Standard Deviations
White Model			
Teacher experience (years)	.020	11.9	4.6
Teacher test score	.117	24.8	1.4
Percent students with nonwhite teacher last year	−.024	13.4	16.0
Black Model			
Teacher experience (years)	.045	11.3	4.0
Teacher test score	.178	24.0	1.8
Percent students with non-white teacher last year	−.026	44.7	19.4

SOURCE: Hanushek, "Production of Education, Teacher Quality, and Efficiency," p. 86.

mance in school. Now we are going to take these results one step further. We are going to ask how large these coefficients are in terms of the achievement-score difference between the low and high performance groups compared in each study. How much would increasing the average test score of teachers teaching black students, for example, contribute to eliminating the difference in exam scores between black and white students? Our numerical operations are, of course, nothing more than simple simulations. But the results of our simulations are remarkably consistent: in no case does a large increase in the characteristics of school inputs allocated to the low-performance group result in equality of performance with the high-performance group. In each case, the increase in resources allocated to the low-performance group by our examples would leave that group with *more* (not equal) resources per pupil than the high-performance group.

Table 8.6 shows the results of these calculations. In each case the increase in the independent variable (usually taken as one standard deviation from the mean) is multiplied by the corresponding coefficient from the disadvantaged group regression to get the estimated increase in exam score. We assume that there is a constant marginal product of increases in quality; that is, we assume that the coefficient does not decline as the mean of the variable is increased.

The first case in Table 8.6 estimates the increase in verbal achievement score (Stanford Achievement Test) of Anglo third-graders from homes where the father has a manual occupation if we "improve" four teacher characteristics by one standard deviation from the mean. This means increasing average test scores of those teaching these low-SES Anglos from a mean of 67 points in the second and third grades to a mean of 85 points. Similarly, the number of years since the teachers' last educational experience would be reduced from more than two years to only a few months. The effect of each of these measures in reducing the exam-score difference between this group and Anglo third-graders from nonmanual-occupation homes is shown in Column 3. Since the coefficients used to estimate changes in exam score are themselves estimated with other variables held constant at their respective means, it is not altogether legitimate to *sum* the changes from the four increases, especially when the changes in the independent variables are large. There

Table 8.6.   Examples of Estimated Exam-Score Increases of Low-Performance Students When Quality of Inputs for Such Students Is Increased

	Change in Independent Variable	Absolute Change in Test Score of Low-Performance Group	Percent of Different Overcome Between Low- and High-Performance Groups
Third-Grade Children of Manual and Nonmanual Occupation Fathers			
Teacher (3rd) test score	+16.0	1.44	15.8
Teacher (2nd) test score	+19.0	1.14	12.5
Years since education experience (3rd)	−1.6	0.91	10.0
Years since education experience (2nd)	−2.6	1.77	19.4
Total		5.26	57.7
Urban and Rural Puerto Rican Sixth-Graders			
Teacher academic preparation	+1.0	0.89	13.1
Teacher experience	+7.0	2.59	38.0
Daily hours attended	+0.5	1.38	20.3
Total		4.86	71.4
Lowest and Highest Socio-economic Class, Urban Puerto Rican Sixth-Graders			
Teacher academic preparation	+1.0	2.61	14.7
Teacher experience	−3.0	2.88	16.2
Percent teachers certified	+0.1	2.81	15.8
Daily hours attended	+0.5	2.60	14.6
Total		10.90	61.3
Black and White Eastmet Sixth-Graders			
Teacher test score	+4.8	1.62	14.2
Teacher experience	−3.1	0.73	6.5

Table 8.6.—continued

	Change in Independent Variable	Absolute Change in Test Score of Low-Performance Group	Percent of Different Overcome Between Low- and High-Performance Groups
Teacher turnover	−4.2	0.56	5.8
Volumes per student	+1.9	0.19	1.7
Total		3.10	28.2
Black and White Northeast Urban Sixth-Graders		Percent Change	
Teacher test score	+3.6	2.7	—
Teacher experience	+4.0	1.2	—
Percent students with nonwhite teacher	−22.3	1.3	—
		5.2	

SOURCES: Tables 8.1 through 8.5.

may be important interaction effects (either positive or negative) which could occur when the means of all these variables are changed simultaneously. Nevertheless, as a first approximation, the sum indicates that the mean score of the disadvantaged Anglo group would be increased from 55.7 to 61.0 points. The *mean* score of children from nonmanual-occupation homes is 64.8,[7] which is still significantly higher.

Hanushek's results are far less hopeful for compensating Mexican-American students. The results of Table 8.1 show that the coefficients of teacher inputs are not significant for the Mexican-American achievement-score equation. This implies that increases in test score and other characteristics of those teaching Mexican-Americans do not have a significant effect on Mexican-American achievement test scores.[8]

[7]Hanushek, "Production of Education, Teacher Quality, and Efficiency," p. 93.

[8]All of Hanushek's equations include a measure of initial endowment—the student's test score in the first grade. The coefficients of schools input variables are therefore probably smaller than they would be if the first grade test score variable were not included. In the other studies discussed here, this "value added" aspect of

The second and third examples deal with equalization of test scores between rural and urban Puerto Rican sixth-graders and between lowest- and highest-SES urban Puerto Rican sixth-graders.[9] The average academic preparation and experience of rural sixth-grade teachers is 3.5 years beyond high school and 8.3 years' experience. Urban sixth-grade teachers have training 4.4 years beyond high school and 15.1 years' experience. The difference in both academic preparation and experience of urban and rural teachers is approximately constant through the six years of primary school, at 1 year of preparation and 6–7 years of experience. The increase proposed here would take place with teachers who teach all six years of rural primary school and would result in nominally equal teacher inputs for urban and rural primary students. The average number of hours attended by urban and rural sixth-graders is already equal (5.6 hours), but we have increased rural hours by one-half hour daily. The result of all this is an increase of almost 5 points in the mean rural Spanish-reading score, from 43.0 to 47.9 points. The mean sixth-grade urban score is 49.8, which is significantly higher.

The situation between the highest and lowest socioeconomic classes of urban Puerto Rican students appears much more difficult to equalize. Average academic preparation (4.4 years beyond high school), experience (14 years), and percent of teachers certified (86 percent) are equal for those teaching lowest- and highest-SES urban sixth-graders. The average daily hours attending school is also equal (5.5). Yet the Spanish reading score for the lowest SES group is 38.4 points and for the highest, 56.2. By increasing average teacher academic preparation by one year, reducing average teacher experience by three years, increasing the percent of teachers certified by 10 percent, and increasing the average daily hours attended by one-half hour, the average Spanish reading score of lowest SES students would be increased by 11 points, or about 60 percent of the difference between the two groups.

---

schooling inputs is not directly accounted for, so the effect on students' achievement score of increases in teacher quality is probably *overestimated*; i.e., the coefficients of various teacher characteristics, not holding students' initial endowment constant, are upward biased.

[9]See Carnoy, "Family Background, School Inputs and Students' Performance in School."

The last two cases compare urban black and white students in northeastern United States. The Levin and Michelson data taken from Michelson's study in the USOE volume (see Table 8.4) indicate that raising the verbal score of those teaching black students by two standard deviations (4.8 points), lowering their average experience and turnover by one standard deviation (3.1 years and 4.2) and increasing the volumes per student (from 1.7 to 3.6) would only overcome about one-fourth of the difference between black and white achievement scores. The new mean teacher verbal score for black students would be 26.6 versus 24.7 for white students; teacher experience would be 6.1 years versus 15.1 for whites; and average teacher turnover would be 1.8 for black students and 6.9 for whites. The number of volumes per student would be 3.6 for blacks and 2.8 for whites. These relatively large changes in school inputs are estimated to increase average black verbal-achievement score from a mean of 23.6 to 26.7. This falls far short of the white mean of 35.1.

Hanushek made similar estimates for a different sample (see Table 8.5) from the Coleman data. Again, using two standard deviations for the change in teacher verbal score and one standard deviation for the change in teacher experience and the percent of students with a nonwhite teacher, we estimate a total change in black verbal achievement as a result of these teacher changes of 5.2 percent (Hanushek's coefficients are elasticities rather than absolute values, so yield a percentage change in exam score). Taking the black student mean achievement as 25, the 5.2 percent translates into a 1.3 point rise in achievement score.

CONCLUSION

Many of the empirical studies presented here in support of our hypothesis were done primarily as a reaction to the Coleman Report of 1966. Coleman reported—erroneously—that once the socioeconomic background of children in school is accounted for, school inputs have negligible effect on students' achievement.[10] The studies discussed here show that it *is* possible to alter the allocation

---

[10]For a discussion of the errors in the Coleman Report, see Samuel Bowles and Henry Levin, "The Determinants of Scholastic Achievement: An Appraisal of Some Recent Findings," *Journal of Human Resources* 3, no. 1 (Winter 1968): 3–24.

of resources in schools to increase the performance of those who are now receiving fewer schooling resources. But the data also make clear that equalizing resources spent on schooling for children of different socioeconomic, ethnic, or racial groups will not equalize academic performance among those groups. Even if substantially higher-quality teaching is made available to the low-scoring than to the high-scoring students, the change would result in only a partial reduction of exam-score difference between the two. In the case of ethnic and racial minorities in the United States, the reduction may well be negligible.

There is a fundamental belief in U.S. educational circles (and among the public at large) that lower-SES children cannot learn as quickly or as well as middle- or higher-SES children. The response to this belief on the part of those who wish to equalize the amount learned by all groups is a strategy of allocating much more resources to these "disadvantaged" slow learners so that they can catch up. The structure of schools would remain the same in this strategy, as well as the teacher-pupil relation and the student's social-role perception. Schools would still have the goal of producing a certain type of citizen, but with a higher achievement or reading score than before. The difficulty, probably the impossibility, of achieving equality in this way is evident from the empirical studies presented here. The strategy, even in failure, would also turn out to be extremely costly relative to the benefits these lower-SES groups would gain in society as a result of higher scores.[11]

The alternative to this strategy is to reject the concept of a neutral school system implicit in the poor learners–good learners theory, and to assume instead that all groups of children can learn equally well but under different conditions. We may find that children's motivation is affected much more by the structure of the learning environment than by the number of years of teacher's academic preparation. The low probability of success of compensatory programs within the existing framework points to the need for new educational strategies for ethnic and racial minorities if equality is to be

---

[11]For attempts to cost out increases in teacher quality, see Martin Carnoy, "A Systems Approach to Evaluating Education Illustrated with Puerto Rican Data," mimeographed (Stanford University, 1971), and Henry Levin, "A Cost-Effectiveness Analysis of Teacher Selection," *Journal of Human Resources* 5, no. 1 (Winter 1970): 24–33.

achieved. The solution may be to change schooling for all children and to create an educational process that does not preconceive social roles or even clearly define what or how a child must learn. This process would require new kinds of tests to measure results and a different kind of teacher to produce them. Education of this type could allow a child's own stereotypes of himself and others to be destroyed and be replaced by personal relationships. The alternative strategy, then, creates equality among groups of children, by believing that all children are equally *capable* of learning and building an educational structure that allows children to express themselves in various ways, all equally acceptable. This alternative would thus start from the premise that the structure of learning in the schools must be changed to produce something called "equality," rather than accepting the present hierarchical, role-reinforcing structure and attempting to overcome its deficiencies with massive infusions of traditional resources.

But is it possible to change the structure of formal public schooling, the relationship between teacher and student, without fundamental changes in hierarchies outside the school? Are not classroom relations modeled on economic and social relations in the society at large? If the schools are to produce workers and citizens to function in societal structures based on well-defined hierarchies and ethnic, racial, sex, and class discrimination, how can these same elements be eliminated from the educational system? Fundamental changes in schooling—as suggested here—will require fundamental changes in the basic structures of the society.

II

The Alternatives Before Us

'OF COURSE, THIS FORCED BUSING IS ONLY A TEMPORARY MEASURE WHILE WE LEARN TO LOVE ONE ANOTHER, OR SOMETHING . . .'

.9. The Case for Community Control of the Schools*

HENRY M. LEVIN

AMONG ALL the major social movements of our time, demands for community control of the schools must certainly be one of the least understood. Perhaps this is the case for most complex issues, but it would seem that a major share of the confusion is due to the sensational, but relatively superficial, reporting of the news media. The press has tended to present this phenomenon in the context of a temporary racial crisis, giving greater emphasis to implications for "law and order" than to the education of minority-group students. An analogy might be made to the journalists who, in reporting the causes for the outbreak of World War I, intensely explored events surrounding the assassination of Archduke Ferdinand, while ignoring the more complex set of economic and political relationships that led to the extensive international conflagration.

In an attempt to provide greater depth and balance to discussion of this issue, this essay focuses on the rationale or justification for the community control movement.[1] Indeed, demands for community

*Henry M. Levin, "The Case for Community Control of the Schools," from James W. Guthrie & Edward Wynne, editors, *New Models for American Education* ©1971. Reprinted by permission of Prentice-Hall, Inc., Englewood Cliffs, New Jersey.

[1]For a more detailed statement of the financial and administrative steps that might be involved in the establishment of such schools, see Henry M. Levin and H. Thomas James, "Financing Community Schools," and Marilyn Gittel, "The Balance of Power and the Community School," in *Community Control of Schools*, ed. Henry M. Levin, (Washington, D.C.: Brookings Institution, 1970).

control cannot be fully understood without first recognizing the situation that presently confronts racial minorities in their quests for equality and dignity. Though two hundred years of slavery have been followed by one hundred years of "freedom," the black American still remains outside the mainstream of American life. By almost all standard measures, his welfare is substantially below that of the American majority; statistics on income, employment, life expectancy, housing, and infant mortality all reflect his unenviable position.

He has migrated from rural to urban areas seeking opportunity, and he has worked hard at the jobs that were available. However, the rapid upward mobility that greeted immigrants from other lands has eluded the black American. In part this is due to his arriving in the cities at a time when opportunities for unskilled labor were fast diminishing and when the large-city political systems had already established themselves without his participation. Thus, he found himself caged by the walls of the urban ghetto with housing and job discrimination handicapping his chances of substantially improving his status. Massive discrimination and racism in both the government and private sectors have prevented any semblance of equal human rights for the black man, and while our society has recently begun to attempt to redress these inequalities, progress has been pitifully slow.

Of all the conditions facing the American black, the worst probably has been his feeling of powerlessness. Given the same high aspirations as his fellow citizens, the black is unable to fulfill them because of discriminatory barriers placed in his path. He is imprisoned in substandard, overpriced ghetto housing, and his choice of jobs is limited. He has neither the occupational nor residential mobility, nor the political power to counter these disabling conditions. Compounding this feeling of impotence is the fact that the very social institutions which were designed to improve his prospects have not been able to do so. It is this frustrating lack of control over his life's circumstances that may well be the most bitter pill to swallow. Without some measure of control over his destiny, his aspirations can never be more than pipedreams.

Thus, the basic problem of the black American is that of gaining control over his destiny, and in recent years a prospective solution to this problem has come into focus. Through racial cohesiveness and self-development, many black men intend to liberate themselves from racism and to gain equality and dignity. Foremost in this drive is the quest to redirect and reform those institutions that seem to have failed black Americans or, worse yet, have inflicted injury and further disadvantages on racial minorities. In the black neighborhoods of large cities, schools have become among the first of these institutions to be challenged.

One point that is not at issue is the fact acknowledged by urban educators and informed laymen alike that city schools have failed to help the black American to improve his status. The indictment of the schools is an especially serious one because formal education has represented the primary social device for more nearly equalizing opportunity among children of different races or social groupings. Yet, while about three-quarters of white males in their latter twenties have completed high school, only about half of nonwhite males in this age bracket have fulfilled a high school education. These data provide only a portion of the picture. Even among those students who do reach the twelfth grade, the average Negro is about three years in standardized achievement units behind the average twelfth-grade white.

The black American, then, enters his adult life with severe educational deficiencies, and the nature of the schooling experience which is provided for him must share some of the blame for this condition. The average black in the large cities attends a school which is less well endowed than that attended by whites. For example, teachers in Negro schools have less experience and lower verbal ability than their counterparts in schools attended by whites. In addition, schools with black enrollments are more likely to be crowded and to experience shortages of supplies and other materials; and historically they have been characterized by lower expenditures.

But inferior resources are only one way in which schools handicap the ghetto child in preparing him for life. Even more destructive to his self-concept and growth is the cultural intolerance reflected by his schooling experience. The materials, curriculum, and teaching methods were developed for children of the white middle class, and they have been largely irrelevant to the experiences and special educational requirements of the black child. Thus, the present schools situated in Negro neighborhoods tend to undermine the black student's identity by ignoring his cultural heritage. That is, in their effort to be "color blind," many schools have ignored color; they demand that the ghetto child reflect the language patterns, experience, and cultural traits of the white middle class. In this sense, city schools have been guilty of massive institutional racism by forcing black students to be captive audiences in a hostile environment, an environment that just did not have their needs in mind. In this respect, city schools tend not to reflect the pluralism that is claimed for our society.

Given the intention by blacks to take responsibility for those institutions which mold their lives and the lives of their children, it is no accident that the schools represent an initial focal point. As one spokesman noted:

> The schools are rather natural and logical vehicles for the first thrust because they represent the white underbelly of society. They are present. They are constant. They are not something that is hidden in a back room in city hall which you can't reach. The principal of the school is at hand. The teachers are there. So there is a very tangible instrument around which action could focus.

In addition to the visibility of schools, there is a widespread notion that in the long run education is a potent power in society, and that those who control schools, control something that is extremely meaningful.

An additional factor in favor of decentralizing control of the schools has been the fact that the black community frequently has the sympathy of a large segment of the white middle class who are also frustrated with the empty promises, administrative rigidities, unresponsiveness, and red tape that seem to characterize many city school bureaucracies. Yet another powerful element underlying the crusade for radical changes in school governance is the fact that the palliatives suggested by educational professionals for improving the ghetto schools have frequently been shown to be difficult to implement at best, and totally ineffective at worst.

Conventional wisdom of the late 1950s and early 1960s suggested that, through racially integrating the schools, educational problems of blacks and other minorities could be solved. In most cities, promises of integration were never fulfilled. Inaction on the issue or, worse yet, gerrymandering of local attendance districts to prevent meaningful integration, created great bitterness among many blacks whose top priority was racially integrated education. The fact that many city school boards could not deliver what they had promised led to much of the present minority distrust of centralized school boards. Where integration did take place, it tended to be token in nature, with black students placed in different "ability" groups or curricula than white students. Indeed, the U.S. Commission on Civil Rights found in 1966 that "many Negro students who attend majority-white schools in fact are in majority-Negro classrooms."

Today, white middle-class outflow from cities in combination with black in-migration and political opposition to busing and other methods of alleviating de facto school segregation have made large-scale integration an improbable event. Of the twenty cities in the largest metropolitan areas in 1966, nine had Negro majorities among their elementary school enrollments, and fifteen had enrollments that were over 30 percent Negro. Thus, true school integration implies transgressing traditional political boundaries and incorporating metropolitan school districts that would encompass city and suburbs. Substantial opposition to this proposal by suburbanites will probably prevent such a development for the foreseeable future. In the meantime, inability of large city schools to adapt to the special needs of "minority" students will become increasingly a failure to adapt to the needs of a majority of students, most of these students obtaining their schooling in segregated environments. Among seventy-five cities surveyed by the Civil Rights Commission in 1966, three-quarters of the Negro students in elementary schools were already attending schools whose enrollments were 90 percent or more Negro.

Indeed many blacks reject integration as a solution not only because it is a phrase that is replete with false promises, but also because it has ideological overtones that are an affront to their dignity. As Floyd McKissick has suggested, the view that quality education can only take palce in an integrated school seems to be based upon the degrading propositon: "Mix Negroes with Negroes and you get stupidity."

A second approach to improving schools in the black ghetto has been that of *compensatory education*. During the early 1960s it became increasingly in vogue among educators to refer to the "educationally deprived" or "disadvantaged" child. In particular, most urban black children were considered to be disadvantaged, because it was said they lacked the home and community environment that stimulated educational motivation, achievment, and the derivation of middle-class attributes. Therefore, additional school resources were to be provided to the disadvantaged child in order to compensate for his middle-class deficiencies.

Unfortunately, the record to date for compensatory education is unimpressive. Most compensatory efforts have focused on smaller class size and additional personnel. The types of teachers, curriculum, school organization, and educational methods that have consistently failed the ghetto child have been largely retained, and little educational progress has been demonstrated. Some school spokesmen have excused compensatory program failures by asserting that most of these attempts have been underfinanced. Perhaps this is true, but one can certainly question how spending more money on such traditional panaceas as the reduction of class size is going to change the qualitative nature of basic schooling processes that did not have the urban black youngsters in mind to begin with.

It is clear that schools as presently constituted have shown little evidence of being able to fulfill the educational needs of the disadvantaged child and particularly the black disadvantaged child. Both compensatory education and school integration have witnessed more failures than successes (with the possible exception of preschool programs), and most future plans for improving the education of black children revolve about these two approaches. In a sense, representatives of the black communities are saying to the educational professionals and the white community: "You've been given your chance, and our schools have not improved." Now blacks want a chance to solve their own educational problems, and the professionals have not been able to counter these demands with genuine alternatives. Instead, the rather tired response has been something to the effect: "Just give us a chance to provide really racially integrated, quality education." In the eyes of the black community, this reply has not only come too late, but it smacks of the same stale remedies that have failed to change the picture in the past. The surge for self-determination in combination with the failure of the professionals to prove themselves has made schools particularly vulnerable. This vulnerability has manifested itself in the increasingly voiced sentiment that the education of blacks can no longer be considered to be the "white man's burden." The black community has rejected this paternalistic approach and wishes to take responsibility for the schooling of its own.

MAKING SCHOOLS WORK FOR MINORITY CHILDREN

Before embarking on a description of how community-controlled schools might improve the schooling experiences of minority children, it is useful to offer a more precise analysis of why the present approach to compensatory education must inevitably fail the culturally different child. Inherent in compensatory education programs is the condescending view that the urban minority child is somehow inferior to the middle-class child. Relative to the white middle-class child, he is "deprived" and "disadvantaged." Therefore, he needs remedial work and compensatory resources to improve his prospects. That is, *remediation* is considered to be the key to the minority-child's emancipation.

That the minority child is different from the middle-class white child is a mere tautology. Yet, in this case the schools assume that the child's cultural differences represent inferiorities that must be eliminated. Inherent in this approach is a total disrespect for the cultures and experiences of black and other minority children. Yet, to a black youngster, his experience is certainly as valid as that of his white counterpart.

There is no reason that a minority child must deny or deprecate his background in order to "learn." Indeed, such forced self-denunciation can only guarantee the development of a serious and widening breech between the school and the child. "Quite the opposite, the schools must capitalize on the cultural strengths of minority children in order to build cultural bridges between the experiences of those children and the goals of the larger society."[2]

[2]This approach is well documented and illustrated in Sylvia Ashton-Warner, *Teacher* (New York: Simon and Schuster, 1963). See also Frederick D. Flower, *Language and Education* (London, England: Longmans, Green, 1966).

But this goal requires taking a specialized approach to educating minority students, one that violates the underpinnings of the present universalistic model. The present method tacitly assumes that the same approach is universally applicable to all children despite the pious rhetoric often espoused about "individualized" instruction. Unfortunately, large urban school systems have shown themselves to be incapable of building educational programs that capitalize on the cultural attributes of minority children. This fact becomes quite clear when one examines the way in which so-called compensatory education programs have been formulated. Most money has been spent on such traditional methods as reducing class size, increasing the number of counselors and remedial specialists, and buying more library volumes. That is, more money has been spent on the same remedies that have not worked well in the past. The inevitable result is a larger version of the same dismal cake. There must be qualitative changes in the recipe in order to improve the quality of education for minority children.[3]

The fact that such qualitative changes have not generally taken place has meant that dollar resources have been misspent. The U.S. Office of Education in evaluating the effect of Title I moneys on reading scores found that ". . . a child who participated in a Title I project had only a 19 percent chance of a significant achievement gain, a 13 percent chance of a significant achievement loss, and a 68 percent chance of no change at all relative to the national norms."[4] Further, projects that were investigated were ". . . most likely to be representative of projects in which there was a higher than average investment in resources. Therefore more significant achievement gains should be found here than in a more representative sample of Title I projects."[5]

In fact, comparing dollar inputs between schools attended by

[3]Certainly this idea is not new. It has been suggested by many persons concerned with minority education. An excellent example is Joan Baratz and Roger Shuy, *Teaching Black Children to Read* (Washington, D.C.: Center for Applied Linguistics, 1969). It has been rarely applied, however.

[4]Harry Piccariello, "Evaluation of Title I," mimeographed (1969), p. 1. To be published in Joseph Froomkin and Dennis J. Dugan, eds., *Inequality: Studies in Elementary and Secondary Education,* U.S. Office of Education Planning Paper 69-2, Office of Program Planning and Evaluation.

[5]Ibid.

minority students and those attended by middle-class whites is an erroneous way of measuring school resource endowments between races. To the degree that money is spent in both cases on teachers, curriculum, and other inputs that are more effective for white children than for black or Spanish-speaking students, dollar expenditures tend to overstate vastly the relative resources available to the latter group. Rather, nominal resources devoted to the two groups of schools must be weighted by their effectiveness to ascertain their true values.

The ludicrous nature of comparing schools attended by majority and minority students on the basis of checklists of physical characteristics or on dollar expenditures is reflected in the following illustration. If black schools and white schools have the same number of teachers with the same preparation and experience, the two sets of schools are considered to be equal according to conventional criteria. Now what if all the teachers have white racist views? Clearly, if black schools and white schools have equal numbers of white racist teachers, the two sets of schools are not equal even through the physicial quantities of teachers are. This example raises additional questions about the present definition of remediation and compensatory education. If we double the number of white racist teachers in black schools, class size will be reduced by 50 percent; yet it is difficult to argue that healthy increases in educational output will take palce. Such a situation is perfectly consistent with the conventional arithmetic of spending on compensatory education. Attention is heavily focused on the amount of traditional resources available to minority children with almost no consideration of the appropriateness or the efficacy of those resources.

MAKING URBAN SCHOOLS MORE RESPONSIVE

For many blacks and members of other racial minorities, community control of the schools is seen as the only path that will succeed in making schools more responsive generally to the needs of the populations they serve. Under existing centrally administered systems, principals, teachers, and parents have found attempts to improve their schools frustrated by cumbersome procedures and regulations which protect the status quo. The school systems are so large that they cannot view themselves as being accountable to particular schools or parents, especially if those schools serve children whose parents lack political muscle. Since departures from tradition must usually be approved in the offices of the central school administration, bold and imaginative proposals for change are throttled by the lack of decison-making power in individual schools and classrooms. In fact, the central school board's obsession for procedural order above other considerations has encrusted schools with a drab and uniform educational approach despite the large variety of educational situations and student needs that are actually present in large cities. To the degree that many of the methods, curricula, and personnel have not been appropriate and have failed to give minority children, in particular, the skills and healthy attitudes that the schools claim as objectives, the failure has become institutionalized and systematic.

The massive inefficiencies and rigidities evident in the existing approach have been documented by so many novelists and journalists that many members of the public simply take them for granted. In one city, schools have waited for two years for textbooks that could have been received within two weeks had they been ordered directly from publishers. Many city schools have reported storerooms full of unused scientific equipment and library books without having the programs, laboratories, and libraries to make use of these materials. Other schools have the programs and physical facilities but lack equipment. In schools of some cities, a simple request for stationery or paper clips must be approved by a dozen different signatories before the request can be filled.

Further, the choice of textbooks and curriculum can rarely be modified by a teacher, no matter how useless or deleterious they may be to his or her pupils. One of the better publicized incidents that illustrates the administrative callousness of large city schools took place recently in a black junior high school. A young white teacher was harassed by her principal, who received support from the office of the central school board, for daring to introduce the Negro play *Raisin in the Sun* into her English class and for encouraging and supporting her pupils' efforts to produce a student newspaper. Her creative attempts to introduce relevant activities were criticized as violations of the "required" curriculum. That she had succeeded in getting her students excited about their English classes was ignored in favor of administrative uniformity. There is evidence that many of our better teachers leave the schools in part because of these same frustrations. In fact, the general failure of compensatory education programs is a monumental tribute to the inability of large-city school bureaucracies to adapt themselves to the needs of the sizable group of black children.

Thus, a major objective of school decentralization is that of making schools more responsive to the particular populations they serve, by making them accountable to the communities from which they draw their enrollments. The unwieldiness of the present highly centralized administrative structure prevents this type of accountability. It is expected that by being answerable to a local rather than city-wide governing board, schools will improve the learning environment for the children involved.

The direct impact of decentralization on schools would be derived from the ability of each community to select the curricula, materials, programs, and personnel that were most appropriate to the specific needs of its students. Experimentation and innovation, then, might lead to school environments that were more receptive to students and more successful in stimulating intellectual and emotional growth than are the present schools. In addition, decentralization would enable schools to handle logistical problems more efficiently by obtaining textbooks and other supplies in appropriate quantities at times when they are needed. Decentralization could also enable schools to obtain outside consulting on specific problems, utilize new types of personnel, such as artists and writers, and contract certain services that might be supplied more efficiently by private firms.

But, in addition to these direct effects, it is possible that the learning process will be enhanced indirectly by a healthy metamorphosis of community education attitudes. That is, the participation of parents and other members of the community in the operation of schools will lead to a more total involvement between the school and its constituency than is possible under the present bureaucratic structure. It appears that parental involvement in schools leads to more favorable attitudes toward education among their children: however, under the present system of highly centralized control, the school appears to be an impenetrable and alien fortress to the community and its parents. The inability of parents to have any meaningful influence in modifying rigid and anachronistic school policies has certainly led to parental frustrations and hostile attitudes that are easily transmitted to their children. It is believed that if the school were accountable to the community by being truly responsive to its educational needs, parents would show greater respect for schools and more favorable attitudes toward education. These attitudes would filter down to their children and would be reflected in the attitudes and performances of the students in those schools.

DECENTRALIZATION AND THE BLACK COMMUNITY

To the black community, the educational rationale for community governance is equally compelling, but the need for change is far more urgent than that suggested in the general case.[6] Not only is the present highly centralized system considered to be educationally inadequate, but also it is viewed as one which must inevitably have racist consequences. That is, the school system can afford to favor middle-class white children at the expense of black children because black citizens simply lack the political power to do any thing about it. In this respect, the schools reflect a type of racism which is ignored by the average white American. Kenneth Haskins, the principal who initially led the Morgan Community School in the District of Columbia, suggested that racism in this sense means ". . . that a public school system that fails black children can be tolerated, while a public school system that fails white middle-class children cannot."[7]

There is a strong belief that this dereliction might be reversed if the administration of those schools in black neighborhoods was responsive to the needs of large groups of black parents who were deeply concerned and involved in the process of education. In this regard, it is interesting to note that the Morgan Community School showed gains in the reading proficiencies of students in its very first year of community control. Only a handful of other public schools in the entire district exhibited such improvement over this period, while most schools showed declines.

[6]While this discussion is generally limited to the black community, it is certainly applicable to such ethnic minorities as Mexican-Americans and Puerto Ricans.

[7]Kenneth W. Haskins, "The Case for Local Control," *Saturday Review* (11 January 1969): 52.

Many black Americans also see a new and important educational focus emerging from community governance. They suggest that schools should be responsible for helping to fulfill the ideals and aspirations of the people served. The constituency of the school must necessarily include all the people of the community since the needs of the students cannot be divorced from the context in which they live. The school should be expected to promote the sense of self-worth and identity of the students served while imparting to those youngsters the ability to influence what happens to their lives. That is, the often noted observation that schools and the larger society tend to destroy the self-worth and identity of black children is considered to be as reprehensible as the academic failures of the schools.

In order to carry out these responsibilities, the community school must address itself not only to transmitting academic or cognitive skills, but also to affective skills, with particular attention given to the formation of positive attitudes. Indeed, community schools must be designed to compensate for the second-class treatment of black citizens in other sectors of society by building educational programs that will help black children to succeed.

But, even beyond that, many black Americans view community control of those schools in black neighborhoods as the beginning of a significant drive toward full equality. This approach springs from the widely held concept that as long as black Americans lack political and economic power, they will not be able substantially to improve their lot. Accordingly, community control of the schools represents the thin edge of a political wedge which would begin to redistribute decision-making power to those whose lives are affected by the decisions, in this case, the black community. Control of the schools is viewed as the first step in effecting a more just distribution of political power and a greater degree of self-determination for black citizens.

As one spokesman explained: "Improving the schools attended by black children is an urgent priority, but it seems to me that the bigger issue is one of how large numbers of people who have been effectively disenfranchised begin to find their way toward being a part of the society." It is interesting to ask, then, if large numbers of black communities did indeed obtain control of their school systems, how meaningful would that phenomenon be in securing complete liberation from the powerlessness that has hindered black advancement? His answer is that it could be very meaningful:

While the answers are not in, it seems very clear that this could be an initial step toward more effective control of other institutions in the community, for it is the success patterns of communities which give those communities a sense of better future instead of futility. Given control of the schools, the community could sense a beginning of political potency. It is this factor which would enhance the community's ability to deal more effectively with other problems such as jobs and housing and which would construct the groundwork for full equality.

In this respect community schools represent a focus around which political and social structures would emerge for black Americans where such structures are presently lacking. The factors that link black men today are the largely negative ones of enduring racial discrimination at the hands of white society. While there is a recent emphasis on black culture, the school represents a tangible institution about which a sense of community involvement and black pride might develop. Responsibility for the schools represents a positive experience which can be shared by all blacks as opposed to the negative one of white racism.

The importance of the school in developing the communal ties that black Americans, and perhaps most Americans, desire so passionately cannot be overemphasized. As Robert Maynard has suggested: "An issue has been raised around which many residents can rally as never before and one in which their mutual, or community, interest is most clearly defined." In this sense it seems that the often cited term, *black community*, in fact, reflects the common attributes which blacks wish to develop and share with each other. Control of schools represents a setting within which these latent and somewhat mystical ties might emerge to form a true sense of community, a sense of a common purpose and destiny.

Thus, the black American views community control as a way of improving and broadening the educational performance of ghetto schools as well as more generally improving the status of black citizens. This would be done by breaking down many of the rigidities that characterize these schools, as well as by introducing programs, personnel, and materials that are specifically designed to transform black children into capable young adults. The historical evidence suggests that presently structured school bureaucracies are incapable of carrying out such changes. Therefore, community control becomes a logical alternative for educational reform.

In addition, may blacks feel that community support for operating schools will provide the nucleus for a community power base; and it is believed that strong and cohesive black communities represent the most effective strategy for obtaining a more equitable share of power in the larger society. While few critics might deny the importance of the immediate educational goals of the community schools, many have reacted strongly to these political implications.

POLITICAL IMPLICATIONS OF COMMUNITY SCHOOLS

The main criticism against community control of schools seems to be that the search for political "liberation" of black Americans has no place in the schools. One wonders whether it is not the ends of obtaining power rather than the means that are being questioned, for the schools have traditionally claimed the goal of preparing students for a participatory democracy. Courses given throughout the standard curriculum are designed to give students the requisite literacy, knowledge, and common set of values that enable them to understand and participate in the political life of our society. But blacks and other racial minorities have been excluded from the power structure. They have been unable to form a coalition or find any other group that will represent their needs and the present objectives of the schools have not served them well. Indeed, present values reflected in the school curriculum are necessary for perpetuating the present distribution of political power; they do not encourage opening the game to players who have not been dealt a hand.

Since a significant portion of the black community feels that only self-development will invest it with the strength to reinforce its demands for a fairer representation in the larger society, it appears consistent that schools in the black community emphasize political goals of black cohesion rather than those of the beneficent democracy. Democratic trappings presently reflected by schools are clearly deceptive to black Americans who still lack political equality and meaningful representation. Thus, from the black point of view, there is necessarily an important educational precedent for relating its educational goals to its political ones.

SOCIALIZATION AND RACIAL SEPARATION

A second and related major social objection to decentralization is that it would institutionalize racial separation. Presumably neighborhoods would represent the initial basis of community, so that blacks would continue to attend schools that were predominantly black and whites would attend schools with white enrollments. Yet a major objective of the schools in a democratic society is that of exposing children to fellow students who are drawn from a variety of social, economic, and racial backgrounds. This goal is considered to be part of the socialization function of the schools, whereby individuals are being prepared to fulfill their interpersonal or social obligations in a multicultural setting. It is believed that exposure to a heterogeneity of cultures, races, and social classes improves understanding and interactions among the various groups and increases social mobility. These end products are considered to be prerequisites for an effectively functioning democratic society.

In this respect the community school appears to be both socially divisive and antidemocratic. But blacks are frequently among the first to point out that the concept of the "melting pot" has been a historical myth as far as black Americans are concerned. The fact is that blacks presently live in a separate society, and neither legal remedies nor the putative good will of the white community have been able to give them housing, education, and other social activities in an integrated setting. In the particular case of city schools, it was not blacks who rejected integration; it was the large-city school boards representing a sizable component of the white community. The vast majority of black Americans have always lived in a separate society, and past efforts to integrate them have not been successful.

But if we assume that a healthy America requires the full economic, political, and social integration of blacks and whites, the real question is how to achieve such a goal. Paradoxically, black cohesiveness appears to be a more effective strategy than any other existing alternative. The reason for its promise is a simple one. This society responds much more quickly to demands from powerful constituencies than it does to requests from weak ones, and black community is the basis for black political potency.

The effects of black separation in getting a larger piece of action are noticeable on the university campuses. The demands of newly formed black student unions for increases in black enrollments, black faculty members and administrators, and courses in Afro-American culture have been met with positive responses at many institutions. In addition these demands have spurred substantial increases in the recruitment of blacks by professional and graduate schools as well as greater provisions of financial aid and counseling services for such students. These gains are particularly relevant because they represent the traditional paths of access to the middle class that have been heavily trodden by whites, but, until very recently at least, have been largely inaccessible to minorities. What the issue comes to in the final analysis is the view by community control advocates that integration and equality will never come until blacks have the power to pursue such objectives meaningfully, and the requisite power cannot develop without black unity.

COMMUNITY SCHOOLS AND WHITE AMERICANS

Is political decentralization of the schools an equally valid response to the educational problems of whites? One of the most serious flaws that characterizes city schools, as well as many other American institutions, is the fallacious assumption that identical treatment of different groups yields the same outcomes for all groups. The fact is that, given the different cultural attributes of racial and social groupings, application of the same educational approach yields highly unequal results. In particular, evidence suggests that the traditional schooling approach has been far less effective for black children and those of some other racial minorities than it has been for children of the white middle class. If this is so, then the same logic must be applied to the choice of remedy. That is, organizational reforms that are drastically needed to improve the status of minority students are not necessarily the most appropriate remedies for curing the educational infirmities of those schools serving white populations.

In this respect, community control of the schools is far more urgently needed by minority Americans than it is by whites. Blacks (and other racial minorities) are a special educational case because their exigencies are not represented by the power structure or by traditional institutional arrangements. The result of their lack of representation is that blacks have been shortchanged in the allocation of school resources, and their needs have been ignored in determining the nature of the schooling experience that is provided for their children. As a consequence, there exists an enormous breach between the context in which the black child lives and the schooling that is imposed upon him. In addition, the central school authorities have shown themselves to be insensitive to other major concerns of the black population. Sites have been selected for new schools that are to be built in black neighborhoods without consulting inhabitants of the local areas. As a result, black residents and businesses have been uprooted despite the availability of suitable alternative sites that would leave housing and other neighborhood buildings intact.

On the other hand, no major contradiction is found between the values represented in the school and those embodied in the white community at large, and whites already have the political power to protect their major school interests. The central school authority is politically sensitive to both school-resource demands and site-selection preferences of residents in white neighborhoods. In fact, in these as well as other major respects, whites already send their children to community-controlled schools. The very failure of policies to reduce de facto school segregation is a tribute to the power of white neighborhoods to keep black students out of their schools.

To be sure, particular whites might not be altogether happy with their schools, but most white Americans can express their dissatisfactions through political channels or through moving to another neighborhood or school district, and many white Americans have the financial ability to send their children to private institutions. The minority American has neither the luxury of obtaining political responsiveness, the income necessary to seek private alternatives, nor the choice of a large number of neighborhoods or communities in which he can obtain housing and better schools for his children. Locked-in to his community, and locked-out of city hall, the minority American's only hope for improving his schools appears to be through their immediate and direct governance. Therein lies the case for community control of the schools.

.10. *The Rise of the "Free School"*

BONNIE BARRETT STRETCH

FOR THE past five years, critics have been telling parents and teachers what is wrong with the public schools. Such writers as John Holt, Herbert Kohl, Jonathan Kozol, George Dennison, and Paul Goodman have described the authoritarianism that structures many classrooms, the stress on grades and discipline at the expense of learning, and the suppression of the natural curiosity and instincts of the young. Many parents and teachers have begun to see for themselves the boredom, fear, and grievous lack of learning that too often accompany schooling—not only for the poor and the black, but for suburban white youngsters as well—and they have begun to ask what can be done about it.

The revolt is no longer against outdated curricula or ineffective teaching methods—the concerns of the late 1950s and early 1960s. The revolt today is against the institution itself, against the implicit assumption that learning must be imposed on children by adults, that learning is not something one does by and for oneself, but something designated by a teacher. Schools operating on this assumption tend to hold children in a prolonged state of dependency, to keep them from discovering their own capacities for learning, and to encourage a sense of impotence and lack of worth. The search is for alternatives to this kind of institution.

In the past two years, increasing numbers of parents and teachers have struck out on their own to develop a new kind of school that will allow a new kind of education, that will create independent, courageous people able to face and deal with the shifting complexities of the modern world. The new schools, or free schools, or community schools—they go by all these names—have sprung up by the hundreds across the country. Through a continuous exchange of school brochures and newsletters, and through various conferences, the founders of these schools have developed a degree of self-awareness, a sense of community that has come to be called "the new schools movement."

The new schools charge little or no tuition, are frequently held together by spit and string, and run mainly on the energy and excitement of people who have set out to do their own thing. Their variety seems limitless. No two are alike. They range from inner-city black to suburban and rural white. Some seem to be pastoral escapes from the grit of modern conflict, while others are deliberate experiments in integrated multicultural, multilingual education. They turn up anywhere—in city storefronts, old barns, former barracks, abandoned church buildings, and parents' or teachers' homes. They have crazy names like Someday School, Viewpoint Non-School, A Peck of Gold, The New Community, or New Directions—names that for all their diversity reflects the two things most of these schools have in common: the idea of freedom for youngsters and a humane education.

As the Community School of Santa Barbara (California) states in its brochure: "The idea is that freedom is a supreme good; that people, including young people, have a right to freedom, and that people who are free will in general be more open, more humane, more intelligent than people who are directed, manipulated, ordered about...."

The Santa Barbara Community School is located in a converted barracks on a hill above the town. The fifty or so children (ages three to fourteen) almost invariably come from wealthy, white, fairly progressive families who want to give their children "the nicest education possible," as one teacher put it. Inside the building are a large meeting room; some smaller rooms for seminars, discussions, and tutorials; a wood and metal shop; classrooms for the younger children; and a small library. Classes for the younger children are based on the Leicestershire model. Rooms are organized by activity centers—a math corner here, a reading corner there. Parents' money has helped provide a remarkable amount of creative learning materials. Children are free to move from one thing to another as their interest shifts, and children of all ages frequently work and play together. For the older kids, the method is largely tutorial: one, two, or three youngsters working with a teacher. Although there is a "core curriculum" of literature, science, and social studies, the classes follow the interests and preferences of the students.

Outside and behind the building is enough space for a large playground, a pile of wood and lumber, a large pile of scrap metal including bicycle and car parts, and an old car, whose motor the older children are dismantling as a lesson in mechancis or physics (depending on whom you talk to). Children of all ages use the wood and metal to carve or weld into sculpture, as well as to fix bikes and build toys. "It's important for kids to learn about tools," explained a teacher. "Most kids don't know how things work. You really have to see a six-year-old in goggles with a welding torch to appreciate what it means."

The parents like the school, although they sometimes worry about how much the children are learning. By "learning" they mean the three Rs, social studies, etc. Parent pressure has led the Community School to place more emphasis on traditional subject matter than many free schools do. Teachers, on the other hand, are more concerned about another kind of learning. They would like to help these white middle-class youngsters develop a better sense of the world, to expose them to styles of life and work besides those of their families. There are frequent trips to ranches, factories, local businesses, and other schools. But these experiences, being interludes, remain essentially artificial to children. What are real are the comforts and concerns that inform their daily lives and that are shared with their friends.

In contrast to this isolation is the Children's Community Workshop School in New York City. Situated in an economically and racially integrated neighborhood, the school makes a conscious effort to keep its enrollment one-third white, one-third black, and one-third Puerto Rican. Because it is intended specifically as an alternative to the public schools, the Community Workshop charges no tuition. It is supported primarily by foundation grants and private donations, but the scramble for money is a continuous one that taxes a great deal of the energy of the school's director, Anita Moses.

Like the Santa Barbara Community School, the Community Workshop bases its structure on the Leicestershire method. And, again like Santa Barbara, it does not hold strictly to that method. There is a great deal of emphasis on the children's own interests, and new directions and materials are being tried all the time. A visitor to the school may find one group of children at a table struggling to build arches out of sugar cubes; another two or three children may be working with an erector set, others with tape recorders and a typewriter. In the midst of all this independent activity may be found one teacher helping one child learn to write his name.

Except for the use of Leicestershire techniques, there is little similarity between the Children's Community Workshop and the school in Santa Barbara. The heterogeneity of the student body makes the educational and human problems far more complex. Where achievement levels and cultural backgrounds vary widely, there is a great deal of accommodation necessary on the part of teachers and parents. At the same time, there can be no question that the children are learning more than the traditional three Rs.

Both the Community Workshop and the Santa Barbara Community School, however, have more structure than many free schools. The tendency in these schools is not to stress conventional intellectual training, to offer it if and when the children want it, and in general to let the youngsters discover and pursue their own interests. The new schools agree fully with Piaget's statement that "play is the serious business of childhood," and a child may as easily spend whole days in the sandbox as in the reading center. The lack of structure, however, leads to a lot of noise and running around, and all this activity may seem like chaos to a visitor. Often that's exactly what it is. It is a difficult skill to attune oneself to individual children, and to build on their individual needs and concerns, and few teachers have mastered it. Often, too, older youngsters, suddenly released from the constraints of public school, will run wild for the first few weeks, or even months, of freedom. But gradually, as they work the pent-up energy out of their system, and as they learn that the adults really will allow this freedom, they begin to discover their own real interests and to turn their energy to constructive tasks.

"The longer they've been in public school, and the worse their experience there is, the longer it takes for them to settle down, but eventually they all do," says Billy Kenney, who has taught at Pinel School in Martinez, California, for ten years. Pinel is an essentially Summerhillian school where classes in subjects such as reading and arithmetic are offered, but the children are not compelled to attend. Based on his experience at Pinel, Mr. Kenney believes that in a school that is solidly middle-class it can be expected that any happy, healthy child will eventually learn to read, write, and do basic arithmetic, whether or not he is formally taught. The experience of other middle-class free schools tends to corroborate this assumption.

The appeal of this philosophy is enormous, judging from the number of students and teachers applying to the new schools—all these schools report more applicants than they can handle—and from the constant flow of visitors who come to watch, ask questions, and sometimes get in the way. A few schools have had to set up specific visiting days in an effort to stem the tide. Three major conferences on "alternatives in education" took place this spring—in Cuernavaca, Mexico; in Santa Barbara, California; and in Toronto, Canada—and people flocked to them by the hundreds to talk to such "heroes" as John Holt and George Dennison, and to talk to one another and learn who's doing what and how. Representatives from foundations, universities, and the U.S. Office of Education also came, eager to know whether the critics' ideas can be given life.

Through the conferences and through correspondence and exchanges of school newsletters, a self-awareness is developing among the new schools, a sense of themselves as part of a growing movement. Much of this increased consciousness is due to the work of the New Schools Exchange, an information clearinghouse that grew out of a conference of two hundred schools a year ago. During its first year, the Exchange set up a directory of new schools, put teachers and kids in touch with schools, and schools in touch with teachers, kids, materials—and even, occasionally, money. In that year, too, eight hundred new names were added to the Exchange list, and the Exchange helped many through the labor pains of birth by offering nuts-and-bolts information about how to incorporate a school, and ways to get through the bureaucratic maze of building, fire, and health regulations.

But the mortality rate among these new schools is high. Harvey Haber of the Exchange estimates about eighteen months is the average life span. This includes those that endure for years and those that barely get off the ground. Money is universally the biggest hassle and the reason most commonly cited for failure. Even those schools that endure are seriously hampered by the constant struggle for fiscal survival that too often must take precedence over education. Most schools are started by people who are not rich, and charge little or no tuition, in an effort to act as an alternative for the common man (the rich have always had alternatives). Teachers work for pennies, when they are paid at all. "How do I survive?" one teacher laughed a bit anxiously. "I found a nice landlord who doesn't bug me about the rent. I dip into my savings, and get my parents and friends to invite me to dinner—often. Then, there are food stamps, of course. Mostly we rely on each other for moral support and help over the really rough places."

This kind of dedication, however, is too much to ask of anyone for any length of time. Working with children in an open classroom with few guidelines makes tremendous demands on teachers, Anita Moses of the Children's Community Workshop points out. Furthermore, teachers must often give their time for planning, for parent conferences, or for Saturday workshops with new teaching techniques and materials. There are intrinsic rewards for this, of course, but extrinsic rewards are also necessary, Mrs. Moses stresses, and those rewards should be in terms of salary.

There are other hurdles besides money—red tape, harassment by various state and city bureaucracies, and hostility from the community at large. In Salt Lake City, for example, a citizens committee tried to close a new Summerhill school on the grounds that the school was immoral and the teachers were communists.

But perhaps the most fundamental factor for survival is the degree of commitment on the part of the teachers and parents. For brochures, newsletters, and other public pronouncements, it is possible to articulate the concept of freedom and its importance to the emotional and intellectual development of the child. But basically the appeal is to a gut-level longing for love, joy, and human community, and often the schools are run on this romantic basis. "If you stop putting pressure on the kids, the tendency is to stop putting pressure on the staff, too," one teacher observed. Schools that fail within a few months of opening tend to be those begun by people merely interested in trying out a new idea. When the idea turns out to be more complex, and its implementation more difficult than anticipated, the original good feeling evaporates and a deeper determination is required.

Parents and teachers who have worked out their ideas together, who have similar goals, who know what they want for their children and why, have a better chance of keeping their school alive. Nonetheless, almost every school follows a similar pattern. If they make it over the physical hurdles of getting money, finding a building, and meeting bureaucratic regulations, they run into the spiritual struggle. Usually, somewhere in the first three to six months, according to Harvey Haber, comes the first great spiritual crisis: "structure" vs. "nonstructure." Having experimented with the idea of freedom, and having discovered its inherent difficulties, many parents and teachers become impatient and anxious. Are the children learning anything, they wonder, and does it matter? Frequently there is a slowdown in the acquisition of traditional academic skills. Children, it turns out, would rather play than learn to spell, and the blossoming forth of innate genius in a warm, benevolent atmosphere fails to occur. Anxious adults begin to argue for more structure to the school day, more direction for the kids, more emphasis on the familiar three Rs. Others insist upon maintaining the freedom, and upon learning to work with children on a new freer basis that really tests its limitations and possibilities.

As Robert Greenway, whose sons were enrolled in the Redwood Association Free School in Sonoma County, California, wrote:

It seems to me that this anxiety that gets aroused about "what's happening to our kids" is understandable and inevitable. In a public school, we turn our children over to the wardens; there is no illusion about the possibility of influence to torture us. . . . But a truly cooperative venture arouses every possible hope about involvement in the growth of our children—and probably every latent frustration about what we think *didn't* happen to us as well. . . . I suggest that, unless we find a way of dealing with the real anxieties and concerns that this type of enterprise arouses, then we'll fail before we've hardly started (I'm responding to my own growing sense of frustration and anxiety, and to the sign of sudden and/or premature withdrawals from the school, and to the growing hue and cry for "more organization").

The Santa Fe (New Mexico) Community School went through this crisis in the middle of its second year, a bit later than most. Parents were willing to go along with the school as long as the teachers seemed confident about what was happening with the children. But when one teacher began to articulate the fears many parents had tried to suppress, the situation came to a head. There was a period of trying to impose more order on the kids, and the kids rebelled and refused to take it. Some staff members were fired, and parents demanded more teachers with bachelor's and master's degrees, but found they could not get them for a salary of $200 a month. There were endless pedagogical debates, and finally some of the parents simply took their kids back to the public school. "Unfortunately, those who left were the ones with the most money," sighed one teacher. "We're poorer now, but the people here are here because they're dedicated."

After the crisis, the school was reorganized. Previously ordered by age clusters, it is now divided into activity centers, and children of all ages move freely from one center to another. On a bright southwestern day a visitor may find a couple of boys sitting in front of the building, slumped against a sun-warmed wall, eating apples and reading comic books. Inside, in the large front room, a group of children may be painting pictures or working with leather or looms. In a quiet, smaller room, someone else is having a guitar lesson. A room toward the back of the building is reserved as the math center; a couple of teachers are math enthusiasts, and many of the older children pick up from them their own excitement for the subject.

In the playground behind the building is an Indian kiva built by students and teachers learning about the culture of local Indian tribes. The Southwest is a multicultural area, and the Community School has tried to draw on all these cultures. There are Indian and Spanish children enrolled, as well as white, and each is encouraged to respect and learn from the cultures of the others.

But despite its efforts to reach into the Indian and Spanish communities, the Santa Fe Community School remains essentially a white middle-class school. The Chicanos and Indians, mainly poor or working class, tend to shy away from such experiments, partly because their cultures are traditionally conservative with highly structured roles for adults and children, and partly because the poor cannot afford to take a chance on the future of their young. Middle-class whites can always slip back into the mainstream if they choose. But for the poor, neither the acquisition of such intellectual tools as reading and writing nor a place in the economy is guaranteed.

These fundamental differences show up clearly in the community schools operated by and for black people. Black people on the whole bring their children to these schools, not merely because they believe in freedom for self-expression or letting the child develop his own interests, but because their children are not learning in the public school, are turning sullen and rebellious by the age of eight, and are dropping out of school in droves. The ideology in many of these schools is not pedagogical, but what one school calls "blackology"— the need to educate the children in basic skills and in pride of race. In the black schools there is much more emphasis on basic intellectual training and much more participation on the part of parents. By and large, parents are the founders of these schools; they are the main source of inspiration and energy. They have the final say in selecting both teachers and curriculum, and their chief criterion is: are the children learning?

As in the white schools, classrooms for the younger children are frequently patterned after the Leicestershire model. But the approach is deliberately eclectic, providing closer guidance and more structured activities for youngsters who need it. The academic progress of the children is carefully observed and quietly but firmly encouraged. "We want teachers who will try a thousand different ways to teach our children," said one mother.

Equally important is a teacher's attitude toward race. Although some schools would like to have all-black faculties—and in a number of cities, parents are in training to become teachers and teacher aides—they must still hire mainly whites. "When I interview a teacher," said Luther Seabrook, principal of the Highland Park Free School in Boston, "I always ask, can you think of a community person as an equal in the classroom?" Many teachers cannot, either because of racial bias, or because of notions about professionalism. Even after a teacher is hired, the going is still rough where feelings run high on the part of blacks and whites, but there is a determination to confront these problems directly through open discussion and group sessions.

The same approach applies to daily work in the classroom. Teachers and aides are encouraged to talk openly about their successes and problems in weekly planning sessions, to admit mistakes, and to try out new ideas. Such sessions are frequently the keystone of the teaching process in these schools. They are the times when teachers can get together and evaluate what has been happening in the classroom, how the children have responded to it, and how the teachers have responded to the children. "It's a tremendous place to grow," one teacher remarked. "You're not tied to a curriculum or structure, and you're not afraid to make mistakes. Everyone here is in the same boat. We get support from each other and develop our own ways of handling things."

There is little doubt that the youngsters prefer the community schools to traditional schools. The humane and personal atmosphere in the small, open classrooms makes a fundamental difference. The children work together writing stories or figuring math problems, working with Cuisenaire rods or an elementary science kit. They are proud of their work and show it eagerly to visitors. There is virtually no truancy, and many youngsters hate to stay home even on weekends, according to their mothers.

But perhaps the greatest achievement of these schools is with the parents. They develop a new faith, not only in their children but in themselves. "Now I know," said a New York City mother, "that, even though I didn't finish high school, it is possible for me to understand what they are teaching my child." In changing their children's lives, these parents have discovered the power to change their own lives, as well. Parents who are not already working as aides and coordinators in the classrooms drop by their schools often to see how Johnny is doing. At the East Harlem Block Schools in New York, stuffed chairs and couches and hot coffee put parents at ease, while teachers talk with them as equals and draw them into the education of their children.

Nonetheless, black schools share many of the problems with the community that white schools have. People are suspicious of new ways of teaching, even though their children obviously are failing under the old ways. Parents who enroll their children out of desperation still grow anxious when they see the amount of freedom allowed. In integrated schools, like Santa Fe or the Children's Community Workshop, there is the added problem of race and class, as middleclass parents learn that all the children are not necessarily going to adopt middle-class values and life styles, that cultural differences are valid and must be accepted.

Some schools are fed up with "parent education;" it takes too much time away from the children. A number of schools already are taking only children whose parents are in sympathy with their aims, parents who won't panic if the child doesn't learn to read until he is eight or nine.

But as a school grows more homogeneous, it faces the danger of becoming an isolated shelter against the reality of the outside world. Instead of educating kids to be strong and open enough to deal with a complex world, the schools may become elitist cloisters that segregate a few people even further from the crowd.

Once again the free schools must ask themselves what they are all about. If one assumes (as many free schools do) that any healthy, happy youngster will eventually learn to read and write, then what is the purpose of school? Is it enough simply to provide one's children with a school environment more humane than the public schools, and then stay out of nature's way?

At a California high school in the Sausalito hills, teachers and students think that that in itself is quite a lot. After going through a typical cycle of kids getting high on freedom and doing nothing for six months, getting bored, and finally facing the big questions—What am I doing? Where am I going?—students and teachers think they have learned a lot about themselves and each other. But as the youngsters return to studying and start to seek answers to those questions, they find the teachers have little to offer besides a sympathetic ear. Some kids return to the public school feeling better for their experience with freedom. (Feeling, too, perhaps, that it didn't work, that they really do need all the rules and discipline their parents and teachers demanded.) Gradually, those who remain have forced the teachers back to the traditional textbooks as the chief source of knowledge.

The humane atmosphere remains, but missing is a curriculum that truly nurtures the independence of thought and spirit so often talked of and so rarely seen. It takes extraordinary ingenuity to build on students' needs and interests. A few brilliant teachers, such as Herbert Kohl, can turn kids on, meet them where they are, and take them further—can, for example, take a discussion of drugs and dreams and guide it through the realms of mythology, philosophy, and Jungian psychology. But what do you do if you're not a Herb Kohl? According to Anita Moses, you "work damn hard." There are other things, too: You can hire a master teacher familiar with the wide range of curriculum materials available. Little by little you can change the classroom, or the school itself, to make it do the things you want it to do. And little by little through working with the children and hashing out problems with help from the rest of the staff, you begin to know what it is you want to do and how you can do it.

But even this does not answer the deeper questions—questions that are implicit in every free school, but that few have faced. Is it only a new curriculum or new ways of teaching that we need? Or do we need to change our ideas about children, about childhood itself, about how children learn, what they learn, what they need to learn, from whom or from what kinds of experience? It is clear that our ideas about teaching are inadequate, but is it possible that they are simply false? For example, children can often learn to read and write without any formal instruction. This is not a miracle: it is a response of an intelligent young being to a literate milieu. It is also clear that children learn many cognitive as well as social abilities from their peers or from children but a few years older than themselves. What, then, is the role of the adult in the learning of the child?

In simpler times, children learned from adults continually, through constant contact and interchange, and through their place close to the heart of the community. Today, the society has lost this organic unity. We live in times when children often see their fathers only on weekends. We live in a world that separates work from play, school from the "real" world, childhood from personhood. The young are isolated from participation in the community. They seem to have no integral place in the culture. Too often schools have become artificial environments created by adults for children. How is it possible to forsake these roles?

Young people are trying. Many will no longer accept without question authority based solely on tradition or age. They are seeking alternatives to The Way Things Are. But the venture into unfamiliar territory generates enormous anxieties. The young are painfully aware of their own inexperience; they lack faith in themselves. But who can help them in their conflicts both within themselves and with the outside world? Surely, this is a function of education. But in today's world there are few adults who can do this for themselves, far less for their children. For who can respond with assurance to the anxieties of young people over sex, drugs, and the general peril in which we live? Who knows how to deal with others when the traditional roles are gone?

And yet it should be possible for adults to relate to young people in some constructive way. It must be possible because the young, in their alienation and confusion, and the culture, in its schizoid suffering, demand it. In the words of Peter Marin, former director of the Pacific High School, a free school in California:

Somebody must step past the children, must move into his own psyche or two steps past his own limits into the absolute landscape of fear and potential these children inhabit. . . . I mean: we cannot *follow* the children any longer, we have to step ahead of them. Somebody has to mark a trail.

Is this what the free schools are all about? Few of them have asked these questions. Few will ever want to. But the questions are implicit in the movement. The free schools offer alternatives—alternatives that may be shaped to meet new needs and aims. At least, they offer a first step. At least, the possibility is there.

.11. Political Knowledge and Experience in Elementary Education*

PHILIP BRENNER

PART II

Now NONE of you really expect this essay to be read by children. You anticipated before turning to it that the essay would be written on a "level" that you could understand, and that the concepts and perhaps language would have little meaning for children. What has come before, in Part I, by the way, is known to all of you for this very reason. Part I is your tacit knowledge—accumulated in various ways —that makes it possible for you to comprehend what I will say. This knowledge is more than vocabulary. The symbols that follow have literary meaning for you because you have had experience with similar symbols.

What I am talking about is not experience with politics. The relevant experience to which I am referring is academic. You deal in words and know how to relate to them. Knowing about politics—not the literature on politics—would require a different sort of knowledge. As politics is more often intuitive than cognitive, more person-oriented than deductively logical, and is bound up with values, not antiseptic formulas, so one cannot experience politics through books. This is the essence of this essay, and the central proposition underlying the Washington Mini School—an experiment which I will

*Prepared for delivery at the Sixty-sixth Annual Meeting of the American Political Science Association, September 8–12, 1970, Los Angeles, California.

shortly describe. My a priori assumption is that knowledge derives from experience, that what we know is what we have experienced.[1]

We find ourselves in the midst of a political crisis. The state, which ostensibly came into being under the original social contract to provide for our safety and protection, brings us to the brink of destruction by rattling atomic weapons and engaging in military adventures, and cannot prevent the increasing white-collar and street crime in society. Political conflicts repeatedly result in continued deprivation of the many for the benefit of the few. The government is unwilling to control modern technology so that it does not lead to chronic conditions.

Children will inherit the crisis. In order to prepare them to grapple with it, there seem to be three strategies. The first would be to ignore the problem. Things will work out by themselves for the best, it could be reasoned. Ostriches who talk this way do not merit a serious response.

Second, we might provide children with a thorough grounding in the skills necessary to build the good society and then send them out to ply their wares. Third, we can give children an understanding of the crisis and let them begin to deal with it immediately.

What are the necessary skills? Well, here we might have the raging type of debate found at the annual meetings of the Association of Secondary School Teachers. In an age of television, is reading as important as knowing how to use the mass media? Is it important to know how to take a square root, or is it more important to learn which operation to perform on a computer so that it can take the square root? Whatever subject matter you choose, though, it is essential to remember that by teaching it in a school, the child is experiencing the nature of the school as well as the subject.

This is what progressive educators have been saying from John Dewey to John Holt and Herbert Kohl. In an authoritarian school, children learn submissiveness as well as mathematics if they are to "succeed." In most schools they learn to direct their energies to future goals—"It will be useful some day, you'll see." They learn that the world is made up of right answers, and that those in authority

[1]The proposition is fully expounded by John Dewey in *Experience and Education* (New York: Collier Books, 1969); and by Eugene Gendlin in *Experiencing and the Creation of Meaning* (New York: Free Press, 1962).

always have the right answers. They learn that they can be reduced to a quantified equivalent, to a graded profile, and that this is the way to judge people. Finally, they learn to ignore their intuition and real feelings, and to replace them with strategies of "faking"—in Holt's terms—in order to receive acceptance and approval.

The response of "progressive" educators has been to make schools less authoritarian, to orient teaching to the needs of children rather than those of a mystical curriculum, to emphasize the process of questioning rather than answering, and to create classrooms that are undifferentiated by grade so as to emphasize individual development. But still this all occurs in a school.

These experiences are isolated from the "real world." Just that phrase "real world" suggests that what happens in school is not real. And we all think that way. In the traditional schools children were kept unaware of the purposes for which they were educated and of the real world. In progressive schools children are told about that world. And the organization of the school is supposed to facilitate the child's entry into the real world as an individual. But the child is kept isolated and it is not clear how he is supposed to transfer what he experiences in a "safe," supportive environment to the real world.

Dewey attempted to resolve the dilemma by arguing that the real world was a world in which the scientific approach was predominant. Thus, what was necessary to impart to children was an experience with this approach.[2] Thereby, in school, children would be experiencing the real world.

My real world, however, is political. In a sense, what children learn in a traditional school is political. Submission to authority, abhorrence of deviance, and the like are political. And the democratic underpinning of the progressive schools is political as well. While I do favor the latter, it is not clear to me that these lessons would not be learned if there were no school at all. What progressive schools have done is to free children from adult authoritarianism in order to allow them to follow their own democratic inclinations—inclinations which we find prevail when children are on their own to arrange games outside school. What is the purpose of school, then, if its political education can be learned as well without it?

[2]Dewey, *Experience and Education*, chap. 7.

Entering into the whirlwind of the real world, children are easily overwhelmed. Either they have been channeled through successive steps of schooling to fit into a preestablished mold,[3] or they have been nurtured in safety, without experiencing the world. Perhaps they have been told about the world and on a glorious field trip to Congress, to the United Nations, to a factory, they have actually seen it. But to know about it is to feel it, to sense what corporate decisions lead to and how they are made, to see the world as political decision-makers see it. Without any experience in the real world, children cannot relate to the reality we think we describe to them. Their perceptions of what we say relate to the body of experience they have had, because it is through experience that we all make meaning from abstract symbols. The experience forms an intuitive base of knowledge—tacit knowledge, in Michael Polanyi's phrase—to which new knowledge can then correspond. Without experiencing politics, reading about politics does not open up vistas; it merely continues children's old experiences with words, or with other nonreal world experiences.

If we are dealing only with symbols, then symbolic instruction may be appropriate. Sensing that a knowledge of mathematics is useful to shopping at a food market may add an incentive to learn the subject. But it is not essential to understand the logic of mathematics that a child have experience in shopping.

Politics is different. It is an activity of the world. It not only involves interpersonal relations, but will govern the lives of children through the economy, foreign relations, police power of the state, and over-all tone of life. By keeping children ignorant of politics, that is, by not giving them experience with it, until they are eighteen or older, we place them in the world at that age with little knowledge for survival. Then we expect them to challenge the crisis immediately and to succeed. They will know their mathematics and interpersonal democracy, but will they have the necessary tacit knowledge of larger political structures to find where they should begin the fight? Will they have a sense of what questions they should ask? Merely teaching children to ask questions is unsatisfactory. Children must have a

[3]Marcus Raskin, *Being and Doing* (New York: Random House, 1971), especially "The Channeling Colony." This book provided the formative ideas for the mini-school, and Raskin worked as a consultant on the project.

sense of what questions are meaningful, and this they can acquire by experience with politics. Schools can offer political knowledge if they are organized to provide experience. And schools should do this so that children are prepared to grapple with political problems.

Now, let me ask a very important question. Have you ever played the game *Monopoly*? If you have, are you now prepared, because of that experience, to tackle the world of real estate? In fact, if you have ever bought a house you know that *Monopoly* provides you with a very distorted picture of what is involved. Of course, the designers of the game may not have intended you to get a picture of reality. But there are some essential elements about *Monopoly* that suggest why games are not an appropriate way to provide children with experience in the real world.

For one thing, the game is not real. The decisions are irrelevant to anything but the game, and children do not learn what the consequences of decisions are in real terms. They may foster the notion that the problems involved are other people's problems, not problems that the children will and do face for themselves. Education should not create distance. One meaning for political knowledge is the understanding of how political decisions relate to everyone and affect everyone.

I have taken off on games because their use has become the vogue in schools, especially in regard to politics. There are games of diplomacy and games of democracy, games for all aspects of political life. But they are not true to life. Players are assigned roles and learn to play these roles. While a child in fact may have little choice in his life's roles, it does not have to be that way. Moreover, the games depict roles in existing institutions. There is hardly any creativity involved. And last, in accepting the rules of the game the children do not learn to question existing political patterns. Yet it is these very patterns that have led to crisis, and to learn how to question them should be the purpose of political education.

What I find perplexing about the introduction of games is the purpose of this innovation. There would appear to be three distinct motivations. (Naturally, some educators might have only one of these purposes in mind while others may be looking to all three. I do not consider a fourth, cynical goal; introducing "relevance" into the curriculum for the sake of assuaging unrest.) The three serious motivations are: (1) to feel politics, by experiencing a simulation; (2) to learn to do politics, by practice; (3) to understand abstract concepts about politics, by seeing them concretely.

The first is the key to the other two, because in order to do politics one must have a sense of political relations, and for someone to conceptualize abstractions that relate to reality, the symbols must have some basis in his real life experience.

For example, war games are somewhat "successful" in testing out new strategies and organization because they are grounded in real experience. Generals have a sense of what the reality is, and know how to relate the game to reality, what to dissect from the practice. Without real experience, however, a game is just a game. Law students find "moot court" to be stimulating, but they also find that any number of moot-court games cannot prepare them for the reality of trial law.

Moreover, if abstract concepts are learned from political games, we are far from certain that these are concepts that relate to political life. They may be concepts about how to win a game. Without knowing what is real, a child cannot begin to sense "principles" about reality from a game.

The motivations of these educators are laudable, though. They point directly to the three types of political knowledge that we can learn: (1) a sense of power relations, political conflict, oppression, bureaucracy; (2) a guide to doing politics, to the "rules" for winning elections, overthrowing governments, making collective decisions; (3) a framework for developing abstract concepts about political life.

The first derives from experience with politics. Clearly, the second is hardly useful unless preceded by a sense of politics, because a handbook of what to do can only be used in cases where you know when to do what. There are techniques for winning elections, but the mix of techniques requires a political sensitivity. And abstract concepts may be in a logical deductive world of their own unless experience tells the person that his deductions are based on reality as well as logic.

So we must begin with the first type of knowledge—experiencing politics—in order to "teach" children about politics. What this means will differ for each teacher and especially for each group of students. Black children who live in slums relate to different aspects of the political world than do white middle-class children. The experience under consideration must start from prior experiences of the children. What I will describe, then, is one proposed experience and how it was operated experimentally last spring. It is called the Washington Mini School.

The Mini School is a private corporation. From January through May 1970, it operated in Washington, D.C., twice each week after "regular" school. There were twenty-three students in the program, seven of whom were Caucasian. They all attended the same public elementary school, and all could be classified as middle- to upper-middle-class in terms of apparent family income. Their ages ranged from ten to twelve.

We decided to work with children in this age group because at this age children begin to redefine their world.[4] Their world is no longer narrowly focused on themselves. They tend to become more curious about the society in general and begin to feel that they are a part of it. Moreover, they tend not to be completely dulled yet by the regimentation and stifling organization of their schools. They still have creativity and curiosity; they are still uninhibited enough to ask embarrassing questions.

Defining "political" very broadly, we wanted children to know about government, communications, private power, why Washington looks as it does, the ways in which people become sick and how they are cared for, the way in which people's leisure time is organized, and how society provides goods for people. In short, we defined "political" as the quality of life, and we wanted children to examine facets of life that would give them a sense of how this quality is determined.

The children were transported to institutions in Washington where various activities take place. At each place we had arranged for people actively engaged in the business of the institution—not tour guides or public relations directors—to talk with them, and where possible to begin work with them. A brief description of these visits follows.

Architecture. An architect spent three days with the children, walking through a neighborhood and asking questions about the nature of the buildings. On the third day they designed a school. The children were far from free yet. They saw "school" only as a building

---

[4]The project was undertaken by Kenneth Fox and myself. Mr. Fox is now a consultant with the Urban Institute.

with rooms, and did not envision new forms. On a fourth day they went to a city planner who explained what he does. This was very unsatisfactory as the children complained that the planner was "like a teacher." That is, he talked to them and did not want to listen to what they had to say.

Congress. Questioning architectural forms appeared to carry over very clearly to the first of two sessions we had in Congress. On the first day the children met with a former congressman in a committee hearing room. It was a large one, and an early question was: "Is this a very important room?" After some questions it became clear that they *felt* it was an important room and that important things took place there because it was large and richly decorated. They did some role playing as congressmen that day, and the next talked with a congressman in his office.

Health services. Working with a community psychiatrist, and a health planner from the city's united fund, the children spent two days talking about what the health needs of a community were, based on their own experiences. They then went to a new comprehensive health center and talked with doctors and nurses, while we consciously raised questions to compare this type of health care with the kind the children have for themselves. They then toured a pediatric hospital and participated in a brain wave experiment with a research physician.

As they did with the other two "subjects," the children met on another day to discuss freely what had gone before. Often these discussions were used by them to talk about what had taken place in their regular school; that is, they were very articulate about an institution which affected them closely, with which they were very involved, and they enjoyed these sessions. They needed the opportunity to talk.

At this point we raised the question with them of what they wanted to know. They had been told that we would do something with television and they all said that it was this that they wanted to do. Some wanted to go to the wax museum, some to the zoo. Two wanted to know about sex. In general, they appeared to see the trips as trips, and were not yet interested in formulating questions.

Art. In an effort to raise questions about art, we spent eight days at the Corcoran Art Gallery and School of Art. The minischoolers talked with the curator, director of the school, and other staff of the museum. One day they worked on drawings with the students of the Corcoran School.

Consumer affairs. A lawyer who has worked on consumer/class action litigation spoke with the children one afternoon and then proceeded to play a game with them to demonstrate that some stores charge more than others.

Television. Arrangements had been made with the University of Maryland to open their studios so that the Mini School could make a television program. The intention was to raise questions about mass media and its potential. The program was canceled after two afternoons during which time the children were escorted through the studios, but did no work on their own.

This had a very interesting result. The children were outraged and we discussed what alternatives were open to them to seek redress. They began to talk about television and obligations of the media to offer facilities for children. Last, the children began to ask questions about other institutions and to make suggestions about how to learn some answers. They wanted to know about the music industry—how records are made; they wanted to see a radio station; they wanted to see a new city—Columbia, Maryland.

The afterschool experiment was intended to answer two questions for us. First, would children respond positively to this type of education? Second, would institutions be accessible and open?

On the first score, it is clear that the children responded positively. They continued to attend, on an average of fifteen to eighteen students each day, although attendance was not compulsory, no fees had been paid, they were using their free afternoon hours when they usually enjoyed play activities, and the program was defined as "educational."

We had little expectation that the children would begin to "experience" politics and acquire a sense of political relations in an afterschool program. As one girl wrote about the hospital visit: "three people took a brain wave test. We learned the work of some of the instruments and the people. It was truly an experience."

Another wrote about the architecture series:

The architect was nice, and I think he knew how to get along with a lot of people. The city planner was not so nice and his wife was rude because she told her daughter all of the answers to all of the slides we saw at the city planner place where we were. The architect had a little place for his designing. The city planner had a big place to work because he needs a place to put all of his designs and a place where he could talk. He plans a city. Not just a house or one building like the architect does.

What these children dissected from the experiences were personal incidents, the tones of the people in the institutions. They remembered and could articulate feelings about small vignettes that were far from central to our experience on the trip. Wrote one boy in regard to the art gallery:

We went to many places where a lot of other things, I can't remember. But! one thing I do was when we went into the nude drawing [studio]. When we went in there was a young lady laying down, there was also a man drawing her she then got up and put a robe on.

The gallery elicited more than just this response, though. It was soundly denounced by every student. Each said that it was boring and that they did not enjoy being there. One day we left one half hour after arriving. What they said they did not like was the lack of art by and for children; art that had meaning for them. They did not like the fact that there was no snack bar, that they could not walk around freely, with some noise, and could not eat candy while walking through the museum.

What they learned about the museum then, was that it is not really made for people. It is a showplace. The director of the museum was very receptive to our presence, as was his special projects coordinator. But both sought to maintain the rules which strongly conflicted with felt physical needs of the children—the need to move about and the need to eat. Questions that were raised by us about who purchases art, what are their criteria, why do students paint what they do, and the like were not arresting for the children. But they did begin to experience decision-making, because of their physical needs, in an institution in Washington that shapes the way many people enjoy leisure time.

Which brings us to the second question—the receptivity of the institutions. All the institutions used had expressed initial strong interest. But most proved to be hostile to a free educational experience. The people in the institutions wanted children to be still and listen. (And the children often commented that when this demand was made, minischool was the same as regular school; that is, they saw regular school as that place where arbitrary, even unnatural demands were made on them.)

The problem was never adequately solved, in part because of organizational difficulties with the minischool itself (an unclear division of labor), and in part because institutions were not ready to open up. What we learned about institutions and the people in them was that a viable solution must rest on mutuality of needs. For example, the architect had been disturbed by the program because he had hoped to meet with other artists in Washington to discuss his and their experiences with the children. He was not concerned only about their education. It would have been possible to accommodate his needs with ours and thereby to maintain his support, although we did not. The point is that in order to work with institutions, the teachers in such a school must first know what the needs of the institutions are, and then work within the framework of those needs so long as they do not conflict with the education of the children. Ultimately, if there were many minischools, institutions would perforce change. Constantly open to scrutiny, giving up part of their resources directly to the education of the young (instead of through taxes as they do now), they would be returned to the people. People who are served by the institutions would gain a sense of control over them.

A full-time minischool—which is being planned—would bring children to institutions for most of a week, perhaps half a day each day. Children would stay with a particular area for five to seven weeks, and would begin to participate in the activities of the institutions. They would return to a home base (probably a storefront) where they could play, read, learn skills, and prepare materials. A "teacher" would be present at the institution to offer both support for the children's curiosity and some questioning, and at the store to provide assistance when needed. Some of the broad areas being planned include:

Health care: the causes of disease, the prevention of disease and accidents, hospitals, health centers, research laboratories, dental care, the costs of medicine, mental health.
Entertainment: the record industry, the sports industry, movie making and distribution—how each of these operate, who operates them, how decisions are made.

Food: how food is marketed and distributed, pricing, nutrition and cooking, food production (e.g., milling), waste disposal, advertising food.

Communication: the nature of mass communications and person-to-person communication, the post office and telephone company, the mass media, making a television program, writing a newspaper.

What did and can children learn from the type of school I have just described? What are the broader implications in terms of political change, in terms of education? What are the difficulties and how are they to be resolved?

There was an expected concern on the part of parents to whom we talked about the full-time program that children would not learn necessary skills. But in fact they will be offered the opportunity to learn skills if they see the need to learn them, and if they are curious. In order to develop a photo lab, they will learn chemistry. If they become curious about medicine, they will learn biology. Learning that derives from real curiosity will "stick" far better than forced learning.

The art gallery also demonstrated that children will begin to learn topics such as art. The minischool children talked about subject matter, color, and design as they went through the gallery and worked with art students.

Of course, the crucial question is, will they learn about political life this way? That is, after all, our raison d'être. This political life we talk about is indeed a large entity. It is the political tone of a society. It is the way in which we treat individuals and the way in which decisions are made. It is the set of priorities we have as a collectivity. To teach children directly about political life—if one would even know where to begin—would be nearly impossible. In many ways it is not even possible to articulate what it is we would want to teach exactly.

Yet we have a sense of what makes up this political life—what its parts are composed of. We sense that institutions are the parts. The way in which institutions operate in toto defines the political life of our society, for ours is a society where institutions predominate. The interdependence of parts in society is an interdependence of institutions, not individuals.

Institutions, too, are made up of parts. Their parts are people with skills. These are the skills which schools teach now—working and playing well with your neighbor, mathematics, obedience, spelling.

By starting at the middle—at the level of institutions—the mini-school can go both ways. It can offer children knowledge about skills while pointing to questions that bear on political life. Children will not acquire a sense of political life after experience with one or two institutions. But slowly a sense will emerge from repeated exposure. As Michael Polanyi explains, we learn our conceptions of whole entities by experiencing the parts.[5] Often we cannot even articulate what the whole is, though we know it well. For example, we can pick out a face in the crowd, yet cannot adequately describe it. All we may be able to do is describe some of its features.

That some concepts do not lend themselves to articulation, but form a tacit knowledge, is difficult for teachers to accept. This is especially true with felt experiences—for which there are no words that represent the experience well. I found in the minischool that there was a constant impulse to ask the children to draw larger implications, to say what they were feeling. It was much like a psychiatrist who hopes to have his patient verbalize thought so that the patient thereby gains insight from the articulation. A minischool requires great faith on the part of teachers that in fact something is really happening, that by accumulating experience children will see connections; that they do not need to be tested to see if they are perceiving reality.

Regarding the face in a crowd, knowing what constituted the face's features would even be less helpful—that is, to know what a brown beard is made of would hardly help us to identify a bearded face. As we get further from the whole, what we focus on has less meaning for us in terms of the whole.

Let us take the example of the General Motors Corporation, a blue chip stock. It is certainly true that many of the stockholders are decent folk. If they perceive that what they do harms someone, they usually stop what they are going. And in the case of institutional stockholders, if they perceive that what another company does is harmful to them they try to stop that company. Yet *Campaign GM* failed because a majority of the stock was voted to uphold the corporation's activities on behalf of pollution, war production, and producing unsafe automobiles. Stockholders simply did not perceive

---

[5]*The Tacit Dimension* (Garden City, N.Y.: Doubleday and Co., 1966); especially chaps. 1 and 2.

that GM's activities were inimical to their own health or to the health of others. They did see that the board of directors was managing their money so as to make a handsome profit. In effect, people cannot see the connection between parts in society. They do not see how their ownership of GM stock, and the desire to make a profit, conflicts with their desire to stay alive on the highway.

If people are taught to question the parts, instead of taught skills so that they can fit into a place in the parts, then the sum of their learning is likely to be a coherent whole. Moreover, by developing a framework based on reality, they could begin to understand new phenomena, they could place it in the appropriate context.

Perhaps most importantly, they would better understand the effects of changes and would then have a better sense of what changes would generate which desired consequences. In this way people could respond to change more positively, and produce change that would maintain continuity while promoting a good society. One goal of a minischool approach is to support and foster people's creativity so that they can create new and alternative institutions.

What is most crucial for a minischool in approaching institutions is that there is an intelligent scheme underpinning the choices. A teacher must choose which institutions the children will examine and he must have a sense of what questions are important; that is, the teacher must have a sense of political life, or at least a sense of how children can begin to perceive it.

While such structuring might be thought to be inimical to free inquiry by children, Dewey has argued that freedom does not come merely by loosening physical bonds. In providing only random, unstructured stimuli teachers would leave children less free, because they would be lost.[6] In having stimuli organized for them, children are assisted in experiencing the world. The function of teachers is to provide this type of assistance.

But how are teachers to acquire the necessary knowledge? One of the difficulties we had in the minischool was that the teachers did not comprehend the world very well; we did not have a sense of what institutions were doing, and how they related to other institutions. While we knew some broad concepts about bureaucracy, the congressional process, pluralist democracy, and the political system, we did

[6]Dewey, *Experience and Education*, chap. 7.

not know about the consequences which flowed from actions in the institutions or how work styles in the institutions related to the activities of the institutions. We had not thought about questions of mundane decision making: who decides what a house will look like; or even that this was the consequence of a conscious decision which reflected values. Mostly we had been taught to look at parts piecemeal; political science had not provoked us to think about parts in connection with each other. We look for commonalities in political science without seeing how the parts work in common. We make abstractions that do not have meaning in reality because we do not have a sense of what that reality is. The political world is one of conflicts over values and we are expected to sense this conflict by being detached. So we teach future teachers to ask the wrong questions and give them no sense of what might be the right questions.

What political science must do, then, if it is to do something about the political education of children, is reorient the questions that are considered important. The focus of a new political science should be to investigate how the parts work together, and which questions we must ask in order to pursue the investigation. The goal of this political science is to give back to people control over the institutions that govern their lives.

.12. Education Vouchers: A Proposal for Diversity and Choice

JUDITH AREEN and CHRISTOPHER JENCKS

EVER SINCE Adam Smith first proposed that the government finance education by giving parents money to hire teachers, the idea has enjoyed recurrent popularity. Smith's ideal of consumer sovereignty is built into a number of government programs for financing higher education, notably the G. I. Bill and the various state scholarship programs. Similarly a number of foreign countries have recognized the principle that parents who are dissatisfied with their local public school should be given money to establish alternatives.[1] In America however, public financing for elementary and secondary education has been largely confined to publicly managed schools. Parents who preferred a private alternative have had to pay the full cost out of their own pockets. As a result, we have almost no evidence on which to judge the merit of Smith's basic principle, namely, that if all parents are given the chance, they will look after their children's interests more effectively than will the state.

During the late 1960s, a series of developments in both public and nonpublic education led to a revival of interest in this approach to financing education. In December 1969, the U.S. Office of Economic Opportunity made a grant to the Center for the Study of Public Policy to support a detailed study of "education vouchers." This

[1] Estelle Fuchs, "The Free Schools of Denmark," *Saturday Review*, 16 August 1969.

article will summarize the major findings of that report and outline briefly the voucher plan proposed by the Center.[2]

THE CASE FOR CHOICE

Conservatives, liberals, and radicals all have complained at one time or another that the political mechanisms which supposedly make public schools accountable to their clients work clumsily and ineffectively.[3] Parents who think their children are getting inferior schooling can, it is true, take their grievances to the local school board or state legislature. If legislators and school boards are unresponsive to the complaints of enough citizens, they may eventually be unseated. But mounting an effective campaign to change local public schools takes an enormous investment of time, energy, and money. Dissatisfied though they may be, few parents have the political skill or commitment to solve their problems this way. As a result, effective control over the character of the public schools is largely vested in legislators, school boards, and educators—not in parents.[4]

[2]For a complete description of the Center proposal, see *Education Vouchers: A Report on Financing Education by Payments to Parents* (Cambridge, Mass.: Center for the Study of Public Policy, December 1970).

[3]For other discussions of the need to encourage alternatives to the present public schools, see Kenneth Clark, "Alternative Public School Systems," *Equal Educational Opportunity* (Cambridge Mass.: Harvard University Press, 1969); James S. Coleman, "Toward Open Schools," *Public Interest* (Fall 1967); Anthony Downs, "Competition and Community Schools" (written for a Brookings Institution Conference on the Community School held in Washington, D.C., December 12–13, 1968); Milton Friedman, "The Role of Government in Education," *Capitalism and Freedom* (Chicago: University of Chicago Press, 1962); Christopher Jencks, "Is the Public School Obsolete?" *Public Interest* (Winter 1966); Robert Krughoff, "Private Schools for the Public," *Education and Urban Society* (November 1969); Henry M. Levin, "The Failure of the Public Schools and the Free Market," *Urban Review* (6 June 1968); Theodore Sizer and Phillip Whitten, "A Proposal for a Poor Children's Bill of Rights," *Psychology Today* (August 1968); E. G. West, *Education and the State* (London, England: Institute of Economic Affairs, 1965).

[4]School management has been increasingly concentrated in the hands of fewer educators and school boards. The number of school districts, for example, declined from 127,531 in 1930, to less than 20,440 in 1968. The number of public elementary schools dropped from 238,000 to less than 73,000 in the same period. The concentration is particularly striking in urban areas. The New York City School Board alone is responsible for the education of more students than are found in the majority of individual states. Los Angeles has as many students as the state of South Carolina; Chicago as many as Kansas; Detroit as many as Maine. Nearly half of all the students in public schools are under the control of less than 4 percent of the school boards. See U.S. Department of Health, Education, and Welfare, *Digest of Educational Statistics* (1969).

If parents are to take genuine responsibility for their children's education, they cannot rely exclusively on political processes. They must also be able to take individual action on behalf of their own children. At present, only relatively affluent parents retain any effective control over the education of their children. Only they are free to move to areas with "good" public schools, where housing is usually expensive (and often unavailable to black families at any price). Only they can afford nonsectarian, private schooling. The average parent has no alternative to his local public school unless he happens to belong to one of the few denominations that maintain low-tuition schools.

Not only does today's public school have a captive clientele, but it in turn has become the captive of a political process designed to protect the interests of its clientele. Because attendance at a local public school is nearly compulsory, its activities have been subjected to extremely close political control. The state, the local board, and the school administration have established regulations to ensure that no school will do anything to offend anyone of political consequence. Virtually everything of consequence is either forbidden or compulsory. By trying to please everyone, however, the schools have often ended up pleasing no one.

A voucher system seeks to free schools from the restrictions that inevitably accompany their present monopolistic privileges. The idea of the system is relatively simple. A publicly accountable agency would issue a voucher to parents. The parents could take this voucher to any school that agreed to abide by the rules of the voucher system. Each school would turn its vouchers in for cash. Thus, parents would no longer be forced to send their children to the school around the corner simply because it was around the corner.

Even if no new schools were established under a voucher system, the responsiveness of existing public schools would probably increase. We believe that one of the most important advantages of a voucher system is that it would encourage diversity and choice *within the public system.* Indeed, if the public system were to begin matching students and schools on the basis of interest, rather than residence, one of the major objectives of a voucher system would be met without even involving the private sector. Popular public schools would get more applicants, and they would also have incentives to accommodate them, since extra students would bring extra funds.

Unpopular schools would have few students, and would either have to change their ways or close up and reopen under new management.

As this last possibility suggests, however, there are great advantages to involving the private sector in a voucher system if it is properly regulated. Only in this way is the over-all system likely to make room for fundamentally new initiatives that come from the bottom instead of the top. And only if private initiative is possible will the public sector feel real pressure to make room for kinds of education that are politically awkward but have a substantial constituency. If the private sector is involved, for example, parents can get together to create schools reflecting their special perspectives or their children's special needs. This should mean that the public schools will be more willing to do the same thing—though they will never be willing or able to accommodate *all* parental preferences. Similarly if the private sector is involved, educators with new ideas—or old ideas that are now out of fashion in the public schools—would also be able to set up their own schools. Entrepreneurs who thought they could teach children better and more inexpensively than the public schools would have an opportunity to do so. None of this ensures that every child would get the education he needs, but it would make such a result somewhat more likely than at present.

Beyond this, however, differences of opinion begin. Who would be eligible for vouchers? How would their value be determined? Would parents be allowed to supplement the vouchers from their own funds? What requirements would schools have to meet before cashing vouchers? What arrangements would be made for the children whom no school wanted to educate? Would church schools be eligible? Would schools promoting unorthodox political views be eligible? Once the advocates of vouchers begin to answer such questions, it becomes clear that the catch phrase around which they have united stands not for a single panacea, but for a multitude of controversial programs, many of which have little in common.

REVISED VOCABULARY

To understand the voucher plan recommended by the Center, it is useful to begin by reconsidering traditional notions about "public" and "private" education. Since the nineteenth century, we have classified schools as "public" if they were owned and operated by a governmental body. We go right on calling colleges "public," even when they charge tuition that many people cannot afford. We also call academically exclusive high schools "public," even if they have admissions requirements that only a handful of students can meet. We call neighborhood schools "public," despite the fact that nobody outside the neighborhood can attend them, and nobody can move into the neighborhood unless he has white skin and a down payment on a $30,000 home. And we call whole school systems "public," even though they refuse to give anyone information about what they are doing, how well they are doing it, and whether children are getting what their parents want. Conversely, we have always called schools "private" if they were owned and operated by private organizations. We have gone on calling these schools "private," even when, as sometimes happens, they are open to every applicant on a nondiscriminatory basis, charge no tuition, and make whatever information they have about themselves available to anyone who asks.

Definitions of this kind conceal as much as they reveal, for they classify schools entirely in terms of *who* runs them, not *how* they are run. If we want to describe what is really going on in education, there is much to be said for reversing this emphasis. We would then call a school "public" if it were open to everyone on a nondiscriminatory basis, if it charged no tuition, and if it provided full information about itself to anyone interested. Conversely, we would call any school "private" if it excluded applicants in a discriminatory way, charged tuition, or withheld information about itself. Admittedly, the question of who governs a school cannot be ignored entirely when categorizing the school, but it seems considerably less important than the question of how the school is governed.

Adopting this revised vocabulary, we propose a regulatory system with two underlying principles: (1) no public money should be used to support "private" schools; and (2) any group that operates a "public" school should be eligible for public subsidies.

THE PROPOSAL

Specifically, the Center has proposed an education voucher system (for *elementary* education) which would work in the following manner:

1. An Educational Voucher Agency (EVA) would be established to

administer the vouchers. Its governing board might be elected or appointed, but in either case it should be structured so as to represent minority as well as majority interests. The EVA might be an existing local board of education, or it might be an agency with a larger or smaller geographic jurisdiction. The EVA would receive all federal, state, and local education funds for which children in its area were eligible. It would pay this money to schools only in return for vouchers. (In addition, it would pay parents for children's transportation costs to the school of their choice.)

2. The EVA would issue a voucher to every familiy in its district with children of elementary school age. The value of the basic voucher would initially equal the per pupil expenditure of the public schools in the area. Schools that took children from families with below-average incomes would receive additional incentive payments. These "compensatory payments" might, for example, make the maximum payment for the poorest child worth double the basic voucher.

3. To become an "approved voucher school," eligible to cash vouchers, a school would have to:

   a. Accept each voucher as full payment for a child's education, charging no additional tuition.

   b. Accept any applicant so long as it had vacant places.

   c. If it had more applicants than places, fill at least half these places by picking applicants randomly and fill the other half in such a way as not to discriminate against ethnic minorities.

   d. Accept uniform standards established by the EVA regarding suspension and expulsion of students.

   e. Agree to make a wide variety of information abouts its facilities, teachers, program, and students available to the EVA and to the public.

   f. Maintain accounts of money received and disbursed in a form that would allow both parents and the EVA to determine where the money was going. Thus a school operated by the local board of education (a "public" school) would have to show how much of the money to which it was entitled on the basis of its vouchers was actually spent in that school. A school operated by a profit-making corporation would have to show how much of its income was going to the stockholders.

g. Meet existing state requirements for *private* schools regarding curriculum, staffing, and the like.

Control over policy in an approved voucher school might be vested in an existing local school board, a PTA, or any private group. Hopefully, no government restrictions would be placed on curriculum, staffing, and the like, except those already established for all private schools in a state.

4. Just as at present, the local board of education (which might or might not be the EVA) would be responsible for ensuring that there were enough places in publicly managed schools to accommodate every elementary school age child who did not want to attend a privately managed school. If a shortage of places developed for some reason, the board of education would have to open new schools or create more places in existing schools. (Alternatively, it might find ways to encourage privately managed schools to expand, presumably by getting the EVA to raise the value of the voucher.)

5. Every spring each family would submit to the EVA the name of the school to which it wanted to send each of its elementary school age children next fall. Any children already enrolled in a voucher school would be guaranteed a place, as would any sibling of a child enrolled in a voucher school. So long as it had room, a voucher school would be required to admit all students who listed it as a first choice. If it did not have room for all applicants, a school could fill half its places in whatever way it wanted, choosing among those who listed it as a first choice. It could not, however, select these applicants in such a way as to discriminate against racial minorities. It would then have to fill its remaining places by a lottery among the remaining applicants. All schools with unfilled places would report these to the EVA. All families whose children had not been admitted to their first-choice school would then choose an alternative school which still had vacancies. Vacancies would then be filled in the same manner as in the first round. This procedure would continue until every child had been admitted to a school.

6. Having enrolled their children in a school, parents would give their vouchers to the school. The school would send the vouchers to the EVA and would receive a check in return.

SOME CAVEATS

The voucher system outlined above is quite different from other systems now being advocated; it contains far more safeguards for the interests of disadvantaged children. A voucher system that does not include these or equally effective safeguards would be worse than no voucher system at all. Indeed, an unregulated voucher system could be the most serious setback for the education of disadvantaged children in the history of the United States. A properly regulated system, on the other hand, may have the potential to inaugurate a new era of innovation and reform in American schools.

One common objection to a voucher system of this kind is that many parents are too ignorant to make intelligent choices among schools. Giving parents a choice will, according to this argument, simply set in motion an educational equivalent of Gresham's Law, in which hucksterism and mediocre schooling drive out high-quality institutions. This argument seems especially plausible to those who envisage the entry of large numbers of profit-oriented firms into the educational marketplace. The argument is not, however, supported by much evidence. Existing private schools are sometimes mere diploma mills, but on the average their claims about themselves seem no more misleading, and the quality of the services they offer no lower, than in the public schools. And while some private schools are run by hucksters interested only in profit, this is the exception rather than the rule. There is no obvious reason to suppose that vouchers would change all this.

A second common objection to vouchers is that they would "destroy the public schools." Again, this seems far-fetched. If you look at the educational choices made by wealthy parents who can already afford whatever schooling they want for their children, you find that most still prefer their local public schools if these are at all adequate. Furthermore, most of those who now leave the public system do so in order to attend high-cost, exclusive private schools. While some wealthy parents would doubtless continue to patronize such schools, they would receive no subsidy under the proposed system.

Nonetheless, if you are willing to call every school "public" that is ultimately responsible to a public board of education, then there is little doubt that a voucher system would result in some shrinkage of the "public" sector and some growth of the "private" sector. If, on the other hand, you confine the label "public" to schools which are equally open to everyone within commuting distance, you discover that the so-called public sector includes relatively few public schools. Instead, racially exclusive suburbs and economically exclusive neighborhoods serve to ration access to good "public" schools in precisely the same way that admissions committees and tuition charges ration access to good "private" schools. If you begin to look at the distinction between public and private schooling in these terms, emphasizing accessibility rather than control, you are likely to conclude that a voucher system, far from destroying the public sector, would greatly expand it, since it would force large numbers of schools, public and private, to open their doors to outsiders.

A third objection to vouchers is that they would be available to children attending Catholic schools. This is not, of course, a necessary feature of a voucher system. The courts, a state legislature, or a local EVA could easily restrict participation to nonsectarian schools. Indeed, some state constitutions clearly require that this be done. The federal Constitution may also require such a restriction, but neither the language of the First Amendment nor the legal precedent is clear on this issue. The First Amendment's prohibition against an "establishment of religion" can be construed as barring payments to church schools, but the "free exercise of religion" clause can also be construed as requiring the state to treat church schools in precisely the same way as other private schools. The Supreme Court has never ruled on a case of this type (e.g., G.I. Bill payments to Catholic colleges or Medicare payments to Catholic hospitals). Until it does, the issue ought to be resolved on policy grounds. And since the available evidence indicates that Catholic schools have served their children no worse than public schools,[5] and perhaps slightly better, there seems no compelling reason to deny them the same financial support given other schools.

The most worrisome objection to a voucher system is that its success would depend on the EVA's willingness to regulate the marketplace vigorously. If vouchers were used on a large scale, state and

---

[5] Andrew Greeley and Peter Rossi, *The Education of Catholic Americans* (Chicago: Aldine Publishing Co., 1966).

local regulatory efforts might be uneven or even nonexistent. The regulations designed to prevent racial and economic discrimination seem especially likely to get watered down at the state and local level, or else to remain unenforced. This argument applies, however, to *any*, educational reform, and it also applies to the existing system. If you assume any given EVA will be controlled by overt or covert segregationists, you must also assume that this will be true of the local board of education. A board of education that wants to keep racist parents happy hardly needs vouchers to do so. It only needs to maintain the neighborhood school system. White parents who want their children to attend white schools will then find it quite quite simple to move to a white neighborhood where their children will be suitably segregated. Except perhaps in the South, neither the federal government, the state government, nor the judiciary is likely to prevent this traditional practice.

If, on the other hand, you assume a board which is anxious to eliminate segregation, either for legal, financial, or political reasons, you must also assume that the EVA would be subject to the same pressures. And if an EVA is anxious to eliminate segregation, it will have no difficulty devising regulations to achieve this end. Furthermore, the legal precedents to date suggest that the federal courts will be more stringent in applying the Fourteenth Amendment to voucher systems than to neighborhood school systems. The courts have repeatedly thrown out voucher systems designed to maintain segregation, whereas they have shown no such general willingness to ban the neighborhood school. Outside the South, then, those who believe in integration may actually have an easier time achieving this goal with voucher systems than they will with the existing public school system. Certainly, the average black parent's access to integrated schools would be increased under a voucher system of the kind proposed by the Center. Black parents could apply to any school in the system, and the proportion of blacks admitted would have to be at least equal to the proportion who applied. This gives the average black parent a far better chance of having their children attend an integrated school than at present. There is, of course, no way to compel black parents to take advantage of this opportunity by actually applying to schools that enroll whites. But the opportunity would be there for all.

PROPOSED DEMONSTRATION

The voucher plan described above could in theory be adopted by any local or state jurisdiction interested in increasing diversity in schools and parental choice in selection of schools. In the long run it is not much more expensive than the present system. But the Center has recommended to OEO that a demonstration project be financed first, carefully regulated to ensure that the proposed rules are followed, and carefully monitored to test the effects of dispensing public education funds in the form of vouchers. The Center has recommended that at least ten thousand elementary school students be included in the demonstration site, and that the demonstration city (or part of a city) should contain a population which is racially and economically heterogeneous. Ideally some alternative schools should already exist in the selected area, and the prospects for beginning other new schools should be reasonable.

In March 1970, staff and consultants of the Center embarked on an extensive investigation of the feasibility of conducting a demonstration project. Superintendents of schools in all cities with a population in excess of 150,000 in the 1960 Census, which were not under court or administrative order to desegregate their school systems, were contacted by mail. Expressions of interest were followed up. Meetings were held in interested cities around the country. Local and state school administrators were contacted, as were interested school officials, teachers' groups, parents' organizations, and nonpublic schools.

As of November 1, 1970, five communities had decided to apply for preliminary planning funds. If one or more of these cities decides to conduct a demonstration of the voucher program, we may have a chance at last to test what contributions a voucher program could make to improving the quality of education available to children in this country. If, on the other hand, the National Education Association and the American Federation of Teachers have their way, we shall have no test at all.

.13. *Why We Must Disestablish School*

IVAN ILLICH

MANY STUDENTS, especially those who are poor, intuitively know what the schools do for them. They school them to confuse process and substance. Once these become blurred, a new logic is assumed: the more treatment there is, the better are the results; or, escalation leads to success. The pupil is thereby "schooled" to confuse teaching with learning, grade advancement with education, a diploma with competence, and fluency with the ability to say something new. His imagination is "schooled" to accept service in place of value. Medical treatment is mistaken for health care, social work for the improvement of community life, police protection for safety, military poise for national security, the rat race for productive work. Health, learning, dignity, independence, and creative endeavor are defined as little more than the performance of the institutions which claim to serve these ends, and their improvement is made to depend on allocating more resources to the management of hospitals, schools, and other agencies in question.

In these essays,[1] I will show that the institutionalization of values leads inevitably to physical pollution, social polarization, and psychological impotence: three dimensions in a process of global degradation and modernized misery. I will explain how this process of degradation is accelerated when nonmaterial needs are transformed into demands for commodities; when health, education, personal mobility, welfare,

---

[1]*Deschooling Society* (New York: Harper & Row, 1971).

250

or psychological healing are defined as the result of services or "treatments." I do this because I believe that most of the research now going on about the future tends to advocate further increases in the institutionalization of values and that we must define conditions which would permit precisely the contrary to happen. We need research on the possible use of technology to create institutions which serve personal, creative, and autonomous interaction and the emergence of values which cannot be substantially controlled by technocrats. We need counterfoil research to current futurology.

I want to raise the general question of the mutual definition of man's nature and the nature of modern institutions which characterizes our world view and language. To do so, I have chosen the school as my paradigm, and I therefore deal only indirectly with other bureaucratic agencies of the corporate state: the consumer-family, the party, the army, the church, the media. My analysis of the hidden curriculum of school should make it evident that public education would profit from the deschooling of society, just as family life, politics, security, faith, and communication would profit from an analogous process.

I begin my analysis, in this essay, by trying to convey what the deschooling of a schooled society might mean. In this context, it should be easier to understand my choice of the five specific aspects relevant to this process with which I deal in the subsequent chapters.[2]

Not only education but social reality itself has become schooled. It costs roughly the same to school both rich and poor in the same dependency. The yearly expenditure per pupil in the slums and in the rich suburbs of any one of twenty U.S. cities lies in the same range— and sometimes is favorable to the poor.[3] Rich and poor alike depend on schools and hospitals which guide their lives, form their world view, and define for them what is legitimate and what is not. Both view doctoring oneself as irresponsible, learning on one's own as unreliable, and community organization, when not paid for by those in authority, as a form of aggression or subversion. For both groups the reliance on institutional treatment renders independent accom-

---

[2]Ibid.

[3]Penrose B. Jackson, *Trends in Elementary and Secondary Education Expenditures: Central City and Suburban Comparisons 1965 to 1968* (Washington, D.C.: U.S. Office of Education, Office of Program and Planning Evaluation, June 1969).

plishment suspect. The progressive underdevelopment of self- and community-reliance is even more typical in Westchester than it is in the northeast of Brazil. Everywhere not only education but society as a whole needs "deschooling."

Welfare bureaucracies claim a professional, political, and financial monopoly over the social imagination, setting standards of what is valuable and what is feasible. This monopoly is at the root of the modernization of poverty. Every simple need to which an institutional answer is found permits the invention of a new class of poor and a new definition of poverty. Ten years ago in Mexico it was the normal thing to be born and to die in one's own home and to be buried by one's friends. Only the soul's needs were taken care of by the institutional church. Now to begin and end life at home become signs either of poverty or of special privilege. Dying and death have come under the institutional management of doctors and undertakers.

Once basic needs have been translated by a society into demands for scientifically produced commodities, poverty is defined by standards which the technocrats can change at will. Poverty then refers to those who have fallen behind an advertised ideal of consumption in some important respect. In Mexico the poor are those who lack three years of schooling, and in New York they are those who lack twelve.

The poor have always been socially powerless. The increasing reliance on institutional care adds a new dimension to their helplessness: psychological impotence, the inability to fend for themselves. Peasants on the high plateau of the Andes are exploited by the landlord and the merchant—once they settle in Lima they are, in addition, dependent on political bosses, and disabled by their lack of schooling. Modernized poverty combines the lack of power over circumstances with a loss of personal potency. This modernization of poverty is a world-wide phenomenon, and lies at the root of contemporary underdevelopment. Of course it appears under different guises in rich and in poor countries.

It is probably most intensely felt in U.S. cities. Nowhere else is poverty treated at greater cost. Nowhere else does the treatment of poverty produce so much dependence, anger, frustration, and further demands. And nowhere else should it be so evident that poverty—

once it has become modernized—has become resistant to treatment with dollars alone and requires an institutional revolution.

Today in the United States the black and even the migrant can aspire to a level of professional treatment which would have been unthinkable two generations ago, and which seems grotesque to most people in the Third World. For instance, the U.S. poor can count on a truant officer to return their children to school until they reach seventeen, or on a doctor to assign them to a hospital bed which costs sixty dollars per day—the equivalent of three months' income for a majority of the people in the world. But such care only makes them dependent on more treatment, and renders them increasingly incapable of organizing their own lives around their own experiences and resources within their own communities.

The poor in the United States are in a unique position to speak about the predicament which threatens all the poor in a modernizing world. They are making the discovery that no amount of dollars can remove the inherent destructiveness of welfare institutions, once the professional hierarchies of these institutions have convinced society that their ministrations are morally necessary. The poor in the U.S. inner city can demonstrate from their own experience the fallacy on which social legislation in a "schooled" society is built.

Supreme Court Justice William O. Douglas observed that "the only way to establish an institution is to finance it." The corollary is also true. Only by channeling dollars away from the institutions which now treat health, education, and welfare can the further improverishment resulting from their disabling side effects be stopped.

This must be kept in mind when we evaluate federal aid programs. As a case in point, between 1965 and 1968 over $3 billion were spent in U.S. schools to offset the disadvantages of about 6 million children. The program is known as Title I. It is the most expensive compensatory program ever attempted anywhere in education, yet no significant improvement can be detected in the learning of these "disadvantaged" children. Compared with their classmates from middle-income homes, they have fallen further behind. Moreover, in the course of this program, professionals discovered an additional 10 million children laboring under economic and educational handicaps. More reasons for claiming more federal funds are now at hand.

This total failure to improve the education of the poor despite more costly treatment can be explained in three ways:

1. Three billion dollars are insufficient to improve the performance of 6 million children by a measurable amount; or
2. The money was incompetently spent: different curricula, better administration, further concentration of the funds on the poor child, and more research are needed and would do the trick; or
3. Educational disadvantage cannot be cured by relying on education within the school.

The first is certainly true so long as the money has been spent through the school budget. The money indeed went to the schools which contained most of the disadvantaged children, but it was not spent on the poor children themselves. These children for whom the money was intended comprised only about half of those who were attending the schools that added the federal subsidies to their budgets. Thus the money was spent for custodial care, indoctrination and the selection of social roles, as well as education, all of which functions are inextricably mingled in the physical plants, curricula, teachers, administrators, and other key components of these schools, and, therefore, in their budgets.

The added funds enabled schools to cater disproportionately to the satisfaction of the relatively richer children who were "disadvantaged" by having to attend school in the company of the poor. At best a small fraction of each dollar intended to remedy a poor child's disadvantages in learning could reach the child through the school budget.

It might be equally true that the money was incompetently spent. But even unusual incompetence cannot beat that of the school system. Schools by their very structure resist the concentration of privilege on those otherwise disadvantaged. Special curricula, separate classes, or longer hours only constitute more discrimination at a higher cost.

Taxpayers are not yet accustomed to permitting $3 billion to vanish from the Department of Health, Education, and Welfare as if it were the Pentagon. The present Administration may believe that it can afford the wrath of educators. Middle-class Americans have nothing to lose if the program is cut. Poor parents think they do, but, even more, they are demanding control of the funds meant for their children. A logical way of cutting the budget and, one hopes, of increasing benefits is a system of tuition grants such as that proposed by Milton Friedman and others. Funds would be channeled to the beneficiary, enabling him to buy his share of the schooling of his choice. If such credit were limited to purchases which fit into a school curriculum, it would tend to provide greater equality of treatment, but would not thereby increase the equality of social claims.

It should be obvious that even with schools of equal quality a poor child can seldom catch up with a rich one. Even if they attend equal schools and begin at the same age, poor children lack most of the educational opportunities which are casually available to the middle-class child. These advantages range from conversation and books in the home to vacation travel and a different sense of oneself, and apply, for the child who enjoys them, both in and out of school. So the poorer student will generally fall behind so long as he depends on school for advancement or learning. The poor need funds to enable them to learn, not to get certified for the treatment of their alleged disproportionate deficiencies.

All this is true in poor nations as well as in rich ones, but there it appears under a different guise. Modernized poverty in poor nations affects more people more visibly but also—for the moment—more superficially. Two-thirds of all children in Latin America leave school before finishing the fifth grade, but these *desertores* are not therefore as badly off as they would be in the United States.

Few countries today remain victims of classical poverty, which was stable and less disabling. Most countries in Latin America have reached the "takeoff" point toward economic development and competitive consumption, and thereby toward modernized poverty: their citizens have learned to think rich and live poor. Their laws make six to ten years of school obligatory. Not only in Argentina but also in Mexico or Brazil the average citizen defines an adequate education by North American standards, even though the chance of getting such prolonged schooling is limited to a tiny minority. In these countries the majority is already hooked on school, that is, they are schooled in a sense of inferiority toward the better-schooled. Their fanaticism in favor of school makes it possible to exploit them doubly: it permits increasing allocation of public funds for the education of a few and increasing acceptance of social control by the many.

Paradoxically, the belief that universal schooling is absolutely necessary is most firmly held in those countries where the fewest people have been—and will be—served by schools. Yet in Latin America different paths toward education could still be taken by the majority of parents and children. Proportionately, national savings invested in schools and teachers might be higher than in rich countries, but these investments are totally insufficient to serve the majority by making even four years of school attendance possible. Fidel Castro talks as if he wanted to go in the direction of deschooling when he promises that by 1980 Cuba will be able to dissolve its university since all of life in Cuba will be an educational experience. At the grammar school and high school level, however, Cuba, like all other Latin American countries, acts as though passage through a period defined as the "school age" were an unquestionable goal for all, delayed merely by a temporary shortage of resources.

The twin deceptions of increased treatment, as actually provided in the United States—and as merely promised in Latin America— complement each other. The Northern poor are being disabled by the same twelve-year treatment whose lack brands the Southern poor as hopelessly backward. Neither in North America nor in Latin America do the poor get equality from obligatory schools. But in both places the mere existence of school discourages and disables the poor from taking control of their own learning. All over the world the school has an anti-educational effect on society: school is recognized as the institution which specializes in education. The failures of school are taken by most people as a proof that education is a very costly, very complex, always arcane, and frequently almost impossible task.

School appropriates the money, men, and good will available for education and in addition discourages other institutions from assuming educational tasks. Work, leisure, politics, city living, and even family life depend on schools for the habits and knowledge they presuppose, instead of becoming themselves the means of education. Simultaneously both schools and the other institutions which depend on them are priced out of the market.

In the United States the per capita costs of schooling have risen almost as fast as the cost of medical treatment. But increased treatment by both doctors and teachers has shown steadily declining results. Medical expenses concentrated on those above forty-five have doubled several times over a period of forty years with a resulting 3 percent increase in life expectancy in men. The increase in educational expenditures has produced even stranger results; otherwise President Nixon could not have been moved this spring to promise that every child shall soon have the "Right to Read" before leaving school.

In the United States it would take $80 billion per year to provide what educators regard as equal treatment for all in grammar and high school. This is well over twice the $36 billion now being spent. Independent cost projections prepared at HEW and the University of Florida indicate that by 1974 the comparable figures will be $107 billion as against the $45 billion now projected, and these figures wholly omit the enormous costs of what is called "higher education," for which demand is growing even faster. The United States, which spent nearly $80 billion in 1969 for "defense" including its deployment in Vietnam, is obviously too poor to provide equal schooling. The President's committee for the study of school finance should ask not how to support or how to trim such increasing costs, but how they can be avoided.

Equal obligatory schooling must be recognized as at least economically unfeasible. In Latin America the amount of public money spent on each graduate student is between 350 and 1,500 times the amount spent on the median citizen (that is, the citizen who holds the middle ground between the poorest and the richest). In the United States the discrepancy is smaller, but the discrimination is keener. The richest parents, some 10 percent, can afford private education for their children and help them to benefit from foundation grants. But in addition they obtain ten times the per capita amount of public funds if this is compared with the per capita expenditure made on the children of the 10 percent who are poorest. The principal reasons for this are that rich children stay longer in school, that a year in a university is disproportionately more expensive than a year in high school, and that most private universities depend—at least indirectly —on tax-derived finances.

Obligatory schooling inevitably polarizes a society; it also grades the nations of the world according to an international caste system. Countries are rated like castes whose educational dignity is determined by the average years of schooling of its citizens, a rating which is closely related to per capita gross national product, and much more painful.

The paradox of the schools is evident: increased expenditure escalates their destructiveness at home and abroad. This paradox must be made a public issue. It is now generally accepted that the physical environment will soon be destroyed by biochemical pollution unless we reverse current trends in the production of physical goods. It should also be recognized that social and personal life is threatened equally by HEW pollution, the inevitable byproduct of obligatory and competitive consumption of welfare.

The escalation of the schools is as destructive as the escalation of weapons but less visibly so. Everywhere in the world school costs have risen faster than enrollments and faster than the GNP; everywhere expenditures on school fall even further behind the expectations of parents, teachers, and pupils. Everywhere this situation discourages both the motivation and the financing for large-scale planning for nonschooled learning. The United States is proving to the world that no country can be rich enough to afford a school system that meets the demands this same system creates simply by existing, because a successful school system schools parents and pupils to the supreme value of a larger school system, the cost of which increases disproportionately as higher grades are in demand and become scarce.

Rather than calling equal schooling temporarily unfeasible, we must recognize that it is, in principle, economically absurd, and that to attempt it is intellectually emasculating, socially polarizing, and destructive of the credibility of the political system which promotes it. The ideology of obligatory schooling admits of no logical limits. The White House recently provided a good example. Dr. Hutschnecker, the "psychiatrist" who treated Mr. Nixon before he was qualified as a candidate, recommended to the President that all children between the ages of six and eight be professionally examined to ferret out those who have destructive tendencies, and that obligatory treatment be provided for them. If necessary, their reeducation in special institutions should be required. This memorandum from his doctor the President sent for evaluation to HEW. Indeed, preventive concentration camps for predelinquents would be a logical improvement over the school system.

Equal educational opportunity is, indeed, both a desirable and a feasible goal, but to equate this with obligatory schooling is to confuse salvation with the Church. School has become the world religion of a modernized proletariat, and makes futile promises of salvation to the poor of the technological age. The nation-state has adopted it, drafting all citizens into a graded curriculum leading to sequential diplomas not unlike the initiation rituals and hieratic promotions of former times. The modern state has assumed the duty of enforcing the judgment of its educators through well-meant truant officers and job requirements, much as did the Spanish kings who enforced the judgments of their theologians through the conquistadors and the Inquisition.

Two centuries ago the United States led the world in a movement to disestablish the monopoly of a single church. Now we need the constitutional disestablishment of the monopoly of the school, and thereby of a system which legally combines prejudice with discrimination. The first article of a bill of rights for a modern, humanist society would correspond to the First Amendment to the U.S. Constitution: "The State shall make no law with respect to the establishment of education." There shall be no ritual obligatory for all.

To make this disestablishment effective, we need a law forbidding discrimination in hiring, voting, or admission to centers of learning based on previous attendance at some curriculum. This guarantee would not exclude performance tests of competence for a function or role, but would remove the present absurd discrimination in favor of the person who learns a given skill with the largest expenditure of public funds or—what is equally likely—has been able to obtain a diploma which has no relation to any useful skill or job. Only by protecting the citizen from being disqualified by anything in his career in school can a constitutional disestablishment of school become psychologically effective.

Neither learning nor justice is promoted by schooling because educators insist on packaging instruction with certification. Learning and the assignment of social roles are melted into schooling. Yet to learn means to acquire a new skill or insight, while promotion depends on an opinion which others have formed. Learning frequently is the result of instruction, but selection for a role or category in the job market increasingly depends on mere length of attendance.

Instruction is the choice of circumstances which facilitate learning. Roles are assigned by setting a curriculum of conditions which the candidate must meet if he is to make the grade. School links instruction—but not learning—to these roles. This is neither reasonable nor liberating. It is not reasonable because it does not link relevant qualities or competences to roles, but rather the process by which such qualities are supposed to be acquired. It is not liberating or educational because school reserves instruction to those whose every step in learning fits previously approved measures of social control.

Curriculum has always been used to assign social rank. At times it could be prenatal: karma ascribes you to a caste and lineage to the aristocracy. Curriculum could take the form of a ritual, or sequential sacred ordinations, or it could consist of a succession of feats in war or hunting, or further advancement could be made to depend on a series of previous princely favors. Universal schooling was meant to detach role assignment from personal life history: it was meant to give everybody an equal chance to any office. Even now many people wrongly believe that school ensures the dependence of public trust on relevant learning achievements. However, instead of equalizing chances, the school system has monopolized their distribution.

To detach competence from curriculum, inquiries into a man's learning history must be made taboo, like inquiries into his political affiliation, church attendance, lineage, sex habits, or racial background. Laws forbidding discrimination on the basis of prior schooling must be enacted. Laws, of course, cannot stop prejudice against the unschooled—nor are they meant to force anyone to intermarry with an autodidact—but they can discourage unjustified discrimination.

A second major illusion on which the school system rests is that most learning is the result of teaching. Teaching, it is true, may contribute to certain kinds of learning under certain circumstances. But most people acquire most of their knowledge outside school, and in school only insofar as school, in a few rich countries, has become their place of confinement during an increasing part of their lives.

Most learning happens casually, and even most intentional learning is not the result of programmed instruction. Normal children learn their first language casually, although faster if their parents pay attention to them. Most people who learn a second language well, do so as a result of odd circumstances and not of sequential teaching. They go to live with their grandparents, they travel, or they fall in love with a foreigner. Fluency in reading is also more often than not a result of such extracurricular activities. Most people who read widely, and with pleasure, merely believe that they learned to do so in school; when challenged, they easily discard this illusion.

But the fact that a great deal of learning even now seems to happen casually and as a byproduct of some other activity defined as work or leisure does not mean that planned learning does not benefit from planned instruction and that both do not stand in need of improvement. The strongly motivated student who is faced with the task of acquiring a new and complex skill may benefit greatly from the discipline now associated with the old-fashioned schoolmaster who taught reading, Hebrew, catechism, or multiplication by rote. School has now made this kind of drill teaching rare and disreputable, yet there are many skills which a motivated student with normal aptitude can master in a matter of a few months if taught in this traditional way. This is as true of codes as of their encipherment; of second and third languages as of reading and writing; and equally of special languages such as algebra, computer programming, chemical analysis, or of manual skills like typing, watchmaking, plumbing, and wiring, TV repair; or for that matter dancing, driving, and diving.

In certain cases acceptance into a learning program aimed at a specific skill might presuppose competence in some other skill, but it should certainly not be made to depend upon the process by which such prerequisite skills were acquired. TV repair presupposes literacy and some math; diving, good swimming; and driving, very little of either.

Progress in learning skills is measurable. The optimum resources in time and materials needed by an average motivated adult can be easily estimated. The cost of teaching a second Western European language to a high level of fluency ranges between $400 and $600 in the United States, and for an Oriental tongue the time needed for instruction might be doubled. This would still be very little compared with the cost of twelve years of schooling in New York City (a condition for acceptance of a worker into the Sanitation Department)

—almost $15,000. No doubt not only the teacher but also the printer and the pharmacist protect their trades through the public illusion that training for them is very expensive.

At present schools preempt most educational funds. Drill instruction which costs less than comparable schooling is now a privilege of those rich enough to bypass the schools, and those whom either the army or big business sends through in-service training. In a program of progressive deschooling of U.S. education, at first the resources available for drill training would be limited. But ultimately there should be no obstacle for anyone at any time of his life to be able to choose instruction among hundreds of definable skills at public expense.

Right now educational credit good at any skill center could be provided in limited amounts for people of all ages, and not just to the poor. I envisage such credit in the form of an educational passport or an "edu-credit card" provided to each citizen at birth. In order to favor the poor, who probably would not use their yearly grants early in life, a provision could be made that interest accrued to later users of cumulated "entitlements." Such credits would permit most people to acquire the skills most in demand, at their convenience, better, faster, cheaper, and with fewer undesirable side effects than in school.

Potential skill teachers are never scarce for long because, on the one hand, demand for a skill grows only with its performance within a community and, on the other, a man exercising a skill could also teach it. But, at present, those using skills which are in demand and do require a human teacher are discouraged from sharing these skills with others. This is done either by teachers who monopolize the licenses or by unions which protect their trade interests. Skill centers which would be judged by customers on their results, and not on the personnel they employ or the process they use, would open unsuspected working opportunities, frequently even for those who are now considered unemployable. Indeed, there is no reason why such skill centers should not be at the work place itself, with the employer and his work force supplying instruction as well as jobs to those who choose to use their educational credits in this way.

In 1956 there arose a need to teach Spanish quickly to several hundred teachers, social workers, and ministers from the New York

Archdiocese so that they could communicate with Puerto Ricans. My friend Gerry Morris announced over a Spanish radio station that he needed native speakers from Harlem. Next day some two hundred teen-agers lined up in front of his office, and he selected four dozen of them—many of them school dropouts. He trained them in the use of the U.S. Foreign Service Institute (FSI) Spanish manual, designed for use by linguists with graduate training, and within a week his teachers were on their own—each in charge of four New Yorkers who wanted to speak the language. Within six months the mission was accomplished. Cardinal Spellman could claim that he had 127 parishes in which at least three staff members could communicate in Spanish. No school program could have matched these results.

Skill teachers are made scarce by the belief in the value of licenses. Certification constitutes a form of market manipulation and is plausible only to a schooled mind. Most teachers of arts and trades are less skillful, less inventive, and less communicative than the best craftsmen and tradesmen. Most high school teachers of Spanish or French do not speak the language as correctly as their pupils might after half a year of competent drills. Experiments conducted by Angel Quintero in Puerto Rico suggest that many young teen-agers, if given the proper incentives, programs, and access to tools, are better than most schoolteachers at introducing their peers to the scientific exploration of plants, stars, and matter, and to the discovery of how and why a motor or a radio functions.

Opportunities for skill-learning can be vastly multiplied if we open the "market." This depends on matching the right teacher with the right student when he is highly motivated in an intelligent program, without the constraint of curriculum.

Free and competing drill instruction is a subversive blasphemy to the orthodox educator. It dissociates the acquisition of skills from "humane" education, which schools package together, and thus it promotes unlicensed learning no less than unlicensed teaching for unpredictable purposes.

There is currently a proposal on record which seems at first to make a great deal of sense. It has been prepared by Christopher Jencks of the Center for the Study of Public Policy and is sponsored by the Office of Economic Opportunity. It proposes to put educational "entitlements" or tuition grants into the hands of parents and students for expenditure in the schools of their choice. Such individual entitlements could indeed be an important step in the right direction. We need a guarantee of the right of each citizen to an equal share of tax-derived educational resources, the right to verify this share, and the right to sue for it if denied. It is one form of a guarantee against regressive taxation.

The Jencks proposal, however, begins with the ominous statement that "conservatives, liberals, and radicals have all complained at one time or another that the American educational system gives professional educators too little incentive to provide high quality education to most children." The proposal condemns itself by proposing tuition grants which would have to be spent on schooling.

This is like giving a lame man a pair of crutches and stipulating that he use them only if the ends are tied together. As the proposal for tuition grants now stands, it plays into the hands not only of the professional educators but of racists, promoters of religious schools, and others whose interests are socially divisive. Above all, educational entitlements restricted to use within schools play into the hands of all those who want to continue to live in a society in which social advancement is tied not to proven knowledge but to the learning pedigree by which it is supposedly acquired. This discrimination in favor of schools which dominates Jencks's discussion on refinancing education could discredit one of the most critically needed principles for educational reform: the return of initiative and accountability for learning to the learner or his most immediate tutor.

The deschooling of society implies a recognition of the two-faced nature of learning. An insistence on skill drill alone could be a disaster; equal emphasis must be placed on other kinds of learning. But if schools are the wrong places for learning a skill, they are even worse places for getting an education. School does both tasks badly, partly because it does not distinguish between them. School is inefficient in skill instruction especially because it is curricular. In most schools a program which is meant to improve one skill is chained always to another irrelevant task. History is tied to advancement in math, and class attendance to the right to use the playground.

Schools are even less efficient in the arrangement of the circumstances which encourage the open-ended, exploratory use of acquired skills, for which I will reserve the term "liberal education." The main reason for this is that school is obligatory and becomes schooling for schooling's sake: an enforced stay in the company of teachers, which pays off in the doubtful privilege of more such company. Just as skill instruction must be freed from curricular restraints, so must liberal education be dissociated from obligatory attendance. Both skill-learning and education for inventive and creative behavior can be aided by institutional arrangement, but they are of a different, frequently opposed nature.

Most skills can be acquired and improved by drills, because skill implies the mastery of definable and predictable behavior. Skill instruction can rely, therefore, on the simulation of circumstances in which the skill will be used. Education in the exploratory and creative use of skills, however, cannot rely on drills. Education can be the outcome of instruction, though instruction of a kind fundamentally opposed to drill. It relies on the relationship between partners who already have some of the keys which give access to memories stored in and by the community. It relies on the critical intent of all those who use memories creatively. It relies on the surprise of the unexpected question which opens new doors for the inquirer and his partner.

The skill instructor relies on the arrangement of set circumstances which permit the learner to develop standard responses. The educational guide or master is concerned with helping matching partners to meet so that learning can take place. He matches individuals starting from their own, unresolved questions. At the most he helps the pupil to formulate his puzzlement since only a clear statement will give him the power to find his match, moved like him, at the moment, to explore the same issue in the same context.

Matching partners for educational purposes initially seems more difficult to imagine than finding skill instructors and partners for a game. One reason is the deep fear which school has implanted in us, a fear which makes us censorious. The unlicensed exchange of skills —even undesirable skills—is more predictable and therefore seems less dangerous than the unlimited opportunity for meeting among people who share an issue which for them, at the moment, is socially, intellectually, and emotionally important.

The Brazilian teacher Paulo Freire knows this from experience. He discovered that any adult can begin to read in a matter of forty hours if the first words he deciphers are charged with political meaning. Freire trains his teachers to move into a village and to discover the words which designate current important issues, such as the access to a well or the compound interest on the debts owed to the *patron*. In the evening the villagers meet for the discussion of these key words. They begin to realize that each word stays on the blackboard even after its sound has faded. The letters continue to unlock reality and to make it manageable as a problem. I have frequently witnessed how discussants grow in social awareness and how they are impelled to take political action as fast as they learn to read. They seem to take reality into their hands as they write it down.

I remember the man who complained about the weight of pencils: they were difficult to handle because they did not weigh as much as a shovel; and I remember another who on his way to work stopped with his companions and wrote the word they were discussing with his hoe on the ground: "*agua*." Since 1962 my friend Freire has moved from exile to exile, mainly because he refuses to conduct his sessions around words which are pre-selected by approved educators, rather than those which his discussants bring to the class.

The educational matchmaking among people who have been successfully schooled is a different task. Those who do not need such assistance are a minority, even among the readers of serious journals. The majority cannot and should not be rallied for discussion around a slogan, a word, or a picture. But the idea remains the same: they should be able to meet around a problem chosen and defined by their own initiative. Creative, exploratory learning requires peers currently puzzled about the same terms or problems. Large universities make the futile attempt to match them by multiplying their courses, and they generally fail since they are bound to curriculum, course structure, and bureaucratic administration. In schools, including universities, most resources are spent to purchase the time and motivation of a limited number of people to take up predetermined problems in a ritually defined setting. The most radical alternative to school would be a network or service which gave each man the same opportunity to share his current concern with others motivated by the same concern.

Let me give, as an example of what I mean, a description of how an intellectual match might work in New York City. Each man, at any given moment and at a minimum price, could identify himself to a computer with his address and telephone number, indicating the book, article, film, or recording on which he seeks a partner for discussion. Within days he could receive by mail the list of others who recently had taken the same initiative. This list would enable him by telephone to arrange for a meeting with persons who initially would be known exclusively by the fact that they requested a dialogue about the same subject.

Matching people according to their interest in a particular title is radically simple. It permits identification only on the basis of a mutual desire to discuss a statement recorded by a third person, and it leaves the initiative of arranging the meeting to the individual. Three objections are usually raised against this skeletal purity. I take them up not only to clarify the theory that I want to illustrate by my proposal—for they highlight the deepseated resistance to deschooling education, to separating learning from social control—but also because they may help to suggest existing resources which are not now used for learning purposes.

The first objection is: Why cannot self-identification be based also on an *idea* or an issue? Certainly such subjective terms could also be used in a computer system. Political parties, churches, unions, clubs, neighborhood centers, and professional societies already organize their educational activities in this way and in effect they act as schools. They all match people in order to explore certain "themes;" and these are dealt with in courses, seminars, and curricula in which presumed "common interests" are prepackaged. Such theme-matching is by definition teacher-centered: it requires an authoritarian presence to define for the participants the starting point for their discussion.

By contrast, matching by the title of a book, film, etc., in its pure form leaves it to the author to define the special language, the terms, and the framework within which a given problem or fact is stated; and it enables those who accept this starting point to identify themselves to one another. For instance, matching people around the idea of "cultural revolution" usually leads either to confusion or to demagoguery. On the other hand, matching those interested in helping each other understand a specific article by Mao, Marcuse, Freud, or Goodman stands in the great tradition of liberal learning from

Plato's Dialogues, which are built around presumed statements by Socrates, to Aquinas's commentaries on Peter the Lombard. The idea of matching by title is thus radically different from the theory on which the "Great Books" clubs, for example, were built: instead of relying on the selection by some Chicago professors, any two partners can choose any book for further analysis.

The second objection asks: Why not let the identification of match seekers include information on age, background, world view, competence, experience, or other defining characteristics? Again, there is no reason why such discriminatory restrictions could not and should not be built into some of the many universities—with or without walls—which could use title-matching as their basic organizational device. I could conceive of a system designed to encourage meetings of interested persons at which the author of the book chosen would be present or represented; or a system which guaranteed the presence of a competent adviser; or one to which only students registered in a department or school had access; or one which permitted meetings only between people who defined their special approach to the title under discussion. Advantages for achieving specific goals of learning could be found for each of these restrictions. But I fear that, more often than not, the real reason for proposing such restrictions is contempt arising from the presumption that people are ignorant: educators want to avoid the ignorant meeting the ignorant around a text which they may not understand and which they read *only* because they are interested in it.

The third objection: Why not provide match seekers with incidental assistance that will facilitate their meetings—with space, schedules, screening, and protection? This is now done by schools with all the inefficiency characterizing large bureaucracies. If we left the initiative for meetings to the match seekers themselves, organizations which nobody now classifies as educational would probably do the job much better. I think of restaurant owners, publishers, telephone-answering services, department store managers, and even commuter train executives who could promote their services by rendering them attractive for educational meetings.

At a first meeting in a coffee shop, say, the partners might establish their identities by placing the book under discussion next to their cups. People who took the initiative to arrange for such meetings would soon learn what items to quote to meet the people they sought. The risk that the self-chosen discussion with one or several strangers might lead to a loss of time, disappointment, or even unpleasantness is certainly smaller than the same risk taken by a college applicant. A computer-arranged meeting to discuss an article in a national magazine, held in a coffee shop off Fourth Avenue, would obligate none of the participants to stay in the company of his new acquaintances for longer than it took to drink a cup of coffee, nor would he have to meet any of them ever again. The chance that it would help to pierce the opaqueness of life in a modern city and further new friendship, self-chosen work, and critical reading is high. (The fact that a record of personal readings and meetings could be obtained thus by the FBI is undeniable; that this should still worry anybody in 1970 is only amusing to a free man, who willy-nilly contributes his share in order to drown snoopers in the irrelevancies they gather.)

Both the exchange of skills and matching of partners are based on the assumption that education for all means education by all. Not the draft into a specialized insitution but only the mobilization of the whole population can lead to popular culture. The equal right of each man to exercise his competence to learn and to instruct is now preempted by certified teachers. The teachers' competence, in turn, is restricted to what may be done in school. And, further, work and leisure are alienated from each other as a result: the spectator and the worker alike are supposed to arrive at the work place all ready to fit into a routine prepared for them. Adaptation in the form of a product's design, instruction, and publicity shapes them for their role as much as formal education by schooling. A radical alternative to a schooled society requires not only new formal mechanisms for the formal acquisition of skills and their educational use. A de-schooled society implies a new approach to incidental or informal education.

Incidental education cannot any longer return to the forms which learning took in the village or the medieval town. Traditional society was more like a set of concentric circles of meaningful structures, while modern man must learn how to find meaning in many structures to which he is only marginally related. In the village, language and architecture and work and religion and family customs were consistent with one another, mutually explanatory and reinforcing. To grow into one implied a growth into the others. Even specialized apprenticeship was a byproduct of specialized activities, such as shoemaking or the singing of psalms. If an apprentice never became a master or a scholar, he still contributed to making shoes or to making church services solemn. Education did not compete for time with either work or leisure. Almost all education was complex, lifelong, and unplanned.

Contemporary society is the result of conscious designs, and educational opportunities must be designed into them. Our reliance on specialized, full-time instruction through school will now decrease, and we must find more ways to learn and teach: the educational quality of all institutions must increase again. But this is a very ambiguous forecast. It could mean that men in the modern city will be increasingly the victims of an effective process of total instruction and manipulation once they are deprived of even the tenuous pretense of critical independence which liberal schools now provide for at least some of their pupils.

It could also mean that men will shield themselves less behind certificates acquired in school and thus gain in courage to "talk back" and thereby control and instruct the institutions in which they participate. To ensure the latter we must learn to estimate the social value of work and leisure by the educational give-and-take for which they offer opportunity. Effective participation in the politics of a street, a work place, the library, a news program, or a hospital is therefore the best measuring stick to evaluate their level as educational institutions.

I recently spoke to a group of junior high school students in the process of organizing a resistance movement to their obligatory draft into the next class. Their slogan was "participation—not simulation." They were disappointed that this was understood as a demand for less rather than for more education, and reminded me of the resistance which Karl Marx put up against a passage in the Gotha program which—one hundred years ago—wanted to outlaw child labor. He opposed the proposal in the interest of the education of the young, which could happen only at work. If the greatest fruit of man's labor should be the education he receives from it and the opportunity which work gives him to initiate the education of others, then the alienation of modern society in a pedagogical sense is even worse than its economic alienation.

The major obstacle on the way to a society that truly educates was well defined by a black friend of mine in Chicago, who told me that our imagination was "all schooled up." We permit the state to ascertain the universal educational deficiencies of its citizens and establish one specialized agency to treat them. We thus share in the delusion that we can distinguish between what is necessary education for others and what is not, just as former generations established laws which defined what was sacred and what was profane.

Durkheim recognized that this ability to divide social reality into two realms was the very essence of formal religion. There are, he reasoned, religions without the supernatural and religions without gods, but none which does not subdivide the world into things and times and persons that are sacred and others that as a consequence are profane. Durkheim's insight can be applied to the sociology of education, for school is radically divisive in a similar way.

The very existence of obligatory schools divides any society into two realms: some time spans and processes and treatments and professions are "academic" or "pedagogic," and others are not. The power of school thus to divide social reality has no boundaries: education becomes unworldly and the world becomes noneducational.

Since Bonhoeffer contemporary theologians have pointed to the confusions now reigning between the biblical message and institutionalized religion. They point to the experience that Christian freedom and faith usually gain from secularization. Inevitably their statements sound blasphemous to many churchmen. Unquestionably, the educational process will gain from the deschooling of society even though this demand sounds to many schoolmen like treason to the enlightenment. But it is enlightenment itself that is now being snuffed out in the schools.

The secularization of the Christian faith depends on the dedication to it on the part of Christians rooted in the Church. In much the same way, the deschooling of education depends on the leadership of those brought up in the schools. Their curriculum cannot serve them as an alibi for the task: each of us remains responsible for what has been made of him, even though he may be able to do no more than accept this responsibility and serve as a warning to others.

.14. Cuban Education and the Revolutionary Ideology

SAMUEL BOWLES

"To build communism, a new man must be created simultaneously with the material base. . . .
Society as a whole must become a huge school."

Ernesto "Che" Guevara[1]

"Revolution and education are the same thing."

Fidel Castro[2]

THE CONTINUING social and economic revolution in Cuba since the overthrow of Batista in 1959 has been reflected in a radical transformation of the educational system.[3] The stagnation of the prerevolutionary economy, the class structure, the relations of production, and the imperialist domination of capitalist Cuba were replicated in the school system inherited by the revolutionary movement. Not surprisingly, then, every major economic and social objective of the revolution has been manifested in some aspect of educa-

---

[1]Ernesto "Che" Guevara, "Man and Socialism in Cuba," *Venceremos! the Speeches and Writings of Che Guevara*, ed. John Gerassi (New York: Simon and Schuster, 1968), p. 391.

[2]Fidel Castro, Universidad Popular, 6th Series, *Educación y Revolución* (Havana: Imprenta Nacional de Cuba, April 1961), p. 271.

[3]This essay is based on observations in Cuba during March, April, and May 1969, as well as a survey of the available literature on education and the economy of Cuba. During my stay in Cuba, I taught at the Instituto de Economía of the University of Havana, and consulted with economists and educators in a number of ministries, in-

272

tional change. Similarly, every major dilemma in the construction of a socialist economy has had a counterpart in the school system.

The boundaries between school and society are never distinct: in revolutionary Cuba they have been blurred beyond recognition. Revolution and education are inseparable facets of the process of social transformation. In this essay I discuss the relation between the transformation of the Cuban economy and the development of Cuban education over the first decade of the revolution. In the first section I survey the major economic and social objectives of the revolutionary movement. I introduce and illustrate the concept of correspondence between economic and educational structures in section two. Sections three and four are a discussion of the expansion and structural transformation of the Cuban educational system. In the concluding section I discuss some dilemmas in the continuing revolutionary development of Cuban education.

CAPITALIST LEGACY—REVOLUTIONARY OBJECTIVES

Four main objectives of the revolutionary movement since 1959 may be identified.[4]

First, the revolutionary government sought to expand and fully utilize the society's productive capacities. The Cuban economy, which had stagnated for the half century prior to the revolution, would be transformed into a rapidly growing system capable of ensuring a growing abundance for all.[5]

Second, economic, political, and cultural dependence on the United

---

cluding Sugar and Education, and with the planning staff of the university. Much of what I have written here is based on classroom observation by my wife and me in schools in all parts of Cuba, and school attendance by our children in Havana. I have received helpful comments and criticism from Robin Hahnel, Valerie Nelson, Janice Weiss, members of the Harvard Union for Radical Political Economics seminar, and the Yale University seminar on the Cuban economy directed by Carlos Diaz Alejandro.

[4]A list of this type, though helpful for purposes of exposition, is necessarily somewhat arbitrary and ahistorical. Some objectives are necessarily left out. The relative importance of the objectives listed here has varied over time. The fourth objective—creation of the new socialist man—received very little explicit attention until the mid-1960s.

[5]Evidence on the stagnation of the Cuban economy in the half-century prior to the revolution is summarized in *Cuba: the Economic and Social Revolution*, ed. Dudley Seers (Chapel Hill: University of North Carolina Press, 1964).

States would be eliminated.[6] National sovereignty would be achieved within the framework of cooperation and mutually beneficial economic relations among socialist countries.

Third, a classless and egalitarian society would replace the rigid class structure of capitalist Cuba. Sexism and racism would be eliminated; the economic, cultural, and political domination of the city over the countryside would end.[7]

Fourth, work would cease to be a painful necessity characterized by alienation and motivated by the fear of starvation or the lure of monetary gain. Productive effort would become a challenging and creative activity motivated by social consciousness and by the desire for self-expression.

The first three objectives scarcely require elaboration. The fourth is somewhat less familiar, even in the writings of the Left, and calls for a more extended discussion.

In both China and the Soviet Union, the road toward communism began with a revolution which overturned the power structure of what was essentially a peasant society. In Cuba, however, capitalist penetration of the economy was virtually completed by the end of the sugar boom which ran from the end of the nineteenth century through the 1920s. By 1930 the small property-holding peasantry was of minor significance in the economy. According to the 1953 Census, about two-thirds of the agricultural labor force worked for wages or salaries.[8] In the same year, 72 percent of the economically active population were employees.[9] Thus, on the eve of the revolution, Cuba was a capitalist country with a largely proletarian labor force and relatively

[6]The extent of dependence of capitalist Cuba on the U.S. is surveyed in James O'Connor, *The Origins of Socialism in Cuba* (Ithaca: Cornell University Press, 1970); Edward Boorstein, *The Economic Transformation of Cuba* (New York: Monthly Review Press, 1968); and Roberto Gonzalez Cofino, "On Cuban Foreign Trade," in *Essays on the Cuban Economy,* ed. Carlos Diaz Alejandro (New Haven: Yale University Press, 1971). The record of U.S. political and military intervention in Cuba is traced by Ramón Eduardo Ruiz in *Cuba: the Making of a Revolution* (New York: Norton, 1968).

[7]Data on social inequalities in pre-revolutionary Cuba is presented in David Barkin, "The Redistribution of Consumption in Socialist Cuba," in *Essays on the Cuban Economy.*

[8]Seers, *Cuba: The Economic and Social Revolution,* p. 80.

[9]*Censos de Población, Viviendas y Electoral, 1953* (Havana: Informe General, 1953).

few independent producers. This fact is central to an explanation of both the opportunities and the objectives of the revolution.[10]

In the first place, Cuba did not face the problem encountered in the Soviet Union during the early part of this century, namely, the transformation of an independent peasantry into an industrial labor force. Although the Cuban economy was still primarily agricultural, the social relations of production were typical of capitalist production. Men and women worked for wages, with no other source of income, and with little or no control over their hours or conditions of work. The economy was characterized by a highly developed division of labor. Moreover, one hundred years of nationalist struggle and decades of radical labor organizing had made Cuban workers acutely aware that their interests were not those of the Cuban and North American capitalist class. For all these reasons, it is hard to imagine that workers had any intrinsic interest in either the product of their labor or in the process of production. Cuban workers worked in order to survive. Even for those with a modicum of security, the rewards of work were to be found in the pay.

The revolution has made one of its main objectives the transformation of people's relation to work. The revolutionary leadership has seen in the capitalist relations of production the degradation of man predicted (albeit parenthetically) by Adam Smith,[11] and described in the mid-nineteenth century by Karl Marx:

What, then, constitutes the alienation of labor?
First, the fact that the labor is *external* to the worker, i.e., it does not belong to his essential being; that in his work, therefore, he does not affirm himself but denies himself, does not feel content but unhappy, does not develop freely his physical and mental energy but mortifies his body and ruins his mind. The worker therefore only feels himself outside his work, and in his work

[10]For a more complete discussion of these points, see Maurice Zeitlin, *Revolutionary Politics and the Cuban Working Class* (Princeton: Princeton University Press, 1967); and O'Connor, *The Origins of Socialism in Cuba*.

[11]"The man whose whole life is spent in performing a few simple operations . . . has no occasion to exert his understanding, or to exercise his invention. . . . He naturally loses, therefore, the habit of such exertion, and generally becomes as stupid and ignorant as it is possible for a human creature to become. The torpor of his mind renders him incapable . . . of conceiving any generous, noble, or tender sentiment. . . ." (Adam Smith, *The Wealth of Nations* (New York: Modern Library, 1937) (first published 1776), pp. 734–35.)

feels outside himself. He is at home when he is not working, and when he is working he is not at home. His labor is therefore not voluntary, but coerced; it is *forced labor*. It is therefore not the satisfaction of a need; it is merely a *means* to satisfy needs external to it. Its alien character emerges clearly in the fact that as soon as no physical or other compulsion exists, labor is shunned like the plague. External labor, labor in which man alienates himself, is a labor of self-sacrifice, or mortification. Lastly, the external character of labor for the worker appears in the fact that it is not his own, but someone else's, that it does not belong to him, that in it he belongs, not to himself, but to another.[12]

The revolution has sought to fulfill what Ernesto "Che" Guevara called "the ultimate and most important revolutionary aspiration: to see man liberated from alienation."[13] The objective—to quote "Che" again—is based on "the Marxist concept that man truly achieves his full human condition when he produces without being compelled by the physical necessity of selling himself as a commodity. . . ." The ultimate goal is to "achieve complete spiritual recreation in the presence of his own work, without the direct pressure of the social environment, but bound to it by new habits. That will be communism."[14] Included as an important aspect of the transformation of the social relations of work is the obliteration of the distinction between manual and nonmanual workers. Onerous manual work that cannot be eliminated—particularly cane cutting—is to be shared by all workers.

Thus the revolutionary movement sought to stimulate economic growth, to escape national dependency on the United States, to achieve equality where inequality had been, and to create the new socialist man in place of alienated labor. Simultaneous movement toward all four objectives has been the revolutionary strategy.

The strategy of simultaneous development is more a reflection of the integral nature of these objectives than an indication of the zealousness of the Cuban leadership. At the heart of the problem of economic stagnation lay the low level of the nation's technological capacities, its uneducated labor force, and its outdated and stagnant stock of productive physical equipment—in short, in the underdevelop-

[12]Karl Marx, *The Economic and Philosophic Manuscripts of 1844*, ed. D. J. Struik (New York: International Publishers, 1964), pp. 110–11 (italics in original).

[13]Guevara, "Man and Socialism in Cuba," p. 393.

[14]Ibid, p. 394.

ment of the *forces of production*. Yet the reason for this stunting of the nation's productive capacities lay in the established relations between worker and employer, in the patterns of ownership and control over the means of production, in short, in the *social relations of production*.[15] And it was the relations of production which, in turn, were the source of the class structure, the alienation of labor, and the international dependency of pre-revolutionary Cuba.[16]

Specifically, the relations of production—between capitalist employers and proletarian workers—defined the class structure.[17] Another characteristic of the relations of production—the exclusion of the worker from control over the production process and its product —was the basis of the alienation of Cuban labor. The last aspect of the pre-revolutionary social relations of production—the domination of many important production, marketing, technological, financial, and other managerial decisions by foreigners, in short, the imperialist division of labor and the resulting vertical stratification of the world labor force along national lines—made a mockery of Cuban sovereignty.[18]

Thus the revolutionary strategy required both an expansion of the forces of production and a radical transformation of the social relations of production. Fidel Castro voiced part of this strategy: "An advance in . . . the consciousness of the people must accompany every step forward in the development of the forces of production."[19] Education was to play a central role in both processes.

[15]See Thomas E. Weisskopf, "Capitalism, Underdevelopment, and the Future of the Poor Countries," in *Economics and World Order*, ed. Jagdish Bhagwati (New York: Macmillian, 1972), for an elaboration of this argument in general, and O'Connor, *The Origins of Socialism in Cuba*, for its application to Cuba.

[16]An extended discussion of the social relations of production, alienation, and class in capitalist societies may be found in Andre Gorz, "Capitalist Relations of Production and the Socially Necessary Labor Force," *International Socialist Journal*, year 2, no. 10 (August 1965).

[17]The class position of the substantial segments of the Cuban population who were neither employers nor employees—the peasant proprietors, the small shopkeepers, the independent professionals, and others—is likewise defined by their role in the productive process, though not by the social relations of production *at the level of the individual enterprise*.

[18]A general treatment of the international specialization in managerial, technical, and laboring functions is in Stephen Hymer, "The Multinational Corporation and the International Division of Labor," in *Economics and World Order*, ed. Jagdish Bhagwati (New York: Macmillan, 1972).

[19]Speech on July 26, 1968, reported in *Granma*, July 27, 1968.

EDUCATION AND ECONOMY:
THE CORRESPONDENCE PRINCIPLE

The importance of education in the transformation of the Cuban economy derives from the influence of education on the material forces of production and its role in the reproduction of the social relations of production.

The contribution of education to the forces of production takes two main forms: the development of future workers of those technical, scientific, and other intellectual capacities needed for efficient production; and the inculcation of values, expectations, beliefs, and modes of behavior required for the adequate performance of adult work roles. Although very few of the intellectual skills learned in school are directly transferable to the workplace, basic scientific knowledge as well as communication skills and mathematical abilities are an essential ingredient in becoming and remaining competent in some jobs, particularly those involving directing and technical functions.

The role of education in shaping personalities, attitudes, and beliefs, on the other hand, is of importance for workers in all types of jobs. The affective content of schooling—the values, expectations, and patterns of behavior which schools encourage—is conveyed primarily by the social relations of the schooling process itself, rather than explicitly in the curriculum. Whether established relations among students are competitive or cooperative, whether relations between students and teachers are democratic or authoritarian, and whether relations between students and their work are creative or alienated, are a better measure of what is taught in schools than would be revealed by a study of texts or curricula. The social relations of schooling in capitalist societies—authoritarian, competitive, and alienating—are instrumental in the generation of a labor force attuned to the social relations of production of the capitalist enterprise.[20]

The expansion of the forces of production cannot easily be separated from the second main function of schooling in capitalist societies: the reproduction of the social relations of production. The reproduction of the social relations of production in each cohort does

---

[20]For an exposition of this view see Herbert Gintis, "The New Working Class and Revolutionary Youth," *Socialist Revolution* 1, no. 3, (May–June 1970): 13–43.

not begin in the school, nor does it end there. Family structure and child-rearing practices form an important part of the early socialization process. Following school, the social relations of production in the place of work exert a continuing influence on personality development. Some types of behavior are rewarded; others are penalized. The nature of the work process limits the range of attitudes, values, and behavior patterns that people can exhibit and still find employment.

Yet the school itself plays a central role, particularly in periods of rapid social change. The generation of an adequate labor force is greatly facilitated if the aspects of the socialization process operate in a complementary fashion. In capitalist countries, the preparation of young people for their future roles in production requires that the social relations of production take a particular form. The control of the educational process is denied to students, and success is measured by an external standard—grades and exam marks—which becomes the main motivation for work, so that any intrinsic interest in the product of one's effort—knowledge—or the process of production—learning—is eclipsed.

We thus arrive at the simplest statement of the correspondence principle: the social relations of production are replicated in the schools.

The correspondence between the social relations of schooling and the social relations of production does not necessarily imply a common education for all children. Rather, in capitalist societies, characterized by a hierarchical division of labor, it requires that the education of a relatively small group—the future technical and managerial personnel—develops the capacity to calculate, decide, and rule, while the education of a much larger group develops the capacity to follow instructions willingly and accurately in boring and alienating jobs. This differentiation of the future labor force is accomplished, in part, through the different amounts and types of schooling children destined for different work roles in the hierarchy of production. Thus, in capitalist societies, the class structure is replicated in the school system: the children of parents in directing and technical positions, tend to acquire an education which qualifies them to move into similar jobs.[21]

[21]See Samuel Bowles, "Unequal Education and the Reproduction of the Social Division of Labor," chapter 2 in this volume.

We can now restate and extend the correspondence principle: as the social relations of production reproduce the social relations of production in each cohort, the class structure is also reproduced from generation to generation. The correspondence between educational and economic structures relates not only to the social relations at the level of the individual enterprise and school, but to the aggregate structures as well. Where the imperialist division of labor results in a class structure dominated at the top by foreign management and technical personnel, we may expect to find a corresponding underdevelopment of the nation's advanced educational institutions.

The correspondence between education and the economy is vividly illustrated in pre-revolutionary Cuba. Economic stagnation was matched by educational retrogression. A cohort analysis of the 1953 Census permits approximate estimates of the level of enrollments for periods as far back as the turn of the century. Abstracting from the problems of differential mortality and emigration or immigration rates by years of schooling, data in Figure 14.1 indicate that the percentage of school-age Cubans who never attended school at all rose over the period 1938 to 1953, while the percentage completing primary school fell.[22]

The impression of Cuban educational stagnation in the thirties, forties, and fifties is further strengthened by a comparison with other Latin American countries. In 1925–26, 63 percent of the primary school age children in Cuba were enrolled in school, a larger percentage (according to a Cuban government report) than in any other Spanish-speaking republic. Three decades later, the level had fallen to 51 percent; all but three Latin American countries had by then a larger fraction enrolled in school, and the Latin American average was 64 percent.[23] By 1958–59, the eve of the revolution, the fraction of the five to fourteen year age group enrolled in primary school in Cuba had fallen further—to less than one-half.[24] Although the percentages attending secondary and higher education grew somewhat over this period, the total enrollments at all levels, as a fraction of the school-going age population, fell.

[22]For a discussion of this, see Richard Jolly, "Education—the Prerevolutionary Background," in *Cuba: the Economic and Social Revolution*.

[23]Ibid., pp. 169–70.

[24]Ibid., p. 227; and Junta Central de Planificación (JUCEPLAN), *Resumen de Estadísticas de Población, no. 3* (Havana, 1968).

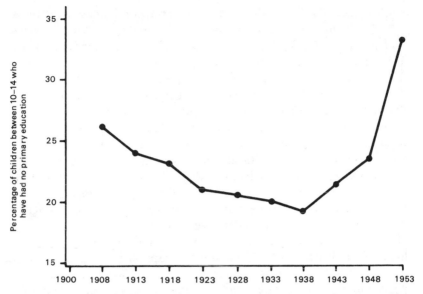

Figure 14.1   Apparent Percentage of Primary School Age Group that Never Attended School, 1908–53 [a]

SOURCE: Richard Jolly, "Education—the Prerevolutionary Background," *Cuba: the Economic and Social Revolution,* ed. Dudley Seers (Chapel Hill: University of North Carolina Press, 1964); based on *Censos de Población, Viviendas y Electoral, 1953* (Havana: Informe General, 1953).

[a] The figure presents data on the percentage, responding as having had no schooling, of the population in each age cohort, as reported in the 1953 Census of Housing and Population. Thus, for example, 33.5 percent of those who were 10–14 years of age in 1953 said that they had not attended school, as did 20.3 percent of those who were 30–34 years of age in 1953.

Cuba's economic dependence on the United States was equally reflected in her distorted and underdeveloped educational system. The concentration of technical, research and managerial functions in the hands of North Americans—often outside Cuba—manifested itself in the sorry state of pre-revolutionary Cuban higher education. Enrollments in higher education had risen over the pre-revolutionary decades, no doubt in response to the politically powerful Cuban upper- and upper-middle-classes' attempts to direct public largesse toward the education of their own children. Nonetheless, Cuba had proportionally fewer students enrolled in higher education in 1958 than less dependent Latin American countries at similar levels of development. The only fields with substantial enrollments were those of little production value—humanities—as well as a few preparing students for professions not dominated by foreigners—undergraduate training in accounting and business administration, as well as law and medicine.

Inequalities in the educational system both reflected and reproduced the class structure and other social and economic inequalities of pre-revolutionary Cuba. Zeitlin's sample of workers, for example, displays a strong relationship between class and educational attainments: the sons of agricultural laborers or peasants were only one-fifth as likely to have completed sixth grade as were the sons of those in nonmanual salaried occupations.[25] Presumably comparison with the sons of capitalists would indicate even greater inequalities. Rural education was particularly underdeveloped.

The social relations of Cuban schooling mirrored the social relations of production in the predominant capitalist sector of the economy: autocratic, teacher-centered education was the rule, discipline, a major (if sometimes vainly sought) objective, students' success depended on their financial resources and on their ability to behave well and to reproduce on exams fragmented bits of knowledge largely irrelevant to their lives and interests.

The correspondence between pre-revolutionary Cuban education and the capitalist economy was complete: the objectives the revolution set for the economy were reflected in parallel objectives in the school system. First, stagnation in education would be replaced by rapid growth in enrollments. Fidel Castro stated this theme with characteristic simplicity: "The levels of development that the country will reach can be measured only by the percentage of young people carrying on advanced studies...."[26] But the expansion of education would serve to do more than expand the material forces of production. Quoting Castro again, "The possibility of a man's being motivated by the content of his work is in direct relation to the individual's knowledge and his cultural level."[27]

National dependency in the scientific and cultural spheres would be

[25]Zeitlin, *Revolutionary Politics and the Cuban Working Class*, p. 141.
[26]Speech of March 13, 1969, reported in *Granma*, March 14, 1969.
[27]Ibid.

eliminated by the expansion of high level educational technical and research facilities. Similarly, the class structure of Cuban education would be destroyed; education would be made available to all: "The revolution cannot reconcile itself with the idea that in the future there should always be a minority in society with a monopoly on technical and scientific knowledge and a majority shut out from this knowledge."[28]

Last, the social relations of Cuban education would be transformed to develop the new socialist man, to help produce "the fully developed individual, fit for a variety of labors, ... to whom the different social functions he performs are but so many modes of giving free scope to his own natural and acquired powers," to borrow a phrase from Marx.[29] The motivation for study would be changed, too, so that "coming generations" would "receive the heritage of education . . . that is totally devoid of selfish sentiment."[30]

I turn now to a survey of the quantitative dimensions of the educational revolution in Cuba.

THE EDUCATIONAL REVOLUTION: QUANTITATIVE DIMENSIONS

Verbal and quantitative description can only weakly capture the diversity and breadth of educational activities initiated by the revolution. In a stable society not undergoing rapid change, the education of adults occupies only a peripheral role (devoted almost exclusively to the transmission of narrowly defined skills) in the entire educational picture. Where a sharp revolutionary break with the past is made, the educational process must extend throughout the population, encompassing the old and middle-aged as well as the young. The role of formal schooling in this process of reeducation of the Cuban population is, for this reason, relatively limited. The potential output foregone by withdrawing any sizable portion of the adult population from directly productive activity in order to attend schools is simply pro-

[28]Ibid.

[29]Karl Marx, *Capital* (New York: Modern Library, 1906), vol. I, p. 534.

[30]Fidel Castro, speech on September 28, 1964, as quoted in Richard Fagan, *The Transformation of Political Culture in Cuba* (Stanford, Calif.: Stanford University Press, 1969), p. 13.

hibitive. Effective channels for education must be developed outside the schools—through labor organizations and the armed forces; through participation in the Committees for the Defense of the Revolution, the Federation of Cuban Women, and other mass organizations; and through direct political education such as that which has invariably surrounded every major political event in Cuba since 1959. Even though formal schooling occupies a comparatively minor role in the education of adults, over 10 percent of Cubans past the school-leaving age are enrolled in formal adult education classes, and a substantial portion of all workers are engaged in continuing or intermittent *superaction* (improvement) courses. Thus, while the statistical information below pertains almost exclusively to formal education, mostly of young people, it should be remembered that this is only a part of the entire educational effort in Cuba.

The structure and quantitative dimensions of Cuban education in 1958–59 and the growth of schooling since the revolution are described in Figures 14.2 and 14.3. Because data are not available for the most recent school year on all types of courses, I present enrollment data for the year 1967–68 in Table 14.1.

Rates of educational expansion at the elementary level, as well as the spread of literacy in Cuba, have far exceeded the performance reported for other Latin American countries. In the course of a decade, the educational system of Cuba has grown from a position of relative backwardness to a position considerably in advance of most of her Latin American neighbors.[31]

Enrollments in higher education have grown considerably less rapidly than in the rest of the educational system. However, over the decade following the triumph of the revolution, the internal structure of higher education changed drastically. The importance of technical and scientific studies has risen. Scientific research related to production has been promoted both in the university and in numerous newly established research institutes. The numbers studying humanities have fallen. In 1968–69 one-fifth of the university students (those en-

[31]Figures for higher and secondary education are not comparable across countries because of substantial study abroad in some countries and differing definitions of secondary education. A glance at Figure 14.2, however, suggests that educational expansion at these levels may not have been as high in Cuba as in a number of other countries.

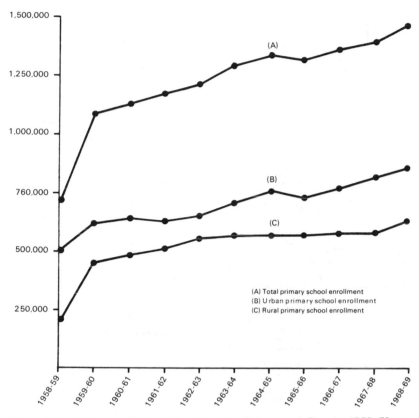

Figure 14.2   Primary School Enrollments, Urban and Rural, 1958–59 to 1968–69

Source: JUCEPLAN (Junta Central de Planificatión) *Compendio Estadístico de Cuba, 1968* (Havana, 1968), pp. 32–33.

rolled in the faculty for workers and peasants) were graduates of adult education programs in elementary and secondary education. Some aspects of these changes are indicated in Table 14.2.

The dramatic expansion of enrollments, particularly at the lower levels, has required the allocation of a major portion of Cuba's productive resources to the education sector. Even abstracting from the ubiquitous on-the-job training programs and the substantial adult education system, about one-fifth of Cuba's total productive capacity

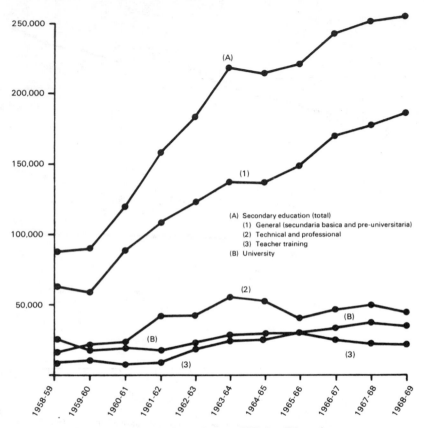

**Figure 14.3　Enrollments in Secondary and Higher Education,
1958–59 to 1968–69**

SOURCE: JUCEPLAN (Junta Central de Planificatión) *Compendio Estadístico de Cuba, 1968* (Havana, 1968), pp. 32–33.

was, in 1968–69 devoted to formal schooling, a figure unsurpassed among the major countries of the world, rich or poor.[32] Education rivals sugar as Cuba's largest productive sector.

It may be thought that an educational expansion of the magnitude achieved during the first ten years of the revolution would be asso-

[32]This figure represents the percentage of the actual and potential labor force above the age of 14 allocated to the education sector. Those allocated to education included all post-primary school students (excluding adult education) and all teachers.

Table 14-1. Enrollments, School Year 1967–68

Type of Education	Number of students
Primary education	1,391,478
Secondary education:	177,087
Secondary basic	160,308
Pre-university	16,779
Technical and professional education	45,612
Primary schoolteacher training	18,121
University	34,532
Adult education	405,612
Workers' technological institutes	46,595
Agricultural and fishing schools for youth	28,832
Construction schools	10,663
Technical Institute	1,626
Ministry of Public Health	6,060
Physical education schools	2,462
Others	7,092
Total	2,352,859

SOURCE: Comité Central del Partido Comunista de Cuba, *La Productividad del Trabajo y Factores de su Aumento*, (Havana, undated), p. 47.

ciated with a lowering of standards. While it is difficult to determine if this has in fact occurred—and many believe that it has—the available quantitative evidence provides no evidence for a quality deterioration. Table 14.3, which gives teacher-student ratios at each level of schooling for the years 1958–59 and 1968–69, suggests that the number of teachers relative to students has increased substantially at the primary level and not declined significantly at any level except in

---

The total labor force estimate of 2.5 million was inflated to include those potential workers currently enrolled in school as defined above. The figure cited is an underestimate of the true percentage of Cuba's resources devoted to education. First, I have excluded almost half a million adults enrolled in primary and secondary school as part of the adult education program. Second, the calculation takes no account of the fact that the potential and actual members of the labor force working in the educational system are, on the average, considerably more educated than the average Cuban worker, and thus represent greater foregone production opportunities than the simple head count calculation above would indicate. The education and labor force statistics are from, *Cuba 1968: Supplement to the Statistical Abstract of Latin America*, eds. C. Paul Roberts and Mukhtar Hamour (Los Angeles: Latin American Center, University of California, 1970), pp. 92–99, 102–03, and 202. The enrollment figures there have been augmented by the enrollment data for special educational programs enumerated in Table 14.1.

Table 14.2.   Enrollments in Higher Education by Specialization,
1958–59 and 1968–69

Faculty	1958–59		1968–69	
	Number of students	Percent of total	Number of students	Percent of total
Faculty of Humanities	4,291	16.8	1,196	3.4
Institute of Economics	6,102	23.8	1,230	3.5
Faculty of Science	1,617	6.3	3,152	8.9
Faculty of Technology	3,323	13.0	6,588	18.6
Faculty of Medicine	3,947	15.4	7,278	20.5
Faculty of Agriculture and Fishing Science	1,202	4.7	2,203	6.2
Institute of Education	5,032	19.7	6,642	18.7
Faculty for Workers and Peasants	85	0.0	7,201	20.3
TOTAL	25,599	100	35,490	100

SOURCE: JUCEPLAN, (Junta Central de Planificación), *Compendio Estadístico de Cuba, 1968* (Havana, 1968), pp. 34–35.

teacher training ("normal schools").[33] Moreover, the curriculum reforms (for example, new math); the establishment of an educational equipment factory; and the widespread introduction of new methods—particularly educational television—have probably had some positive effect on the quality of schooling.

THE EDUCATION REVOLUTION: NEW FORMS

The revolutionary content of Cuban education is conveyed primarily outside the classroom. It is in the fields and the factories, at least as much as in the schools, that one finds the development of a new concept of education and the evolution of new social relations of production in the process of education itself. I will outline here some of these changes.

First, chronologically and also in symbolic importance, is the cam-

[33]Of course, the rapid increase in the number of teachers implied by these data may have been associated with a fall in the level of formal training among the teachers, particularly in the early years. I have no evidence on this problem.

**Table 14.3.   Students per Teacher at Various Levels of
Schooling, 1958–59 and 1968–69**

Primary school S/T:	
1958–59	41.3
1968–69	29.8
Total secondary school (general) S/T:	
1958–59	14.0
1968–69	16.5
Total secondary school (technical and professional) S/T:	
1958–59	12.3
1968–69	12.9
Total secondary school (teacher training) S/T:	
1958–59	12.9
1968–69	18.2
University education S/T:	
1958–59	24.3
1968–69	7.9
Total S/T:	
1958–59	35.3
1968–69	21.4

SOURCE: JUCEPLAN (Junta Central de Planificación), *Compendio Estadístico de Cuba, 1968* (Havana, 1968), pp. 30–33.

paign against illiteracy, waged during the Year of Education, 1961. The fact that the first major social objective of the revolution was universal literacy is symptomatic of the paramount importance placed on education. The task of the literacy brigades was to locate and to teach the one-quarter or so of the Cuban population which was illiterate. This objective was virtually accomplished (the illiteracy rate reported at the termination of the campaign was 3.9 percent[34]) through the efforts of over a quarter of a million literacy teachers, or *alfabetizadores*. The *alfabetizadores* were drawn heavily from the school system itself: over 100,000 students joined the campaign when schools were closed for the year on April 15, and almost all of the professional teachers in the country participated. As most of the illiterate population lived in rural areas, the *alfabetizadores*—disproportionately from urban areas—spent extended periods away from

[34]UNESCO, *Methods and Means Utilized in Cuba to Eliminate Illiteracy* (New York, 1965), p. 29.

home, often living with the *campesinos* and others whom they taught. While the educational stagnation of the previous four decades could hardly be wiped out in a single year's mobilization, the near-eradication of illiteracy on the island placed Cuba considerably ahead of the other Latin American nations.

A second revolutionary aspect of recent Cuban educational policy is the *escuela al campo* ("the school goes to the country") program. The educational value of productive labor has repeatedly been emphasized by the revolutionary leadership. In part, as recognition of this, and in part, to augment the agricultural labor supply, entire schools move to the countryside for extended periods to harvest crops and do other agricultural work. Secondary schools may spend as much as twelve weeks in the country, housed in simple camps and doing hard agricultural work side by side with the *campesinos*.

Not only are the schools moved to the work place—the productive life of the nation has been integrated into the curriculum. The major vehicle for this third aspect of the transformation of Cuban education are the *círculos de interés*. These "interest circles" are analogous in many respects to extracurricular activities in U.S. high schools, but are oriented exclusively around productive activities—animal science, soil chemistry, and oceanography are typical interest circles.[35]

Although not all secondary schools have active programs of interest circles, they are spreading rapidly. Ideally, they are a bridge between the school curriculum and the students' later life of productive activity. Where the school is itself a productive unit engaged in agriculture, the chemistry class can devote itself to soil analysis with an interest and motivation reflecting both the wholeness of the educational experience and the real contribution being made to the productive capacity of the nation.

By tying the educational experience more closely to the economy, the *círculos de interés* perform a very important function. A society which has foregone the use of wage incentives needs an alternative

---

[35]A list of *círculos de interés* at one school which I visited follows: Agriculture, Biochemistry, Cane, Animal Sciences, Citriculture, Electricity, Physiosanitation, Photography, Fruits, Geodesy and Construction, Mechanics, Agricultural Mechanics, Meteorology, Oceanography, Petroleum, Food Chemistry, Radio-electricity, Hydraulic Resources, and Soil.

means of encouraging young people to enter occupations in short supply. Thus the *círculos de interés* provide a means of informing young people about the content of various occupational pursuits, while at the same time stimulating student interest in careers likely to make a major contribution to national development.

A fourth aspect of the revolutionary changes under way in Cuban education relates to the role of the students themselves in the process of education. Shortly after the triumph of the revolution, students were encouraged to study in groups, that is, to pursue collective rather than individual study. The process of expanding knowledge and competence was seen as a group effort, and elements of competition in the classroom were to be minimized.

Although recently the importance of individual study has been re-emphasized,[36] the collective spirit is maintained in the monitors program. Each class selects a student or a group of students in each subject to help the rest of the class with their studies. Thus in one class I observed there were three monitors for the history lessons. Their role was primarily in leading group discussions among students, helping individual students who were having difficulty, taking charge of classes being taught by educational television, and similar activities. In one school I sat in on a sequence of geography classes: one, a seminar of ten or so students working (under the guidance of a teacher) on a project concerning the economics of West Africa,[37] another, a televised unit supervised by a monitor, and a third in which a monitor was lecturing and answering simple questions on the main economic characteristics of various African nations. This particular school was hardly typical, as it specialized in group work and the extensive use of monitors, but most Cuban educators with whom I talked see this type of teaching as spreading throughout the entire school system over the next few years. I will devote some attention to the "average" classroom below.

Similar in spirit with both the *escuela al campo* and the *círculos de interés*, though at a more advanced level, is a more recent pro-

[36]Jose Llanusa, *Desarrollo de la Educación a lo Largo de los 10 Años de Proceso Revolucionario* (Havana, 1969).

[37]In the class I asked a student to imagine that he was visiting a West African nation and was asked for advice as to how to overcome their economic backwardness. "I would advise them," he replied, "to have a revolution."

gram: the universalization of the university.[38] The detailed implementation of this objective has yet to be worked out, but the outlines are reasonably clear. The scholarly work of students in universities should be integrated with the productive activities of the nation. Students studying economics already spend a considerable amount of time attached to various ministries with economic responsibilities, doing applied research and attempting to improve programs. Sociology students carry out community studies concerning the process of adjustment to life in the new towns. Those in the school of engineering work on irrigation projects or on terracing. Hardly a faculty in the University of Havana is not involved in at least one major development project. Even the students in the faculty of letters are involved; they carry out rural surveys of the cultural and educational aspirations and needs of the *campesinos*. But the universalization of the university is a two-way street. All students are to be workers, and at the same time all workers are to be students. There are plans to set up faculties of the university throughout the island, some located in industrial plants and other productive units. Ultimately, the central physical facilities of the university are to be devoted exclusively to advanced research, with instruction, in the traditional sense, decentralized in a number of widely separated units.

EDUCATION AND THE REVOLUTIONARY OBJECTIVES

Having surveyed both the expansion and structural transformation of Cuban education, it is now possible to assess the extent to which educational policy has served the revolutionary objectives: increased economic productivity, sovereignty, equality, and the creation of the new socialist man. I will discuss each objective in turn.

There is every indication that the allocation of a sizable fraction of the nation's resources for education has made a major contribution to the forces of production. The strategy of economic growth, chosen by the revolutionary government, required both a substantial number of highly skilled workers and the spread of general education throughout the population. The introduction of scientific agriculture and advanced technologies of production as well as reliance on a centralized decision-making structure, requires a substantial amount of technical,

[38]Castro, speech of March 13, 1969.

organizational, and administrative expertise.[39] Moreover, the motivation of labor to work for collective rather than personal objectives—a central part of the growth strategy—presupposes the workers' acquaintance with enough of the economy and history of Cuba to understand the social value of his or her effort.

While the needs for educated labor were great, the supplies were meager, reflecting the low level of schooling prior to the revolution. Moreover, even the low levels of technical skills and general education in the Cuban labor force on the eve of the revolution were seen to be further depleted. The immediate post-revolutionary years saw a drastic reduction in the available supply of highly educated labor. In the first three years following 1959, it seems likely that about 250,000 Cubans left.[40] A very substantial percentage of these were professional workers. About one-third of the doctors emigrated, as did perhaps 15 percent or more of the technical and professional personnel.[41] In addition, the nationalization of foreign firms was accompanied by the departure of significant numbers of alien management and technical personnel.

Evidence from other countries—some with economic characteristics similar to Cuba's—suggests that the economic returns to increased schooling are quite considerable. Studies of the contribution of schooling to economic growth carried out in these countries indicate that the rates of return to most levels of schooling are high, particularly at the primary school level.[42] The low level of supply, the high level of demand, and the evidence available from other economies all point to the same conclusion: far from being a costly luxury, the expansion of enrollments and the allocation of a major part of Cuba's productive resources to education have made an important contribution to the forces of production. If the experience of other countries is relevant to the Cuban situation, we can also surmise that

[39]For an exposition of the importance of basic education in a program of agricultural modernization, see Theodore W. Schultz, *Transforming Traditional Agriculture* (New Haven: Yale University Press, 1964).

[40]Jolly, "Education—the Prerevolutionary Background," p. 177.

[41]Ibid.

[42]George Psacharopoulos, "Rates of Return to Education Around the World," *Comparative Education Review* 16, no. 1 (February 1972); and Samuel Bowles, *Planning Educational Systems for Economic Growth* (Cambridge, Mass.: Harvard University Press, 1969).

the allocation of the lion's share of educational resources to the lowest level—on mass literacy and primary education—was also in the interests of increased productive capacity, despite the fact that the very rapid expansion of basic enrollment necessitated a slower growth of higher education. Further, the emphasis, at all levels, on mathematics, technical skills related to production, and science has also, no doubt, made an important economic contribution. While the direct economic benefits of technical education at all levels may be somewhat exaggerated and the high costs not fully appreciated,[43] the shift in emphasis is justified in direction, if not in degree, when one takes into account the low level of technical competence in the pre-revolutionary labor force.

The contribution of the educational system to production might have been even greater had a more systematic approach to educational planning been adopted. Educational policy and economic planning, until recently, have not been seen as part of an integrated resource allocation problem. Economic policy has had to respond to the educational levels and skills of the labor force. The shift in growth strategy from import substituting industrialization, to export expanding sugar and other branches of agriculture in the early 1960s, was dictated in part by a growing awareness of the excessive supplies of technically trained labor required by the process of industrial expansion. While the manpower demands implied by some particular projects have been estimated—for example, the expansion of the nickel complex—no comprehensive long range plan for the matching of labor demands and educational output has even been attempted. Only the crudest guidelines are used in determining the allocation of resources and the enrollment of students at the level of higher education.[44]

The hiatus between economic and educational planning might have been justified had it been necessitated by a systematic pursuit of objectives more important than expanding the forces of production.

[43]Cf. Philip J. Foster, "The Vocational School Fallacy in Development Planning," in *Education and Economic Development*, eds. C. Arnold Anderson and Mary Jean Bowman (London: Frank Cass & Co., 1966), pp. 142–166; and Bowles, *Planning Educational Systems for Economic Growth.*

[44]Organización y Sistemas, Planeamiento y Estadísticas, *Proyecto de Informe Sobre Organizacion y Planeamiento de la Educación de la Universidad de la Havana* (Havana, 1969).

Yet this has hardly been the case. The level of admissions and gradua-tions at each level of schooling is determined more by the commit-ment to accept those who qualify, and the failure to deal with the dropout and retardation problems, than by any rational economic calculation. The annual allocation of the graduates of each type of educational institution to fill work vacancies is a bargaining process among the various ministries, each attempting to gain a sufficient share of the total supply. The number of graduates available is re-garded, for all practical purposes, as determined by considerations not directly related to manpower needs, and is taken as given.

Thus, it would be a mistake to describe the positive contribution of schooling to production as the outcome of careful economic planning. Rather, the fact that the post-revolutionary educational re-source allocations have contributed greatly to the forces of produc-tion may be attributed to the broader ideological commitments of the revolutionary leadership. The emphasis on education itself, and par-ticularly on primary education, derives not so much from economic calculations as from a commitment to achieving greater social equality and to bringing all of the people into the cultural and political mainstream of the nation. Likewise, the attention given to tech-nical and scientific subjects is not the outcome of a manpower plan in which workers with particular skills in these fields were predicted to be in demand, but rather, flows from a more general conviction that scientific and technical knowledge will provide solutions to Cuba's economic problems.

The rapid expansion and transformation of Cuba's educational system has done more than expand the forces of production. The old dependency on the United States for technical skills, research fa-cilities, management, and other professional services has been broken. The formation of research institutes in virtually every major area of production and the expansion of technical and scientific studies at the highest level, have laid the human resource base for Cuba's sovereignty. Although no firm data are available, impressions gained from my extensive observation in production units, research organizations, and educational institutions suggest that by the late 1960s at least, foreign scientists, technicians, and other highly skilled workers play an insignificant role in the Cuban economy, less im-portant, certainly, then before the revolution.

The school system has also played an important part in breaking down the class structure and other forms of social inequality. There can be little doubt that the selective nature of the process of promotion in schools has been drastically altered. Many more blacks, many more children of rural workers, and many more women now achieve high levels of educational attainment. This has occurred, in large measure, through a shift in school resources from the cities to the countryside. Indicative of the emphasis on rural education are programs such as the literacy campaign, and the fact that the fraction of primary school students in rural schools has risen from less than one-third in 1958–59 to more than two-fifths in 1968–69.[45] In part, the large numbers of people from previously oppressed groups now attending schools beyond the primary school level is explained simply by the fact that schools are open to them, they are free, and the prospect of entering highly skilled and responsible positions in society exists, if the appropriate schooling is obtained. Explicit programs of "compensatory education" are not in evidence. The major contribution to educational equality in the Cuban schools seems to have come from the new egalitarian milieu of a society in which racial and social class barriers to attainment—both in schools and in the larger society—have largely been swept away.

This radical transformation has been both implemented by and reflected in the new forms of schooling outlined in the previous section. Students generally learn lessons from what they do, and what their teachers do, as well as from what they read and study. In a society in which manual work is, to a great extent, shared by all, the conventional class distinctions become blurred. And the school activities themselves—students and teachers alike working side by side with the *campesinos*, workers attending school—contribute greatly to the obliteration of class lines based on manual vs. nonmanual work distinctions. Moreover, in the *escuela al campo* program, the leadership of the camp often goes to those who work well, not to the monitors or others who excel at intellectual tasks. The occasional inversion of the hierarchy of the school social system itself teaches an additional lesson for equality. Finally, an important point was made by the closing of the school system to release students and teachers for the

---

[45] JUCEPLAN, *Compendio Estadístico de Cuba, 1968* (Havana, 1968), p. 33.

literacy campaign in 1961: the further pursuit of education for those fortunate to be in school was not as important as the effort to bring the illiterates of the population into broader communication with the rest of society.

It need hardly be stressed that voluntary work in the countryside by white-collar urban workers teaches some of the same lessons, both to the *campesinos*, who chuckle at the incompetence of the city people when it comes to cane cutting, and to the city people themselves who learn to respect the work of the *campesinos* and begin to develop the capacity to bridge the old class divisions. The contribution to equality is furthered by the fact that when a Havana office goes to the country to participate in the harvest, the staff lives in a highly egalitarian camp situation, with the minister or chief of the office sharing the same accommodations and work load with the file clerk. The hierarchy of the camps is based on who cuts the most cane, a capacity not necessarily bearing any relation to one's position in the office bureaucracy.

Of course, vestiges of class and racial distinctions remain. These may be seen, for example, in the apparently lower level of school attendance among rural children, the significantly higher dropout rates among these children (Table 14.4), and the qualification of rural as compared to urban teachers, shown in Table 14.5. Women are still far from achieving an equal place in Cuba's educational institutions and in the society at large. The fact that these problems remain should not obscure the gigantic strides which have been taken toward equality since the revolution. But their existence points to the need for continued movement toward a more equal education.

Education is central to the process of creating the new socialist man. If the schools of the pre-revolutionary period socialized workers for a competitive, alienating work environment, new forms of education would have to be provided for the development of the new man. Schooling is both a complement and a spur to changes taking place directly in the production sphere. The aim is to alter the social relations of production so as to render the work process itself intrinsically rewarding, either through the creative joy of participating in it, or the sense of social fulfillment involved in doing a needed job. Of course a transformation of this magnitude is a long process, involving not only changes in attitudes and in the social relations of production, but

Table 14.4.   Dropout Rates, Urban and Rural, 1968–69

Grade	Percentage who neither Repeat Grade nor Proceed to the Next Grade[a]	
	Urban	Rural
1	6.6	14.3
2	7.6	11.7
3	3.4	17.7
4	15.2	15.4
5	3.7	35.3
6	5.5	17.8
Estimated percent of incoming class that will not drop out before graduating:	64.4	19.4

[a]Dropout rates are calculated by adding the number of students "passed" from the previous grade level, the number of students failing to pass the actual grade level the year before, and subtracting from that figure the actual enrollment figure for the grade level.

SOURCE: Jose Llanusa, *Desarrollo de la Educación a lo Largo de los 10 Años de Proceso Revolucionario*, (Havana, Cuba, 1969), pp. 84, 95.

concomitant changes in the techniques of production and the products produced. Strenuous efforts are being made to eliminate—through mechanization—the most onerous and unrewarding work activities, such as cane cutting. And in the economy, wage incentives are being deemphasized, although very gradually.[46]

Can schooling help to advance these fundamental changes in both the social relations of production and the consciousness of the Cuban people? Many of the new forms of education, discussed above, are directed precisely at such a transformation. The obligation to serve society was taught by example in the literacy campaign; the social value of productive work is taught in the *escuelas al campo*; an interest in the process of production rather than in the monetary reward is stimulated in the *círculos de interés*; and a spirit of cooperation rather than competition is embodied in the practices of collective study and the monitor system.

But, while much has changed, much also remains the same. The structure of the classroom itself seems to have resisted the winds of revolution. In the vast majority of classes which I visited, the method

[46]Piece rates were still in use in 1969 in some agricultural occupations.

Table 14.5. Educational Background of Primary School Teachers, 1968–69

		Urban	Percent	Rural	Percent	Total	Percent
Professional teachers		21,679	74	4,120	22	25,799	54
Student teachers		32	0	54	0	86	0
Maestros populares (teachers of the people)							
Having received the emergency training course for	Introduction	501	2	2,780	15	2,381	5
	1st	2,092	7	7,508	41	9,600	20
	2nd	1,115	4	2,431	13	3,546	7
maestros populares	3rd	523	2	556	3	1,079	2
	Total	4,231	14	13,275	72	17,506	37
Not having taken the course		3,335	11	964	5	4,299	9
Total *maestros populares*		7,566	26	14,239	77	21,805	46
Total Number of Teachers		29,277	100	18,413	100	47,690	100

SOURCE: Jose Llanusa, *Desarrollo de la Educación a lo Largo de los 10 Años de Proceso Revolucionario*, (Havana, Cuba, 1969), p. 50.

of instruction could best be described as catechistic, an authoritarian teacher-centered approach characterized by a single teacher talking at a class of passive students. Little genuine motivation or interest was evinced by the students—and this is hardly unexpected, given the limited role granted the Cuban people in shaping and instigating their own educational activities. Worse still, exams and grades still seem to be a central element in the motivation of students, thus maintaining a structure of rewards external to the process of learning and analogous to wages in a capitalist labor market.[47]

DILEMMAS IN CUBAN EDUCATION

Pursuit of a rapid expansion of the forces of production, simultaneously with radical changes in the social relations of production, is bound to involve some degree of conflict among objectives and require some sacrifice of one objective in favor of another at times. While the objectives of the Cuban revolution—both in the society at large and in the school system specifically—have, by and large, been complementary, conflicts have arisen in some important areas. The way in which these conflicts have been resolved over the decade since 1959 provides an insight into the revolutionary process and the real commitments of the revolutionary government. The ways in which new conflicts will be resolved will greatly shape the future course of the revolution.

The decision to emphasize primary schooling and other basic education, rather than higher education, illustrates the first of these dilemmas. Although the development of Cuba's own technical, scientific, and administrative capacities would have been better served by a more rapid expansion of higher education, the primacy of the egalitarian objectives dictated the decision to invest a large portion of the nation's educational resources at the lowest level of schooling.

---

[47]Of course the grades themselves may be of little importance in achieving material comfort after graduation, as the relationship between personal earnings and scholastic achievement (however measured) may be virtually nonexistent by the time most of today's students reach adulthood. And to the extent that grades are an adequate measure of competence, one might reasonably desire good grades as an indication of one's ability to contribute to the development of the larger community.

While the overall emphasis in educational resource allocation bespeaks a strong commitment to equality, and perhaps even a desire to thwart the development of a technocratic elite, other policies seem to run against the commitment. In a society committed to rapid scientific and technological advance from a position of educational backwardness, the need to fill high-level scientific positions has posed the temptation to give special educational opportunities to especially talented students. A secondary school for an intellectual elite has been established in Havana, and as of 1969, plans were under way to establish others in the remaining provinces. Students at this school are chosen primarily on the basis of their scholastic performance. Teaching and other resources were superior to any which I observed elsewhere at the secondary level, and student performance was impressive. The students at the school seemed well aware of their social obligation to share the skills and knowledge being embodied in them at society's expense. Yet even in a socialist society, a school system which stratifies children at an early age on the basis of their measured abilities and likely future roles in the production process will tend to reproduce a class structure and a sense of hierarchy in the consciousness of its students. The elitist elements built into this type of education, intensified by an almost romantic faith in the scientific expert, are clear.

The issue of "ability grouping" of students, as well as pressures for early vocationalization of education, appear to raise a second conflict—that between the expansion of the forces of production and the pursuit of a classless society and the new socialist man.[48] The elitist implications of a vocationally segregated or "ability-grouped" educational system need not be decisive if they are strongly countered in other areas of social policy. Nonetheless, extension of this kind of schooling beyond its presently limited sphere could seriously threaten the egalitarianism of the revolution.

A third dilemma centers around the problem of reducing the im-

[48]I say "appears to raise" because most Cuban educators with whom I talked saw the objectives as conflicting in this case. However, evidence concerning the efficacy of ability grouping in the United States is contradictory. Even from the standpoint of teaching measurable cognitive skills, it is difficult to make a compelling case for a system of finely graded ability groups.

portance of external rewards based on grades and exams, a problem which has occupied the attention of a number of Cuban educators. The solution, however, seems a long way off, and there is no obvious way out. Complete resort to moral incentives in the economy must be based on the development of a new set of values and commitments among the workers—on the development of "socialist consciousness." And a major source of this socialist consciousness must be the schools. Yet, in many respects, the social relations of the schools themselves still recall the alienating relations of the pre-revolutionary capitalist labor market. But to eliminate the system of external rewards in the schools prior to the development of a new set of values among the students, would surely lead to a slackening of effort. Such a fall in "output" is analogous to that which would be associated with a premature policy of non-material incentives in the economy. Breaking this vicious circle is one of the main challenges facing Cuban planners.

I believe that the revolutionary government is correct in seeking a solution to these educational dilemmas primarily outside the classroom: in the camps of the *escuelas al campo*; in the voluntary work brigades; in the communist communities on the Isle of Youth; and in the experience of living in the revolutionary society itself. But here we are faced with another problem. To produce the workers with the skills and competence necessary to make effective use of the new agricultural and other technologies requires serious study as well as changes in values. One cannot totally dispense with teaching and learning the basic cognitive skills. And yet by nearly everyone's admission, not much serious study goes on in the work camps or other non-classroom activities. Recognition of this problem is implicit in the recent speech of the minister of education stressing the importance of individual (as opposed to collective) study and emphasizing the academic aspects of student evaluation.

The above dilemmas of Cuban education are but a reflection of the dilemmas of the Cuban economy: can forms of work organization and technology be devised which represent *both* an advance in the forces of production and a step toward a social relations of production which enhances rather than inhibits personal liberation and self-development? Can educational forms and techniques be developed which will allow the effective transmission of the needed productive skills as well as the development of values and commitments consistent with the revolutionary ideology?[49]

The answer to both of these questions, I believe, is yes. In education, the grounds for optimism are particularly strong. The structure of the school as we know it in modern capitalist societies was not developed primarily to teach children productive skills but rather to fit them into the social relations of production in capitalist enterprise.[50] The development of the technical and cultural level of the population has undoubtedly been retarded—not advanced—by the teacher-centered, authoritarian educational processes which have successfully initiated future workers to the social relations of the capitalist factory or office. There is no reason to believe that overthrowing the structure of the school inherited from capitalist Cuba will necessarily curtail the contribution of schooling to the forces of production. Thus, the continuing search for new social relations of schooling—at once both productive and liberating—seems likely to bear fruit if it does not succumb to immediate pressures to gear the school system solely to producing the manpower requirements of economic growth. The search for these new social relations of education is the central challenge now facing Cuban educators in their attempt simultaneously to create what Che termed "the two pillars of socialist construction: the formation of the new human being and the development of technology."[51]

[49] A major failing of the Russian revolution in its early period was the almost exclusive stress on the development of the technical and other cognitive capacities of children. In the hope of stimulating rapid economic growth, proposals for an extended period of general education were rejected in favor of a relatively early segregation of students for vocational training in their likely future production roles. The aim of transforming behavior patterns so as to be more consistent with the idealistic and humanistic strands of socialist thought seems to have been largely ignored, apparently because of Lenin's ascendancy on these matters over more humanistically inclined educators such as Bogdanov. The failure of social (nonmaterial) incentives and the ultimate resort to an inegalitarian system of wage incentives must be ascribed at least in part to this shortcoming of education in the decade following the October Revolution. See Frederic Lilge, "Lenin and the Politics of Education," *Slavic Review* 27, no. 2, (June 1968): 230–57.

[50] For an exposition of this view see Michael B. Katz, *The Irony of Early School Reform* (Cambridge, Mass.: Harvard University Press, 1968); and David Isaac Bruck, *The Schools of Lowell, 1824–1861: A Case Study in the Origins of Modern Public Education in America* (unpublished senior thesis, Department of Social Studies, Harvard College, April 1971).

[51] Guevara, "Man and Socialism in Cuba," p. 394.